ONE HIT WONDER

THE *Real-life Adventures*
OF AN AVERAGE GUY AND
THE *Lessons He Learned*
ALONG THE WAY

Kevin R. Kehoe

IZZARD INK PUBLISHING
PO Box 522251
Salt Lake City, Utah 84152
www.izzardink.com

Library of Congress Cataloging-in-Publication Data

Names: Kehoe, Kevin R., author.
Title: One hit wonder : the real-life adventures of an average guy and lessons he learned along the way / Kevin R. Kehoe.
Description: First edition. | Salt Lake City, Utah : Izzard Ink Publishing, [2021]
Identifiers: LCCN 2021041034 (print) | LCCN 2021041035 (ebook) | ISBN 9781642280722 (hardback) | ISBN 9781642280715 (paperback) | ISBN 9781642280708 (ebook)
Subjects: LCSH: Character. | Kehoe, Kevin R. | Motivational speakers—United States—Biography. | Authors, American—Biography.
Classification: LCC BJ1521 .K36 2021 (print) | LCC BJ1521 (ebook) | DDC 158.1092 [B]—dc23
LC record available at https://lccn.loc.gov/2021041034
LC ebook record available at https://lccn.loc.gov/2021041035

Designed by Ashley Tucker
Cover Design by Susan Olinsky
Cover Images: CoolPhotoGirl/shutterstock.com; verOnicka/shutterstock.com

First Edition
Contact the author at info@izzardink.com
Hardback ISBN: 978-1-64228-072-2
Paperback ISBN: 978-1-64228-071-5
eBook ISBN: 978-1-64228-070-8

Table of Contents

FOREWORD	v
PREFACE	ix
An Old Story	1
The Early Bird Gets the Worm	9
We All Work for Someone	15
Build a Door	23
Cosmic Moments	33
It's Good to Be King	43
Helen's Boys	51
Friends Forever	61
No Place Like Home	69
Welcome to My Universe	77
Listen to Your Mother	87
One-Hit Wonder	93
Best Day Ever	101
Obsessed	107

No Good Deed   115

Under the Bus   123

Somewhere Over the Rainbow   133

The Zone   143

Good Men   151

Nine Lives   159

That Guy   173

Stupid, Stupid, Stupid   181

Banned for Life   189

Sticks and Stones   197

White Lies, Dark Side   207

Penny's Pens   219

The Heisman   227

Mount Fuji   235

No Harm, No Foul   247

Crazy Beautiful   255

Twisted Sister   265

Drinking the Kool-Aid   275

Marriage Advice   283

No Such Thing as a Free Lunch   291

Look Up, Not Down   299

Showing Up   307

Sometimes the Dragon Wins   315

Coda   321

ACKNOWLEDGMENTS   329

FOREWORD

The mark of a good book is that the reader can't put it down, and when you do, you can't wait to get back to it. The mark of an outstanding book is that its words and ideas stay with you, and you find yourself thinking about them and their implications for the way you live your life. Spoiler alert: *One Hit Wonder* is an outstanding book. Outstanding books are written by outstanding writers. In my experience, outstanding writers are those who are vulnerable enough with their subject matter to connect it directly to you and me. They are willing to open up, dissect, and share what they've learned from their experiences and compose a story that "sticks" with the reader. And this is what Kevin Kehoe has brilliantly done in *One Hit Wonder*.

I know Kevin, having partnered with him as a speaker as part of his educational programs for his customers. Though I don't know him very well, I know him well enough as someone who's worked next to him to know that he's authentic. He lives his values. He cares. He's a thinker. He doesn't accept facts at face value.

He reflects. He has extremely high standards. And he's passionate about his customers, employees, and projects.

When he asked me if I would write this foreword for the book, I eagerly accepted. You see, he shared the idea of this book with me several years ago, and I even reviewed an early draft and provided feedback. As a result, I was a supporter of the book from the beginning, and I'm glad to see that it is finally becoming a reality. When he asked me to write the foreword, he advised me that I might be the most famous person he knows—since I've written a book before—and that might help sell the book. But what he really wanted was someone who could weave together the thoughts and experiences of the people who have known him for decades, in order to provide you, the reader, with some insight into the personality behind the stories you are about to discover.

Kevin's friends see him as just *one of them* – an average regular guy. Each has a different story, but all share a similar assessment of the man who played some part in their lives. Kevin's requested that I merge these into the foreword. I gladly accepted his challenge. So, to understand the author of *One Hit Wonder* is to know a guy who, as a former star wide receiver on his college football team, made the effort to help out a new guy on the team—one he did not know at all and who was desperate to find campus housing—and arranged to get him a dorm room right next to his. They became lifelong friends.

He's described as a guy who is humble and grounded with a clear sense of self, and who has used this ability and clarity to positively impact others and help them in their lives.

He's a guy who was once spotted for the first time, by a now life long friend, dancing on an elevated platform in a crowded disco in Japan, watching Kevin do his best John Travolta impersonation, and wondering, "who is that idiot?"

He's the guy who made a dejected business client laugh, and in doing so, not only changed the client's perspective but taught him to revise his business management approach, which resulted in a turnaround in the client's fortunes, and produced a lifelong friendship.

He's the guy described as trustworthy, courageous, disciplined, contrarian, and as someone who "goes his own way." He is "big picture" and has grace under pressure. He's known for his simple philosophies: Work hard, make your own destiny, help others achieve success, fight for what is right, face your fears, admit your mistakes, and move on smarter and humbler.

He's the guy who wanted to learn how to surf—something much harder to do than it looks—and proceeded to scratch and claw his way to success, enduring countless beatings and sinuses packed with saltwater to become a decent surfer.

He's the guy who, during a short presentation, shared everything one business owner needed to know about how to run his company, thus laying the foundation for—all of the success the owner achieved in the following years, as well as creating a lasting personal friendship.

He's a guy—according to a coworker—who as a speaker can capture a room and hold an audience in the palm of his hands, motivating the listener to think bigger and more positively.

If you ask him what his mission is, he will tell you that it is to leave the planet a better place than he found it . . . in some small way. If you ask him about his personal values, he can rattle them off quickly and with a description of what each means to him—excellence; service; sacrifice; integrity; responsibility; and generosity.

Finally he's a guy who—as one friend put it—takes you to places where you might not go on their own. When things are important, he goes all in. He creates, fails, and perseveres. He is living proof of what any of us ordinary people can accomplish through discipline, diligence, effort, and courage.

It's a privilege to know him, and to learn from him on his journey of giving birth to this book: *One Hit Wonder*. I'm glad you have it ahead of you because, if you're like me, I know it will affect you in a positive way. So, to all of those "one-hit wonders" out there—this book is for us.

Robert "Cujo" Teschner

Bestselling author of *Debrief to Win: How America's Top Guns Practice Accountable Leadership…and How You Can, Too!* Retired F-15 and F-22 fighter pilot and commander; colon cancer survivor.

PREFACE

*Preface: an introduction to a book,
typically stating its subject and aims*

"Kehoe, you should write a book." That's how my book project got started. I like a good story. I like to hear other people's stories. I've always been interested in where they've been and the things they've done. And I like to tell a few stories of my own, especially the funny ones, the dumb ones, and, yes, in some cases . . . the meaningful ones. That's how this book came to be.

I came to be in Queens, New York, in 1955 when Helen and Roger had their first of six children and gave me the name Kevin. It's a name I like for some reason. But most people with whom I've worked or played closely, in sports or business, just call me Kehoe. And today they often call me Mr. Kehoe. This is something I like, too, as that was how we referred to adults when I was young. We called them "Mrs." or "Mr." I guess I am old school.

I started writing two years ago, but, after writing just a few stories, I wondered, who the heck will read any of this stuff? It's just a collection of stories by some guy nobody knows. What's the point? Someone said that I needed to have a theme for the book. I needed something to tie it together for the reader. What, though? I thought about my own life and what animated and drove me to do these things I was writing about. That answer was pretty simple. I've always tried to be the good guy and the hero. I don't mean this in any exulted and egotistical kind of way. I've tried to be the guy who shows up, and, win or lose, tries to do the right thing. It may not be the best theme, but it's mine. I spent a lot of time thinking about and writing these stories with that theme in mind so I might relay what I learned along the way, trying to be that guy. So with that background, here's my introduction, for better or worse.

I'm not famous. I was born on the right coast but lived most my life on the other one. I haven't been everywhere, but I've been a lot of places. I'm not the smartest guy on the planet, and I've been around long enough to know that, and keep trying anyway. I don't know famous people, but I like the people I do know. I'm an average guy with some thoughts about how to live and maybe even be happy in a world where, too often, by the time you're my age, you've either exhausted all patience with people and want to buy a cabin far out in the woods, or you've learned to accept people for who they are and live with that. How's that for a sentence?

My stories are written here, in thirty-seven chapters, each chapter a separate event with some small insight about life and people. They might make you laugh or cry, and you might even see yourself in them. I'm willing to bet you have good stories, too. I am also willing to bet that some of your stories will sound like mine, except with the names and places changed. I think we all share many of the same experiences over the course of a lifetime. How could we not, actually? That's because, despite our inhabiting a planet crowded with more than seven billion of us, there's a fairly narrow range of human behavior that makes what happens in day-to-day life somewhat predictable. And if things can be somewhat predictable, it might just help to develop a few simple rules of thumb to help us make sense of the world and the people in it. And believe it or not, Waylon Jennings provided me with one of those simple rules of thumb. Yes, that Waylon Jennings, the great country singer and philosopher.

You might be thinking, Waylon Jennings a philosopher? I first came across Waylon's words on a motorcycle trip some twenty years ago. You see, once or twice a year my friend and I would hop on our bikes, point them in a general direction from Southern California—north, south, or east—and ride wherever we felt like for the next five or six days before returning home to the real world. We just wanted to get away from people and the city. We'd often log more than 2,500 miles on these five- or six- day trips. We took roads less traveled, avoiding freeways, and often found ourselves riding on great roads with postcard scenery and no traffic. At the end of each day, we'd stop in some small town, find the local saloon, and spend a few hours drinking tequila and shooting pool.

That's where I met Waylon, not actually in person, but in a jukebox, and became acquainted with his philosophy of people. His words, paraphrased here so I can't be sued by his record company, suggest that we spend a lot of time in life looking for *answers* about people, the who and why they are the way they are. Waylon said it just wasn't that complicated because the most important thing to know is the difference between *yo-yos, bozos, bimbos,* and *heroes.* Not a deep analysis, I admit. But maybe deeper than you think because if you accept his idea, it clarifies life's unfortunate reality . . . and that is that not everyone is good or wants to be, and even when they are, people are just people, sometimes strong and dependable, and at other times not so much. It occurred to me that there was a lot of truth to this, and that to save heartache and false hope, it's not such a bad idea to open one's eyes and have some kind of mental process like . . .

Step one: Observe a person.

Step two: Determine the person's type in your mind: yo-yo, bozo, bimbo or hero?

Step three: If yo-yo, try to avoid.

Step four: If bozo, try to avoid.

Step five: If bimbo, try to avoid.

Step six: If hero, get to know.

Step seven: If avoidance is not possible for steps three through five, then just proceed with caution. . . . and maybe read on in this book to avoid some of the dumb things I did and maybe even gain an insight or two into living according to some code or rules of thumb.

I like the hero archetype. I don't mean *the run into a burning house kind of hero* here. That's a different kind of *hero in the moment.* I mean the day-in and day-out, honest, simple, and dependable people who make the planet go forward. They are humble and dependable and often lead mostly quiet and ordinary lives. They make life easier for everyone. They can be trusted to do the right thing. I'm no *run into a burning house kind of hero.* But I think I can be trusted to do the right thing, or at least try to, and failing that, try to make it right. And once in a while, these quiet heroes have their moment – a moment of personal satisfaction of a job well done. That is the moment of the one-hit wonder for me.

Most of us feel like we are *no-hit* wonders, much less *one-hit* wonders. We feel like we toil in obscurity and that other people are luckier than we. We even think one-hit wonders are just flashes in the pan, having only one thing defining their lives. But like the quiet hero, the one-hit wonder is no accident. Here's what I mean. You're driving along in your car and you hear a song on the radio. You remember it was a big hit back in the day and that you really like the song. But you have trouble recalling the artist, so you ask the others driving with you, "Who wrote this song?" Someone says, "That was so-and-so. They were a real one-hit wonder." And it's said in a way that implies it was the only thing that artist ever did. I know. I've had this conversation. I've felt this way.

Now, shift scenes and flash to another car, where one of the passengers *is* the artist who wrote the song. That artist is listening to the same radio station at exactly the same moment. What are they thinking? I bet they're having an entirely different experience. They're remembering a younger time when they had hopes and dreams and worked hard, writing lots of different songs over many years, most of which never made it to the charts, but this *one* did. They're recalling how great it was to hear their song played on the radio for the first time. They're remembering *all* that they did, and "failed" at, to have that *one* moment of personal satisfaction. They recall a job well done. And now, here they are, years later, having the satisfaction of knowing that people still love the song and radio stations still play it.

Who would not want to experience something like that? The one-hit wonder captures a terrific irony about life. They may only be known for their one hit, but they are remembered for it, forever. That's what you get for being a hero . . . moments and memories and maybe even a legacy. I'm no hero. I don't even have one song I've written that's worth listening to. But I've tried to live like one. . . . for my mom and dad, my brothers and my sister, my wife, my daughter, and those with whom I've played and worked. So, here's to Mr. Jennings, and to all the unseen and uncelebrated heroes of the world. Here's to their stories and yours. Allow me to add mine and share some of what an average guy learned along the way about people and life.

CHAPTER 1

An Old Story

"The unexamined life is not worth living."
—Socrates

We all have to start somewhere to get somewhere else. And for the trip to reach some conclusion, it must begin with some *intent*. That intent must be directional and involve some belief in getting to the destination. Therefore, it is my belief that where we end up in life has little to do with birth order—whether you were born into wealth or not, your gender, the color of your skin, your looks, or your forty-yard dash time . . . though I can make a really strong argument for the forty-yard dash time. After almost seven decades of living on this planet, I've reached a simple conclusion: where we end up in life is rooted in the way we think about ourselves and the self-beliefs we hold to be true. So, if you never take the time to examine who and what you are and what you believe, you may shortchange yourself and miss out on the many opportunities life presents that can make you feel worthwhile and, ultimately, happy with who you are. The unexamined life is a recipe for the alternative.

I mention the forty-yard dash time as a possible exception to this rule. I am, of course, making something of a joke of this, but I am also making a point. I played football in college. I was very good. I wasn't fast, but I had other skills. I had good hands, an ability to get open, and I was hard to tackle. In other words, aside from the lack of an electric forty-yard dash time, I had all the skills essential for playing at the highest level. But I never did. I thought, and pro scouts agreed, that my lack of speed was a disadvantage. But in retrospect, what I lacked wasn't so much pure foot speed. What I lacked was the belief that I could play the game at the highest level *despite* that one disadvantage. So, I concluded I did not belong *there*, in the NFL.

This is one of the oldest stories in the book. It's the story we too often tell ourselves—that we are not good enough and that we don't belong. That story, repeated often enough, simply becomes our reality, and in my case that conviction and belief resulted in my watching other guys on TV, doing on Sunday, what I had hoped and dreamed of doing. The stories we tell ourselves, to a great extent, are accurate predictors of the arc of our lives.

Whether I would have made it to the NFL, had I tried harder, is immaterial. But because I didn't believe I could play *there*, I didn't pursue it. I simply accepted the belief that I wasn't fast enough and therefore not good enough. Maybe this was accurate and maybe it wasn't. But, at that time in my life, that was my story, and I stuck with it. Years later, at a team reunion, I was speaking with some of my former teammates and coaches, and I related this narrative about the NFL to them. I discovered that they were surprised I felt that way. *They* all thought that I had enough talent to have had a legitimate shot at making the NFL. *They* thought I was good enough. I've come to some realizations about this massive difference in what we believe about ourselves and what others think. The first is, the power of our brains to open and close doors for us. And the second is a tougher realization: Did I use that self-story and belief as an excuse not to try? This is a harder thing to come to grips with. But just as Socrates wrote over two thousand years ago . . . *A life unexamined* . . . I would be lying to myself if I didn't confront this possibility.

The stories we tell ourselves become our reality, even when those stories fly in the face of the facts. We become only as good as we want to be. And to become what we might be often requires over-coming some disadvantages—we all have them. And a big part of that is learning to un-tell the false stories we hang on to. It's more than the pop psychology of changing a negative narrative into a positive one. It's deeper than that. It means changing the way we think. And this is very, very hard to do. I know.

Let me give you an example. Starting in my midtwenties, I be-came an amateur long-distance runner and ran many races for the next decade. I ran everything from 10Ks to marathons. I trained almost every day, whether the sun shone, rain fell, or snow covered the ground. One day a runner friend suggested that we enter the city's annual one-mile race. A one-mile race is not a long-distance race. It's a speed race—a sprint compared to a 10K or marathon. I thought I'd give it a try, so I signed up and paid the entry fee. I spent the next few weeks doing my version of speed work in hopes of just being competitive enough so as not to embarrass myself and finish last in what was a 125-man field of guys my age. When we lined up for the start, I could see all the other runners simply by looking to the left and right of me. We were all spread out at the starting line on a wide boulevard, looking down the long straightaway to the finish-line banner one mile distant. I was nervous. We took off at the gun, and I ran "my race" at the speed I had practiced on the track. The first half mile was a bit of a blur for me as we all jostled for position. But at the half-mile mark, I picked my head up to see where I stood. I was a little disoriented by what I saw. I was *leading* the race. I was beating 125 runners with less than half a mile to go.

At that moment, a thought entered my head: *I should not be here, in the lead.* In every other race I'd ever run, I finished somewhere in the middle of the pack. And just two minutes later, instead of leading the rest of the way and finishing first, I finished fourth. It all happened so fast, as I ended up chasing the first-place guy to the finish line by less than two seconds. How did I lose, and why? Certainly, the talent of the other runners had something to do with the final result, but the thought that entered my head that *I should not be here* played a role as well. My brain told me that I did not belong *there* in the front, and . . . well, my brain turned out to be right. The reality is, I most definitely could have won that race. But I didn't. This is what I'm talking about. . . . where you end up is rooted in the way you think and what you believe.

My wife thinks I'm pretty smart. But I tell her that I'm just a guy with average talent and intelligence. This is not negativity. In my mind, it's my *reality*. And there it is. I just wrote it right there in that previous line. That is a rooted belief. That's my self-story. I think one thing about me—she thinks another. My teammates and coaches thought I was NFL material, and I did not. Who's right? I think you know the answer to that. It's more than a lack of confidence, but that accounts for some of it. We like to think that life's so-called "winners" are naturally self-confident people, but it's just not true. They, too, are filled with doubts and have to overcome . . . to become what they might be. Okay, maybe someone like Michael Jordan is an exception. But he's not the norm. As a result, I've come to believe that real self-confidence, not the inflated fake power-of-positive-thinking self-confidence, is the hardest thing to develop.

The question becomes, then, Why is it so hard to do this? First, I think that defeats and disadvantages drain away self-belief and resilience, making it a real effort to get them back once they're lost. Second, I think that most of us undervalue ourselves. We somehow expect perfection and invest too much time comparing ourselves to others . . . a process that always winds up in a dead-end alley. We can judge ourselves harshly and hold ourselves to standards most others never would. There will always be those who are lesser and greater than us in — something. Might it not be better to look inside ourselves, instead of outside at others and discover what's already inside *there*... and work with that? That would mean that what might actually be universally true is that we each bring something unique to the world, where comparisons mean nothing.

I talk to my mom a lot these days. She is ninety-two. She's a good listener. We talk about life and other things. She believes in her children. I don't know why, but many years ago she sent me a quote which I've carried with me ever since. I take it out and read it a few times a year, just to remind myself what is *real*. It's a quote attributed to Marianne Williamson, a best-selling author, which I paraphrase here. . . . and I understand why my mother likes it so much.

[O]ur deepest fear is not that we are weak. Our deepest fear is that we are powerful beyond measure. It is our light, not our darkness, that most frightens us. We ask ourselves, Who am I to be brilliant, gorgeous, talented, fabulous? Actually, the question is, Who are you not to be? We are, each of us, a child of God, and our playing small doesn't serve the world. So, as we accept that and grow and show that to the world, we liberate not just ourselves from our own fears, we by example liberate others.

I particularly like the part about how *playing small* doesn't serve the world. Playing big scares many of us. It feels like an ego trip or something. We prefer humility. But playing small isn't humility. Williamson implies that it might be—hiding. I remember when I was in college, I said something to my friend Lorraine one evening after a hard and disappointing week. I said, "My shit is only together on a day-to-day basis." She laughed. Looking back, I realize how true that statement is for all of us. We're up one day and down the next. We question and wonder, often spiraling into a "rathole" from which escape is difficult. We can also overexamine things, and by doing so, focus on the moment and fail to see our own real *trend line*. I know I overthink the peaks and valleys and miss the direction of my trend line, like a stock market trader can do, missing the longer trends and arcs of the market.

It is the trend line that truly represents the *arc of a life*, not the daily ups and downs. And if the line is arcing is in the right direction, it's a good sign that we are believing the right things about ourselves, and a good predictor of where we will end up. It's the trend line that matters. That's at least what I've come to believe. It helps me remain confident, to continue to have the strength to overcome, and to stay excited about the future. My mother's quote reminds me to play bigger and believe. We never attain perfect confidence and peace. Life throws too many curveballs when you're expecting something else. So like any batter, I've adopted a few swing thoughts to keep me from having a long-running, confidence-draining batting slump. It's self-talk that I've adopted over the years to remember that life, like baseball, is a long season, and there are good and bad days.

If I don't ask, I won't get.

Don't overthink things.

I'm closer to the prize than I think I am.

Someone's going to win today, so why not me?

Too serious? Maybe, but I don't think so. We're talking about having a happy life, right? It's never too late to have one, you know. Look in the mirror and make the change. We owe that much to the planet, as Marianne Williamson said.

CHAPTER 2

The Early Bird Gets the Worm

"Some of us wake up. Others roll over."
—Mark Twain

I was raised in an Irish Catholic family. We went to church. I served as an altar boy when the Mass was still said in Latin. I knew the Baltimore Catechism, inside out. But I wasn't really a prayerful person until much later in life when I discovered that bad things can happen for no reason at all, and you must find a way to deal with the reality that life is short. I don't know what you do to start your day, but these days I get up early, say a prayer, and make a plan to make the most of the day. Maybe I do this because one of the nuns, Sister Maurice, told us in grade school that the early bird gets the worm. Those words have remained with me over the years. In fact, I actually believe them. I'll be honest—I haven't always been so committed to this morning routine, but as I've aged, it has become more important. I honestly enjoy the ten minutes I invest in doing it.

Here's how it works for me: I pray first for those I know who are suffering and in need of mercy and hope. I think about them as I pray and hope they can feel my prayer wherever they may be. Then, I ask myself two questions: "Today comes once. *Who am I going to be?*" The big picture first; then I pose the second question: *"What am I going to do?"* Trust me, there are days when my answers are close to something like, "nobody . . . and nothing. I'm going to be a slug today, and binge-watch TV." Those days happen. But generally, I'm more ambitious than that because at my age I know that I'm running out of my allotted days, and therefore I'm careful about wasting them. And it's not in my nature to do nothing. In fact, my wife says I'm like the old US Army TV advertisement: *We get more done before breakfast than most people do in a day.* I have slowed down, however, and you'll see why in the chapters ahead. Cancer played a big role in that.

The summer of 2016 marked the lowest point in our battle with it. I'd just come out of a fifth surgery that was immediately followed by another aggressive round of chemo. I felt like hell. I was hurting, physically and mentally. Cancer and, more to the point, cancer treatments will beat up your body, but they can also destroy your spirit. And it was during that summer that my days became so difficult that I finally said to my wife,

"If this the way my life is going to be from here on out, then God can have it—I don't want it."

My wife began to cry. And I was immediately sorry I'd said it. But that's how I felt at the time. It wasn't the best thing I've ever said, but I wasn't my best self then, either. For the next week, after I said that, all I could think of was the look on my wife's face and her tears. I continued to struggle, but I began to reconsider what I'd said about not wanting to live. And even though each day was difficult, I willed myself to get up and do . . . *something*. When you're really miserable, it's easy to focus all your energy on your misery. It's all you think about, and that can be the entry point to an endless and dangerous downward spiral into a rathole.

My wife and I were watching TV one evening during those days, when I, channel surfing as I am prone to do, landed on a station where the movie *The Shawshank Redemption* was playing. We'd tuned in on the scene, if you've seen the movie, where Andy and Red are sitting in the prison courtyard. Andy is depressed about the murder of his friend, which took place in an earlier scene. He turns to Red, and says, "I guess it comes down to a simple choice, really: get busy living or get busy dying." I didn't say anything to my wife right then as we watched the movie, but I thought to myself, "That's damn right!"

The following morning, I restarted my morning routine, the one I mentioned at the beginning of this chapter, the one I'd been neglecting for weeks. I said a prayer for a guy we'd met in the chemo center who was worse off than I was. Then I asked my two questions: *"Today comes just once. Who am I going to be?" "What am I going to do?"* And I got up and got moving that day, and then, the next day, too. I began to string days together, despite my misery. I began to forget my misery and think about something else, and I started to build a little hope.

For those of you who have experienced suffering, you know it is a hard teacher. It can bring out the worst in you or potentially your best. You can run from the lessons or you can deal with them. In hindsight, during that summer, I was in the process of coming to grips with the fact that the good life I'd taken for granted for so many years was not *ever* coming back. I was angry about that, for sure. For a guy who had once easily gotten up *early to get the worm* and outwork the guys in the army, I was having a hard time just getting out of bed. This was quite a comedown for me, and my expectations for myself. It was humbling, too. I now knew what real suffering meant and the crushing hopelessness it can bring.

Without being too dramatic, my battle with this cruel disease was teaching me to see people and life through a very different lens . . . a lens of *mercy* for those who suffer. That movie scene and my misery brought me to a realization. I could see who was really suffering and who most needed *mercy*: it was my wife. I had to give her relief . . . ease her pain . . . give her hope. That was the moment I got my ass completely out of bed. And today, I mark it as the moment my *real* battle with cancer began, a full two years after the original diagnosis. After that, everything changed for us. I had a new purpose. No matter what, I'd deal with the setbacks—and there were many —by asking the doctors, "Tell me what I need to do to grow old with my wife."

But cancer wasn't the only thing going on in my life at the time. I still had to run a company and keep as many commitments as I could to keep that moving forward. More than anything, I wanted my old life back and to feel normal again. During the summer, I had to cancel many appointments and commitments. I decided to get back in the game and keep a commitment I'd made a year before to deliver a short keynote presentation that October. I thought I'd try to share some of the lessons I'd learned that summer, hoping the audience might be able to apply them in their business lives. And that's what I ultimately did, and here's what I said:

"I once thought that my business life and my personal life were separate things. Then, two years ago, I was diagnosed with Stage 4 cancer. I am here to tell you that those two lives overlap and bleed into each other. After a half-dozen surgeries, more chemo than I like to recall, and enough radiation that my wife, Lorraine, swears I glow in the dark, I've reached some conclusions

and learned some lessons that might be useful to you in your business life.

First, it's not enough to simply surround yourself with good people. You have to let good people surround you and be humble enough, when the time comes—and it will—to be willing to utterly rely on them. I had to utterly rely on my wife, family, friends, and doctors. This was something that was not easy for me as I like to be in control and was proud of my self-reliance.

Second, bad news comes in bunches. And the way you respond to that can make things better or worse for everyone around you. A raft of bad news taught me that when I got hopeless, others felt that and lost hope, too. I made a decision that when I got bad news, I'd simply say, "Just a bump in the road, Kevin." The people around you need to see that you believe things will get better.

Third, I learned to pray for God's grace. I am not born-again, yet I know there is a God. I know because those prayers and God's grace sustained me though some very dark times before I was granted some relief. There is no scientific explanation for some of what I've experienced. There is in life an intangible element of—faith—that can lift you up and foster in those around you a belief to fight the battle with you.

The game of business is won not only in the head but in the heart. That's at least what I've concluded. Thank you."

"Who am I going to be today?" is a great question because it challenges us to be better. We are our best selves when we think big and dream. And the answer to the first question helps focus the answers

to the second question: *"What am I going to do today?"* These would be a list of actions that advance us closer to the dream. Why am I telling you this? While it's true that the early bird gets the worm, that only happens when the early bird knows where to look and knows how to catch it when it's found. Dreams without foundations are simply exercises in frustration or, worse, delusion. I know. I was always a better doer than I was a dreamer until it occurred to me one day that I was really busy going nowhere. I knew how to make a list and get things done; what I needed to do was to think bigger if I wanted all my efforts to have any meaning at all.

My wife and I watched the rest of *The Shawshank Redemption* during the evening of that summer of 2016. Near the end of the picture, there is a scene where Red, struggling to adapt to life outside prison, travels to the field and big oak tree that Andy had told him about in the prison courtyard. He digs up the box Andy left for him and reads the note. It says: "If you're reading this, you've gotten out. And if you've been willing to come this far, maybe you're willing to go a little further."

We all need something to live for. If we don't have that, we need to find it. I found it that summer. I will do whatever it takes for the opportunity to grow old with my wife . . . and I do that one day at a time. It's a question we all have to answer every day, isn't it? If I've come this far, am I willing to go a little further? Get busy living? Sister Maurice was right. The early bird *does* get the worm. Sometimes all it takes is to get yourself out of bed.

CHAPTER 3

We All Work for Someone

"You're not the boss of me."
—Julia Marie Kehoe
(my one and only child from my first marriage)

My little girl, Julia Marie Kehoe, the one I raised as a single parent before my second marriage, is approaching thirty years old now. She and I have experienced all of the ups and downs that parents and children experience in life. There were very good and very bad days. But these days, things are pretty good. She is happy and that's all I care about. I consider myself fortunate in that regard. I also consider myself fortunate that I was able to work at a job that I enjoyed. And it makes me smile that now, she, too, is having the same experience in her career, and I can't say enough about how important it is to do what you love.

I've worked in the hotel, restaurant, business consulting, and software industries. Most of my career was spent in business consulting, but perhaps the most rewarding job was my last one in software. The stories of how I got into and out of these various careers are good ones, and I share them throughout the rest of the book as they are the experiences that imparted many of the lessons I learned about life and dealing with people. But the first lesson I learned in business, and it applies to both one's personal and business career, is that . . . we all work for someone. This was especially true when I was the "boss" of my own consulting and software companies. The world might be such a better place to live in if we all understood this essential truth . . . we are our best selves when we're serving something larger than ourselves.

I was a single parent for the first decade of my daughter's life. It was a big job for which, like most parents, I had no prior training. All I knew about parenting came from what I'd experienced growing up in my own large family. We were taught values and manners by my parents, among other things. And when I got divorced, raising my daughter, Julia, got complicated because my values and manners weren't always exactly aligned with my ex's values and manners. If you've found yourself in this situation, you learn to appreciate how important it is for both parents to be on the same page with a child. The fact is, it makes it harder to teach your children, and it's confusing for the child, when you're not on the same page. Whatever the case may be . . . same page or not, you must still teach as best you can.

I mentioned that we all work for someone, for a reason. I learned that lesson early on in life—as you will see in a future chapter—and one day I had the opportunity to teach that same lesson to my daughter. I didn't consciously create the opportunity. She did that herself. It happened in our kitchen right before dinner. She and I had developed a routine where we would prepare dinner together. I'd be the boss of the dinner prep, and she was my helper.

One evening, according to our routine, I said, "Hey, let's get dinner ready now."

"I'm not hungry."

"Okay, you may not be now, but you will be later, so let's get it started."

"I'm doing something right now."

"Well, then drop that, and you can return to it later."

"No."

"What do you mean, no? We need to get dinner ready."

"I don't have to, and you're not the boss of me!"

Julia was about seven years old at the time. I can't say I was shocked, as I knew that at some point she and I were going to have this very conversation. I'd had it with my own parents. I knew it was a normal part of growing up and not some major crisis, so I just sighed and thought about how I was going to deal with this "not the boss of me thing" without its escalating into an argument.

"Okay," I said. "Do me a favor. You know that sticky flip-chart paper in my office that we use to draw on sometimes? Can you go get a piece of that and stick it to the refrigerator here for me?"

At the time, I ran my business consulting practice out of our home. My consulting practice focused on things like business strategy, organization structure, leadership, and management of people. I was something of an expert on these things, and my clients engaged me to help them define organization charts, job descriptions, goals, and other related systems. Julia went to my office and retrieved a sheet of paper and stuck it on the refrigerator door.

"Okay," she said. "Now what?"

"I want to draw you a picture," I replied.

"Cool, I like pictures," she said.

"A picture of our little family," I said.

"Okay, nice. Can I help?"

"Sure," I said. "But let me get started first."

I drew a square box. Then I drew another square directly under the first one, leaving some space between the box above and the box below, and then I connected the two boxes with a line from the top box down to the bottom box.

"What is this?" she wondered, starting to frown a bit.

"Well, this is our family."

"It doesn't look like a family picture."

"Just wait a sec. I'm not done yet." I said.

I then labeled the top box with the word "ME" inside it and the bottom box, directly below it, with the word "YOU."

"You remember what Daddy does for work, right?"

"Yeah, kinda. You're a consultant or something."

"Yep. And this picture here is called an organization chart. I draw them all the time for people when I go to work. The chart is really important because the picture shows how people work together and their jobs and responsibilities . . . and who reports to whom. Without one of these, people might argue and fight all the time and forget that they are on a team and have a job to do so that everyone can be happy."

My daughter was then, and is now, very smart. I could see she was getting the point and was none too happy about it. I plowed on.

"This, you have to agree, is the chart for our family organization." I pointed to the top box labeled "me" and said. "This is me." Then I pointed to the bottom box labeled "you" and said, "And this is you. So, as you can see, sweetie, technically, I *am* the boss of you."

"Very funny," she said. "Why do you get to be the boss?'

"Good question! You see all this around you? The house, your bedroom, that food? Where did all that come from, do you think?"

"You?"

"Exactly. That's why I'm the boss . . . and I will remain so until such time that you start your own family or leave this home of ours. And when that happens, you get to have your name in that top box."

"It doesn't seem fair that you get to be the boss of everything," she said.

"I'm not. When I go to work, my clients are the boss of me. In fact, in a way, I work for you, too. I'm responsible for your entire life right now. It's a big job. The truth is, honey, we all work for someone." And that was that. There were no questions or further discussions about it that day. We just made dinner, and I later tucked her into bed and read her to sleep . . . as I always did in those days. That chart stayed on the refrigerator for almost a month.

Almost twenty years later, I ended up hiring my daughter as a sales rep in my software company. She interviewed like everyone else and got the position because she was the best candidate. Was I proud? Of course I was. But I did have a business to manage, and she was just one of about ten people on a team reporting directly to me. I was, then, the founder and director of sales and marketing. I had gathered my team for a planning session in our conference room. The goal of the meeting was to clarify goals, job responsibilities, and our department organization chart as we were hiring a lot of people quickly.

I started the meeting by posting a sheet of sticky flip-chart paper on the white board and began "drawing up" the department organization chart. This exercise can be a bit dry, so I was looking for a way to make it a little more interesting. As I considered how I might do that, I flashed back to that night years before in our kitchen when it was just my daughter and I "drawing up" *our* family chart. I stopped and turned back to my team.

"Let me tell you about organization charts." I then related the story about my daughter and me and that night in our kitchen. My daughter, of course, was in the room, listening to the story. When I finished, one of my other reps looked across the room at my daughter and asked,

"Really? Did that really happen?"

I was watching her. I had no idea if she would recall the conversation. She was just seven years old when it happened. But I could see that she had a smile on her face. She nodded to the guy, and said, "That's the way it happened."

As a parent, you tend to believe, based on many of your child's actions, that they never hear a damn thing you've said. I smiled, too. Here she was—a young adult sitting in a room with other young adults doing adult things, when, from my perspective, it was just yesterday that she was a child and we'd had that talk.

I looked at her and said, "It was a pretty good talk then?"

"Yeah, it was all right."

I looked at the rep who'd asked my daughter the question, and said," Whaddya think? That I just make this stuff up?"

"No, but what were you doing having an organization-chart discussion with a seven-year-old?

My daughter piped up and said, "He was always like that . . . giving me 'lessons.' And the lesson of that one was that we all work for someone."

I said, "That was true then and it's true today. You work for me, but I also work for you guys. That's what's required to be part of a family or a team and do well."

I smiled at my daughter again; then I turned back to the white board and got back to work, she and I now in our new adult world decades removed from those childhood days. I also couldn't help but think about how much I missed those days, a lifetime ago for her, but what felt like only moments for me. And I thought that maybe I had done a good job as her parent and teacher. And maybe even for all I knew there were other lessons that I'd taught her, that I didn't know about, that guided her life now. I could only hope. We all work for someone. I'm glad that some of the work I did for her paid off. I know it has, as she is a great worker and team member.

CHAPTER 4

Build a Door

"If opportunity doesn't knock, build a door."
—Milton Berle, Comedian

It took me a few of years of *kicking around* in the business world before I discovered the job and career that became my life's work. Looking back, I probably kicked around longer than I might have otherwise, if only because I was never one of those people who knew what they wanted to be growing up. In fact, I never even really thought about "what I wanted to be when I grew up" at all. It was a little bit of a shock when, upon graduation from college and without any firm plans, I had to actually choose to do *something*. And because I had no real plan, I landed in the restaurant business because it was one of the only things in which I'd had any experience and that I knew paid decent money. I'd been a bartender in college in a pub on campus during the school year and, on occasion, I'd tended bar at a few clubs during the summer on the South Shore of

Long Island, where I lived at the time. That was the sum total of my credentials. I had a college degree and bartending experience.

Let me explain what I mean by *kicking around*. More than a few times it meant that I got kicked out the door. I've been fired from a job six times in my life. I can't recall all the details of all these terminations. But I do recall the first time clearly. It was soon after college graduation. I was hired as the night manager of a club. I was responsible for opening and closing each night. Another part of the job was making certain the club was cleaned at closing—the bar, the seating areas, and the restrooms. One evening after I inspected all these places, some guy must have gotten back into the men's room and thrown up all over the place. When the owner came in the next day and saw this, he called and told me not to bother coming in for work that night. And out the door I went. I thought the termination was unjustified, but he was the owner. As it turned out, he'd actually done me a favor as I soon landed another better-paying job.

After this experience, I got a few new jobs where twice again I was shown to the door. I was upset by the terminations as I felt I wasn't at fault, and that it had more to do with employers who simply did not appreciate my talents. Yes, that's my version of dry humor. But the facts were the facts, and the common denominator in all my terminations was of course—me. Then came the termination that altered the arc of my business career. It took place in 1985. I had been hired into a family business that was involved in the construction industry. I didn't know much about construction, but I supposed they hired me because of my business degree, which I guess they thought could help them. I had just graduated with an MBA. I really did try to help them. I worked really hard. I tried to do the right thing. What I did not appreciate and understand was the power of the personal histories among relatives, and the dysfunctions within a family business. What I mean is, the decisions you or I might make in a nonfamily business rarely involve personal considerations alone. If someone is not performing and doing their job, we'd simply tell them that. And if they did not improve within some agreed-upon time period, we'd have little choice but to show *them* the door. In a family business, it doesn't work that way. Specifically, it's really hard to fire your brother, or tell him he's a loser, especially when he's a shareholder.

And that's what was happening in that business. I attempted to do what one might do in a nonfamily business. The really weird thing was that the family was only too happy to have me do the dirty work of telling other family members to *pull their weight*. I did not love this responsibility, but this was what I was hired to do. But when I told one of the brothers that he wasn't pulling his weight, he went right into the other brother's office—the guy who had told me to tell his brother that he wasn't pulling his weight—to complain about *me*. I did not actually hear the words that were said, but I assume it was something like, "Someone has to go, and it's either him or me." Guess who got shown the door later that day?

I was out of work again. I wasn't happy, but I wasn't too worried, either. I thought the market was good, I had an MBA degree, I had skills and credentials. I was certain that with all my talents my job search would be a brief one. And that is exactly what did *not* happen. I was out of work for a very long time. So long that, by the time I did find a job, I had less than $100 left in my bank account. What follows is the story of that job search, the one that changed my life, that ended my kicking-around days, and put me in the career I was likely born to be in. Am I being dramatic? Maybe, but my life was never the same after that job search.

It's been a while since I've been unemployed . . . decades, in fact. But I can still clearly recall what it feels like to be unemployed. For anyone, and certainly for me, being out of work for any period of time leaves psychic scars that can last a lifetime. I would do almost anything not to repeat that experience. It's a depressing and unnerving experience at the same time. It's depressing because you feel like a loser——someone kicked you out the door and rejected you. It's unnerving because you still have to pay bills without income. And if you don't have a large bank account——which I did not at that time—it's scary watching your money disappear with no idea when you will be able to replace it.

One month after I'd been let go from my job, not only did I not have a new job, I had zero prospects of getting one anytime soon. That frightened me. I had a personal "come to Jesus" moment and I realized that my situation was serious. Whatever it was I had done in my job search up to that time, it was clearly not working. I decided that I had a problem. Something different needed to be done—and quickly. I decided right then to make finding a job . . . my job. That meant treating my job search like I would treat a real job, had I had one. I decided I had to go to work every day, all day, and work overtime if necessary!

The next day, I got up at 7 a.m. I showered, dressed, and went to the "office" I had set up in my apartment. I had a desk, a phone, a computer, the newspaper, and a few reference books on loan from the library. These books listed potential employers and their contact information. On the very first day, I made a list of everyone I knew, and I called them. I told them I needed work and enlisted their help. After that, I would call these people every week to give them an update, in hopes of keeping my search at the top of mind for them. Then I'd respond to a few ads in a newspaper that appeared promising. But I soon came to the conclusion that responding to the Help Wanted ads was a waste of time. From then on, I used the reference books to identify a company, learn a little about the company, find a contact name at the company, then send the person a cover letter and my résumé, requesting an interview.

Let me put this in perspective so you can understand the logistics involved in that job search. This was the mid-1980s. I had a landline phone. Cell phones had yet to be invented. I had a first-generation IBM PC: the one with two slots where you inserted the Word (*not yet invented*) application into one slot and the document disk into the other. This disk was the place where you were able to store a few documents—résumé and cover letters—before you used up all the storage space and needed a new floppy disk. I had a dot matrix printer. I printed cover letters and résumés. I inserted each into an envelope, put a stamp on the envelope, and went to the post office at day's end to mail them all. There was no such thing as widespread use of email. When I wanted to know more about a company and needed to conduct research, I drove to the library, found the information I needed, and made copies of it. The Internet as we know it now was still decades into the future. Google was not a word anyone had ever heard of.

I worked from 7 a.m. to 5 p.m. every day, Monday to Friday, and sometimes on weekends to catch up on research. I dared not go out anywhere for fear of running out of money. I followed this routine for the next nine months. It was like living on a roller coaster. I'd have days when I felt that I was close to landing a job, only to learn the next day that the position had been filled, or that they really liked me but *they had nothing right now*. I'd go on interviews for hours, only to be told that my skill set was not a good match. I met hundreds of new people. I met people for whom I'd never want to work. I met people who gave me false hope. I had multiple interviews with a few companies, working my way up the corporate pecking order only to be disappointed. I even had a final job interview with a guy who smoked a cigar during the interview, wore green braces with big yellow dollar signs on them, and with his feet on top of his desk, balled up my résumé and threw it at me, hitting me in the chest while he asked me, "So why should I hire you?" I didn't get that job, either.

By the fifth month, I was losing hope of ever finding a job. It sounds odd in hindsight when you've never *not* had a job, but after five months of disappointment with zero prospects, I was convinced I'd never get hired anywhere. I was falling into a dark hole of despair. Desperate, I went through my networking list one weekend and I found a name that I had not yet contacted – my accounting professor from SMU. I called him that Monday and he answered the phone. Thank God, I thought, as the idea of spending another week playing phone tag with another person would have almost driven me over the cliff. I told him my story, and how no one would hire me. He listened, and then he said something that I had never even considered. He said that I'd be doing my job search for a long, long time unless I could provide a prospective employer with a clear picture of how my talents could help them. It was so blindly obvious, but I had never considered this very simple idea. I was so focused on finding a job, that I forgot the guy hiring was looking for someone who could add value to his/her company.

"You need to package your talents so you can present them to the people who are looking for that package," he said.

"Okay, that sounds good, but what *are* my talents?" I asked him.

I was so clueless that I didn't know what my talents were, or how to "package" them (*whatever that meant*), or even how to identify the kind of employer who was looking for people with that kind of package.

My professor said, "Kevin, I only know you as a student, but my impression of you, based on what I saw in class, is that you are a good problem solver."

"Okay," I said. "What does that mean?"

"You have a talent for seeing into the heart of a problem, keeping it simple, understanding the pros and cons, and most important, you have a way of getting people to buy into what you think."

Boom! The last thing he said resonated with me. I *was* good at getting people to buy into what I thought. I had done that a lot. In fact, I liked doing that kind of thing—problem solving and persuasion.

"Okay. Who does that kind of work, and to whom should I be speaking?" I wondered.

He said, "That's what consultants do every day. You should be talking to consulting firms. They're always looking for guys like you."

Boom again! I felt like some door had opened. We were on to something here. My next question was: "What's a consulting firm?"

I had no idea that people did such a thing for a living and got paid for it, or that there were actual companies who hired people to do that. I don't know if Dr. Neil Churchill, professor of accounting at Southern Methodist University, with whom I was speaking, thought I was a total moron at that moment. But he patiently explained what a consultant did and the types and names of companies that did it as well. I was amazed. How had I never heard of this? Dr. Churchill thought for a moment and then added, "In fact, I was talking with a friend at a consulting firm here in Dallas last week, and I think they are looking for someone. Would you like me to make an introduction for you? Maybe there's something there."

What does a man dying of thirst in a desert say when someone offers him a glass of cool water? "Ah, no thanks . . . I'm good." I said, "Yes, as soon as it's convenient for you. Thanks." He made the call that week. A week later I had a phone interview. And two weeks later the company flew me to Dallas for two days of interviews.

Now the pace of my search and my attitude picked up. Armed with this information, I now focused my search exclusively on consulting firms. There were lots of consulting firms, I discovered. I contacted every firm I could find in the library's business reference books. I started knocking on these new doors, and I began to get interviews. I began to build some momentum and some faith that there was a light—and a job—at the end of the tunnel. Heaven knows, I was ready to have a job and money coming in, as I was running short on funds. And my office, by that time, had become not only my home but my prison. After almost eight months of conducting my job search, I was ready to climb the walls of my office. I am able to work well enough alone, but I function much more happily working alongside other people, where I can bounce ideas off others as part of a team.

Almost nine months after those two brothers in that dysfunctional family business showed me the door, I received two job offers from two consulting firms within days of each other. It always seems to be that way in life, doesn't it—famine or feast? I was thrilled and beyond relieved that I could pass from the life I was living to a life with people in the real world, making some money. Choosing between the two offers was a "good" problem to have after the "bad" problem of unemployment I'd lived with for nine months. I ultimately decided to go with the people in Dallas to whom Dr. Churchill introduced me made me the final offer. A month later, I moved to Dallas, a city I very much like, and I worked with a good group of people for almost two years before I made another career mistake, leaving that consulting firm to work for a client of the firm—who ran a family-operated business. You'd have thought I would have learned my lesson.

I paid dearly for that error in judgment, too, but I can only blame myself for screwing that up, as it could have been a very good situation for me. I committed many of the same mistakes I'd made in the first family business—the one that sent me into my job search hell, before resurrecting me into a world I had no idea even existed. This time I was shown the door again within a few months. But I deserved it. Maybe I was just thick as a brick. Maybe I tried too hard. At that time in my life, I guess I just pissed off the wrong people. I've only myself to blame.

A few years later, I finally solved my employment problems by starting my own business. And I was lucky enough to remain self-employed for the last three decades of my working life. It's nice never having to look for a job. But self-employment is not an easy life, either. I had to work even harder than ever, singing for my supper for all those years I was on my own. But I was better equipped for that type of life than I was for any other. When those doors closed on me all those years ago, and no others opened, I had to build my own door. I had help, as Dr. Churchill showed me a door I hadn't known about. Yet it was up to me to knock on it, open it, and as I later discovered as a self-employed consultant, be ready to make my own door and kick it in.

If I learned anything from all my "kicking around," it might be this. It can take a long time to discover what we are uniquely "good at" and an even longer time to situate ourselves. It took several trips to hell to get *that* through my head. And I learned that no one is waiting for you to knock on their door and give you your dream job. You have to hustle and work for everything. I'd rather it wasn't this way. But it seems to be. It could be worse, though, as I often think that maybe I was better off in the long term compared to those people who always knew what they wanted to be. The hard lessons from those days toughened me, enabling me to handle loss and defeat without losing my mind. On the other hand, I wonder what happens to the people who always knew what they wanted to be—their whole life planned and their career job secured—when they were shown the door. That would be hard. Would they have the resilience to bounce back, or would they be crushed? When life doesn't open a door for me, I've learned to build one. In fact, I rely on that now.

Final Note: Here are the stats from that nine-month job search in 1985. Yes, I did keep track of all of this. Over the course of those nine months, I made formal applications to 111 companies, I participated in 353 interviews (*most of these were face-to-face*), I mailed out over 1,000 résumés, and only heaven knows how many phone calls I made. It was the hardest job I ever had.

CHAPTER 5

Cosmic Moments

"*Funny how falling feels like flying, for a little while. . . .*"
—Crazy Heart, *the movie*

It's easier to hate your job than it is to change it. It's like that with
most everything in life. It's easier to stay than it is to leave, no matter how awful the circumstances. I can vouch for that. I was once a
night-shift manager at a Manhattan restaurant. (No, I was not fired
from this job. Read on . . . .) As the manager, I was always the last
guy out every night. I had to wait until the dishwashers finished
up before I went home. I will tell you that although I didn't love
the restaurant business, I didn't hate it, either. At that time, it was
a job, and it paid me okay money. And I might have stayed at the
job longer than I did, were it not for what happened one really cold
wet February morning after I locked up for the night. That day
and into the night, we'd experienced some of that really rotten New

York winter weather that I was growing to despise. It's the kind of weather where the day's temperatures start at thirty-eight degrees with a cold drizzle, then it all changes and gets colder, turning wet snow into sleet. Then in the afternoon it warms again, turning to rain before the thermometer plunges into the twenties and freezes everything into an ice sheet.

It was around three a.m. by the time the dishwashers clocked out. It had been a busy night. I had just locked the restaurant back door and made the dash to my car so I could get out of the weather and sit on the frozen seat. I fired up the engine and turned on the heater and defrosters to warm things up enough to melt the ice on the windows and make the job of chiseling it off just a little bit easier. After I scraped most of the ice from the windows, I hopped back in the car, put it in gear, and . . . nothing. The car did not move. I got back out and checked the tires to see if they were spinning on the ice. They weren't spinning. That wasn't a good sign. At least if they had been spinning, I could get some sand, and rock the car back and forth out of the ice. The car was running, but it would not move. It was now about 3:30 a.m. It's freezing cold and dark and I'm stuck. I kept trying to get the wheels to spin, but the car would not budge. At that moment, I thought that I might have had a transmission problem. I gave up my attempts to move the car, and let myself back into the restaurant and called a towing company. Since the city never sleeps, a tow truck guy arrived pretty quickly. The driver got out. I showed him what was happening and he said it might be some kind of transmission problem. He looked things over and hooked my car to his truck. My car was running and in gear at this time. When he engaged the lift and raised the back wheels, the wheels began to rotate. It wasn't a transmission problem after all. He then lowered the car on top of the ice and, when he did, the car gained traction and moved.

He looked over at me. "I think your transmission is fine, sir. It looks like you were just locked solid in that ice." I'd never heard of such a thing before, and neither had he. But there we were at 4 a.m. and finally, after a rotten long day, some good news! I didn't need a tow truck guy after all. We were good, right? But this was New York. And there was no way the tow truck guy was going to unhook my car, shake hands like they might do in the Midwest, and say something like, "Hey, no worries, friend. Just happy to help you out. I'll be on my way, now. You drive safe, ya hear." I had to pay the seventy-five-dollar "show up" fee, in cash, or the car stayed on the hook and would be towed back to his garage. I paid the man his money and got my car off his hook.

It was 4 a.m. and I was cold, tired, and seventy-five dollars poorer when I thought to myself, "*What the hell am I doing here (in New York and the cold)?* There must be some better place to live on the planet where it's warm." Even though I didn't know exactly where that place might be, I knew it had to exist. There just had to be a place where it was warm every day, where the people were friendly, and where I didn't have to manage dishwashers until 2 a.m. every morning. I decided right then and there that I was *done* with New York City and that I would find that warm place.

That place turned out to be South Florida. I was looking at the advertising posters on a travel agency window when I concluded that was the place to go. Now the challenge was how to get there, when to go, and what to do when I got there. These were important questions because I was planning on something much longer than a two-week vacation. I was going to relocate, and the car that was frozen to the ice that morning was not going to make the journey. I decided to buy that Suzuki GS 750 motorcycle I'd been drooling over even though I couldn't afford it. I called a friend who I knew had a motorcycle, worked on Long Island, and was tired of his job also. "What do you think about riding to Florida and maybe staying a while?"

"What's 'a while'?" he asked. "Are we talking about a couple of weeks down there?"

"No, I'm thinking longer than that," I said.

"Like a month or more?" he asked.

"Yeah, like longer than a few months for sure. For a while. Do you want to go or not?"

"I'm in." He finally agreed. A week later, I handed in my resignation. I was twenty-three years old, and my parents, who still considered me pretty young, weren't thrilled about my plan. In fact, I think they were scared to death by it. I'd never been very far from home in my entire life. But in the end, they made no effort to stop it. After selling or putting into storage everything I could not load onto my motorcycle, Greg and I saddled up and headed south on Route 95. Right here would be the proper place to relate all the details of that ride, but I honestly don't recall much about the four-day ride except:

- I would find a pay phone and call home every night, and my sister and little brother would place a pushpin on a map of the East Coast, charting my progress.

- We stayed in a motel one night that was located in such a sketchy area somewhere in North Carolina that we parked the bikes *inside* the ground-floor motel room.

- We had a run-in with a Georgia state trooper who pulled us over for speeding, but somehow only gave us a warning instead of a ticket (this was not the last time this happened to me).

- We rode through constant rain from the moment we
  crossed the Florida state line until we stopped in Fort
  Lauderdale at a little place called the Aviator Bar & Grill
  on Sunset Boulevard.

We pulled into a parking space in front of the Aviator to get a beer or two. But we stayed way longer than two beers. In fact, we stayed long enough to decide that we'd ride no farther. That night we rented an apartment a few blocks away, near the ocean, and we moved in.

I needed work, as I did not have more than a month's worth of money to live on. I knew all about the restaurant and nightclub businesses, and since South Florida was the mecca of such things as collegiate spring break and the "cocaine cowboys" night life, I wasn't too worried about finding work. Within a week I did find work as a bartender and daytime kitchen assistant to the assistant to the assistant head chef at a five-star restaurant on the Intracoastal Waterway. I was excited. . . . no more dishwashers and no more winter. I went to work and fell into my new lifestyle. I soon discovered that in Fort Lauderdale there was a party every night if you wanted that, or if it found you. I was tending bar at one of the nicest restaurants in Fort Lauderdale, too. It was a place to see people and to be seen. As a result, I got to know a lot of people, especially other bartenders from around town. They'd bring their dates in for a nice dinner, and I'd *take care* of them at the bar. So, when I went to their places of business, they'd reciprocate. It got to the point where I rarely paid for a drink anywhere. And this, ultimately, became a problem.

I said that I fell into my new life. I really did, feet first, and up to my neck. My new lifestyle was so much better than the life I'd led in New York. I was making and spending more money that I had ever gotten in New York. I would work most days in the kitchen, then shower, change, and tend bar four or five nights during the week, and then I'd go bar- and club-hopping— getting lots of free stuff. I was flying high. And on days when I wasn't tending bar, I'd go to the beach until sundown, come home, take a nap, dress, and then go to the clubs from 11 p.m. until 2 p.m. I lived this life for most of the next two years until one night . . . .

That night was a warm Florida night rather than the cold New York one of almost two years earlier. I was sitting at a table in a packed dance club, doing what I typically did. I was chatting up and dancing with a few women with my friend Greg. We'd all just returned to our table when a new song came over the sound system. The song was the B-52's "Rock Lobster." I will never forget it. I motioned to Greg that I'd be sitting the song out and that he should go back on the dance floor again, if he wanted. I was left alone at our table with one of the women we'd met there, and that's when I picked up my drink to take a sip. And that's when I had another one of my cosmic moments. I remember it today, as clearly as I recall the tow truck moment.

As I raised the drink and was about to take a sip, I looked straight through the glass and out the bottom of it like I was looking through a telescope. I was looking into my own little private abyss. I just stared through the glass and my Black Russian. I then lowered the drink and looked around the dance club and at the woman sitting next to me, and I said to myself, "*What the hell am I doing here?*" I recall not having a good answer, just a powerful feeling that what I was doing was not *the right thing for me*. The moment passed, and the woman I'd been chatting with was staring at me. "Are you okay?" she asked. "You kinda zoned out there. Do you still want to dance?" I was a bit disoriented by the telescope moment. I looked back at her, excused myself, and said something like, "I gotta go."

And I got up and left. That was the last time I was in that night club. I drove home and I went to bed.

When I woke up the next morning, I felt different. I felt like I needed to leave Florida. And then I did something I hadn't done since college. I went to the local library. I'm not sure why I decided to do that. I approached the librarian and I asked, "How do I get information that would help me apply to business schools. I'm thinking of getting an MBA degree." She indicated that I should follow her, and she pointed me to the reference section and the books I would need to gather information about graduate programs and their application processes.

Two months later, for the second time in two years, I sold whatever I could not load onto my motorcycle, and this time I rode back *north* on Route 95 to New York and my parents' home. I found work again in the city while I waited to hear from the schools. I was finally accepted into a graduate business program. But it wasn't the program I wanted to be in. I had returned to New York with the intention of going to school in New York. But that's not what happened. I ended up getting accepted and then going to a place I'd never really considered when I was growing up in New York. I ended up going "out west." A little over a year after that night, with the B-52's blasting in the background, I entered business school—at Southern Methodist University in Dallas, Texas.

It's strange how we recall some things in great detail and how we forget large swaths of our lives completely, like that major transition to a new life out west. Those days, too, are a blur to me, just like the ride to Florida had been. All I can remember about that year is that:

- I failed to get into my first-choice schools—NYU and Columbia—and this turned out to be a major blessing in disguise.

- I had to take the GMATs twice because my scores, combined with my GPA from college, were not good enough to gain entry almost anywhere . . . and I hate taking standardized tests.

- I was the best man in my brother's wedding in Rochester, New York, the very day before I was scheduled to start classes at SMU. As a result, right after leaving the wedding, I had to fly to Dallas where I arrived after midnight and found myself at the front door of the residence of the professor from whom I would be renting for the next year while he was on sabbatical. He was not happy to see me on his doorstep at 2 o'clock in the morning.

Those two moments, one in New York and the other in Florida, were like messages from the "cosmos," that ultimately changed the arc of my life. Those moments compelled me to make significant, and necessary, life course changes. Some voice outside or inside me was loud enough to be heard above the roar of my life and made me come up with an answer to that age-old question, *"What the hell am I doing here?"* It's funny how falling feels like flying—at least for a while, until you realize you are *falling* and not flying. We are all good at fooling ourselves, so much so that sometimes what we think looks like the light at the end of a tunnel is actually the headlight of a freight train coming at us. I'm lucky I listened and made the changes I needed to make. Maybe if more of us checked in with the cosmos, we'd discover we're headed in the wrong direction, and that we are actually falling when we think that we're flying. But who am I to say?

Final Note: Thirty years later, on the same stretch of road on Route 95 in Georgia, where I had been pulled over going to Florida on my motorcycle, I was stopped by a state trooper in my rental car for speeding. He was so tall that when he came to my driver side of the window, all I could see of him was his badge and belt buckle. "Do you know how fast you were going?" he asked. I told him I had a pretty good idea – it was over eighty-five miles per hour. Then he said, "I can provide you with my most recent calibration report that certifies the accuracy of my radar equipment." I assured him that would not be necessary, as I was certain that since he had pulled me over, he must be confident that it was pretty correct. He just smiled at me when I said that. He disappeared back into his patrol car to write me up. He returned a few minutes later and handed me a piece of paper. "This is a warning," he said. "I suggest you slow down because up ahead the local troopers in the next county won't be so lenient with you. You have a good night, sir." And there's proof that lightning can strike twice in the state of Georgia!

CHAPTER 6

It's Good to Be King

"When I sit, you sit. When I kneel, you kneel.
Et cetera, et cetera, et cetera!"
—The King of Siam in The King and I

The phrase "It's Good to Be King" comes from a few different sources:

- A Tom Petty song from his 1994 album *Wildflowers*

- A *Stargate SG-1* episode

- A 2004 book by Michael Badnarik

- A 1981 Mel Brooks film, *History of the World Part I*

I was thinking of Mel Brooks when I wrote this chapter. Regardless of the source, the phrase shares the same general conclusion.

And that is . . . that despite the obvious negative aspects of "being the king," it's on the whole a pretty good gig.

I am the oldest of six in my Irish Catholic family. There are five boys and one girl, and she is number five in the birth order. And as we like to say, we are the products of the traditional rhythm method of Roman Catholic birth control . . . an oxymoronic practice that actually seems to guarantee a steady and uninterrupted flow of kids, rather than the opposite.

In my case at least, birth order instilled in me a lifelong comfort with, and desire, to be in charge... of everything. To this day, I like being the boss and I like making decisions. Not that my decisions are always good ones but they are decisions nonetheless. In fact, the thing I missed most when I sold my business was that I was no longer in the middle of, and in charge of, everything. And I'm also a bit like the character in the movie *Night Shift* where Michael Keaton's character tells Henry Winkler's in their first scene together, "I'm an idea man, Chuck. I get ideas all day long... I can't control them." It's true. I *am* an idea guy. I tend to see the bigger picture first, before I get into the details and parse the data. I've never been a purely analytical decision maker, though these days I do look at the data. But I still am primarily an intuitive decision maker. That is good evolution for all those involved working with me, because intuitiveness is far better than the impulsive decision maker I once was. If you are going to succeed at being the boss, you have to be ready and comfortable making decisions.

Being first in the birth order is a both a blessing and a curse. I think most firstborns in larger families would agree with this. It's a blessing because you never wear hand-me-downs, you get the best seat at the dinner table, and there are more pictures of you in family photo albums than of anyone else. The photo album collection in our home was no exception. Whenever we'd break out the slide projector, usually after a holiday dinner (this was a kind of family tradition with us), there would be lots of pictures of me. And after showing about fifty slides—and this never failed to happen—someone would ask:

"Hey, where are the pictures of Tim and Jeremy?" Tim and Jeremy are my two youngest brothers. While there were lots of pictures of me, like pictures of my first nap, pictures of my second bottle, my third step, and so on, only occasionally would a photo of one of the younger kids grace the screen. And when that happened, someone would say.

"Hey, there's one of Tim. . . . When was that, Mom?"

My mother would shrug and say something like, "I'm not sure. Maybe he was six or seven and we were at your uncle's wedding or something."

"You don't remember, Mom? You only have two pictures of him, and you don't remember when you took them?" Every slide show followed the same script. It was a great family tradition filled with both gentle and not-so-gentle teasing like that.

For example, someone would opine that the lack of any pictures of the youngest kids suggested that it could not be proven beyond a reasonable doubt that they were actually members of the family. In fact, the lack of photos appeared downright suspicious—like some truth was being hidden from us by our parents. After considering all that, we'd take another sip of wine, and move on to other possibilities that explained the lack of photos, such as:

"Maybe they were adopted from some other out-of-control, rhythm-practicing Catholic family, who had abandoned them, and we, being good Catholics, had taken them in and given them a home. That would explain the lack of pictures, right?" It was like we worked for the *National Enquirer* where *inquiring minds wanted to know.* You had to have thick skin to survive in my family.

There are, however, the downsides of being the firstborn. You see, when the firstborn arrives, the parents are new to the parenting game. They, in fact, have zero credentials and experience, and essentially have to develop those skills by practicing on the firstborn. They are, in essence, working out their parenting "bugs" (like micromanagement) on the oldest. In software terms, the firstborn experiences the beta version of the parents. The youngest gets the final version with all the upgrades and fixes. As a result, the oldest hears "no" a lot, the youngest hears something more like "sure . . . whatever."

Then, at some tipping point, usually driven by the sheer number of kids who require some form of management, parents—out of necessity and fatigue—enlist the firstborn as a middle manager—to help them manage the menagerie. And as anyone who's worked in middle management knows, middle management is the worst job in a company . . . it's all responsibility without the authority.

If I was expected to be a middle manager, with lots of responsibility and little authority, I intuitively felt that fair compensation was required in exchange. Let me explain what I mean. We had a Sunday tradition when we were growing up. We'd go to the bakery after Mass. We'd order the same thing: two dozen baked rolls and eight crumb-buns. If you're unfamiliar with a crumb bun, it's a pastry with a yellow cake base, which is covered by a thick layer of white sugarcoated crumbs on top. The crumbs alone are so delicious, I've often wondered why bakers even bother making the yellow cake, and instead simply sell boxes of the crumb topping. The bakery we visited every Sunday made real crumb buns, not those commercial-grade supermarket ones you have to settle for everywhere outside New York City. These crumb buns were *made that day* New York crumb buns. I've lived all over America and traveled the world, and I've never found crumb buns that compare with the ones from that bakery. I've asked the question, why that is, and I've been told . . . *it's the water*. Whatever that means.

I'd always accompany my Dad inside the bakery as his helper. This was critical because not only did I get to place the order and get a free cookie from one of the nice old ladies behind the counter who thought I was cute and well-behaved (I was), I got to control the box of crumb buns on the ride back home. That was my job. It always was. I controlled the box. It's not that I wanted the work. I considered it fair compensation for performing my middle-management duties.

On the drive home, I held the box firmly, making sure that none of my brothers would get at it and open it and strip the crumb-bun tops clean of the crumbs. The crumb topping is so delicious, that the temptation to do just that was overwhelming for them. You see, the crumbly white-sugar topping is easily detached from the yellow cake. And detaching the crumbs from the cake is easily accomplished simply by shaking the box. Everyone knew this. So, on the ride home, I would shake the box, gently loosening the crumbs, knowing that when we got home, I would be the one to open the box and place the crumb buns on the table before we said grace. And I would get to harvest and enjoy all those loose crumbs in the box. My brothers weren't happy about this. And the ride home usually sounded something like this:

"Dad, Kevin's shaking the box again."

"Kevin, stop shaking the box."

"Dad, he's still doing it."

"Kevin, stop doing it."

"He's still doing it, Dad."

"Hey, stop. Don't make me come back there."

My Dad said that a lot, but over the all the years of vacations in the Oldsmobile Vista Cruiser dragging a Cox pop-up camper around, and all those trips to the bakery, he never once *came back there.*

So, when we got home, I took charge of the box, and invoked my *kingly privilege* and rights to the crumbs. I considered those crumbs justifiable combat pay for all the crummy duties and responsibilities without authority I was expected to carry out because I was the oldest.

You think it's easy being a king, but that is far from the truth. There are rules to the king game, and principles necessary for the king to rule wisely and create minimal conflict with his subjects. Machiavelli outlined these rules in his book *The Prince*, written in the sixteenth century. He wrote that to be an effective king, the king had to rule with a firm hand. If the king did not rule with a firm hand, his subjects might rise up, rebel, and quarrel among themselves, causing him no end of grief. So, Machiavelli codified these rules into four kingly principles:

1. It's better to be feared than to be loved.

2. Your position (first in birth order) is important, but you must also be ready to act (and not just rely on the power of myth that your position provides).

3. Your subjects don't like hearing the truth (in this case, that the crumbs were mine and not theirs).

4. The loyalty of subjects must be constantly scrutinized and any resistance firmly addressed.

I hope you know that I'm being tongue-in-cheek here, by citing Machiavelli. I didn't actually know about Machiavelli when I was managing the crumb buns all those years ago. I only read

Machiavelli in high school, years after the events I document here. But I somehow knew the rules even then—intuitively. After all, I was born into the position—firstborn. Listen, being the boss or king of anything can be a tough-love business. And so it's not for everyone. In fact, my brother, Michael, never bought into the idea that I was in charge. We fought . . . constantly and about everything. It was an obvious struggle for power, and I had to invoke Machiavelli's Fourth Principle with him— a lot. Today, of course, we are friends. I trust him with my money and everything else, as he's been my financial guy for over three decades. But back then he was just a rebel, and a firm hand was required. And any failure on my part to put down his rebellion would have led to open revolt throughout the ranks, and it would have put my Sunday crumb-bun monopoly at risk.

Of course, kings cannot be tyrants. They won't last long if they act that way. A good king must understand what life is like as a subject. He must understand what it's like to be a follower, not just a leader. I my case, I understood this because I was a follower, too. My parents reminded me that they were the boss of me, and expected much from me within the family. I had to know the rules and obey not only my parents but a long list of teachers, nuns, and priests. I learned to follow the rules, which I hope has helped me later in life laying them down when I became a boss. I suppose I succeeded at being a good follower as my parents gave me greater latitude and fewer responsibilities as the years went by in regards to my younger siblings.

So much so, that when the sixth and last child arrived, my mother felt confident enough that I could be trusted to pick up the management slack and help take care of him, providing my mother some much-needed rest. In fact, my mother admitted, years later, that she would wait for me to come home from school, hoping my team practice would be short, and hand number six off to me, saying, "Here, you take him for a while." And, of course, I did.

To be a good king, or boss, or parent, it helps to know how to be a good follower. It helps to know what it's like *not* to be the king. Machiavelli was very clear about this when he wrote, *woe be unto the king who rules unfairly, for his will be a short and painful reign.* A good king is a fair king. But it is essential that the king *wants* to be the king and to *bear* the responsibilities that go with the benefits and compensations. Maybe that's why, to this day, I like being in charge. I guess I was born into it, and hopefully as I've learned to follow, I've acted wisely as the king. That's why, despite the downsides of kingship, I have to agree with Mel Brooks: *It's good to be king.* I can't imagine any other way of living.

CHAPTER 7

Helen's Boys

"Remember who you are."
—*Mufasa in* The Lion King

It's easy to "get lost" in life, unleashed from your moorings, and drift aimlessly about. I was like that for a time, and I share those details later on in the book. But it took a trip to Ireland to help me understand exactly what my moorings were, and that knowledge has helped ground me. This is how it happened, but let me start from the beginning with my mother. My mother's name is Helen. She was the second of five children born to Irish immigrants in New York City in the late 1920s. Her mother was an au pair for the Colgate family (think "toothpaste"), and her father was on the New York Police Department and for a time walked a patrol beat in Harlem. He was known as "Red" to the people in the neighborhood. My mother remembers this well, as when she walked with him on his beat in the 1930s, people would greet him like that on the street. He got the NYPD job in the typical way people coming over from Ireland did in those days. He graduated from kitchen and construction jobs to the pinnacle in employment for immigrants at that time: a job in the police or fire department of New York City.

My mother's father and mother met and married in America. My mother attended Catholic schools. Upon graduating, she wanted to go to college, but instead, as was customary then, she married Roger, my father, and started a family. They had six children together and remained married until my father passed away suddenly in 1997. They were married for forty-four years. I am the oldest child of first-generation Irish immigrants. Many of these immigrants to America left their small farming villages for something better here, and most found it. Ancestry.com results confirm that I am 99.5 percent Irish. I'm from those same counties in Ireland where my maternal grandparents were born, places where farming was a primary occupation. My father's background has many similarities, but it's my mother's roots that are at the center of this story.

No one in the family tree bears the name Kevin. Why they chose "Kevin" for me, the firstborn, I do not know. But I *do* know that Saint Kevin was an important Catholic bishop from a time in Ireland that preceded even St. Patrick's. Perhaps that played some role in the name they selected for me. I like the name very much. I am a product of Catholic schools also. And for some reason I cannot completely explain, I have always been an early riser. I can go to bed at 3 a.m. and still be awake by 7 a.m. These days, I'm usually up by 5:30 a.m. I'm like a farmer—as soon as the sun hits the horizon, I'm moving. I've always preferred mornings to nights. I like how the start of a new day feels. My earliest memories of my early mornings revolve around our black-and-white Zenith TV set. I can still picture exactly where that TV sat in our downstairs playroom.

I even remember watching the entire weekend of coverage of JFK's assassination and burial on its ghostly black-and-white screen.

The TV set was great for me because I was often up at 5 a.m., sitting in the playroom alone with nothing to do. The Zenith provided something to do. I'd awake, get out of bed with my little green blanket, and go downstairs and turn on the Zenith while everyone else slept. I'd turn it on and off, fascinated by that little white dot in the center of the screen that would light up first, then slowly expand into a picture that would come into focus. I did this because, before 5:30 a.m., there was no programming at all at that time in the morning.

It's difficult for younger people to envision the lack of TV programming options in the late 1950s and early 1960s. There was no 24/7 around-the-clock programming, nor were there many shows from which to choose. We had six channels available in New York: CBS, NBC, ABC, WPIX, WOR, and WNEW. In other words, when I turned on the TV before 5:30 a.m. all I saw was the "white snow" screen . . . and that dot. There was nothing to watch. I'd wait, though, until the picture of a waving American flag appeared, accompanied by the playing of the national anthem. This signaled the start of the programming day. The last shows on at night aired sometime after midnight, at which time the white-snow screen reappeared. I wasn't awake then, so I don't know for certain.

The first program to air on Saturday morning was called *The Modern Farmer*. It was on WNEW (the then government-supported educational channel), I think. Each episode explored some aspect of modern industrialized farming. I'd tune in to watch tractors and harvesters move about fields, sowing and reaping. I watched farmers take soil samples and calculate crop yields and fertilizer application rates. I was enthralled by all of it, and of course, as there were not any other programming choices at that hour, I watched it. I've never dreamed of being a farmer but when I watched that show, I felt like I "knew" something about farming even though we lived in New York and the closest farm was far away. In fact, I think I saw my first farm animals at six or seven years old on a family vacation. I walked up to pet one of the goats, and it spat at me. Since that time, I'm wary of goats and keep my distance. They have weird personalities.

Growing up Irish American, I'd heard stories of Ireland, and decided at some point that if the opportunity arose, I would travel there. I wanted to visit counties Kerry and Leitrim, the places my grandparents were from. And in 1988, I finally made the trip. I went with my younger brother, Tim. We planned to drive around Ireland for two weeks, visit the ancestral grounds, and drink some Guinness. Ireland is a different culture, obviously, but because of my upbringing it wasn't entirely foreign to me. The Irish can be dryly sarcastic and droll, but direct when they want to be. And we got a taste of that at the airport rental-car counter upon arrival, when the agent inquired about our itinerary:

"Where might you be going?" he wanted to know.

"We're going to Leitrim first," we said.

He looked at us. "Leitrim? Why would you go to that godforsaken place?"

We were off to a good start. We had a car, and we had directions. We were traveling in pre-GPS days. And if that wasn't challenging enough, the roads in Ireland in those days were notoriously poor and largely unmarked by signs. That meant the going was slow, and when we got lost, as we often did, we had to rely on verbal directions or outdated maps. We were headed to the Rooney farm, in Leitrim, where my mother's father had been born. The farm was still in the family, owned and managed by his spinster sisters. It was located in the Iron Hills near the small village of Kiltyclogher, which itself was part of a larger old English castle estate called Manor Hamilton.

Kiltyclogher is located hard against the border of British Northern Ireland. It's the birthplace of Seán Mac Diarmada, one of the seven signatories to the 1916 Proclamation of the Irish Republic and leader of the Easter Rising for which he was later executed by the British. His statue stands in the village center near—what was once—a barricaded bridge that crossed over a small river into Northern Ireland. When we arrived in 1988, it was during the time of "the Troubles," and the bridge was closed and painted over with anti-British IRA slogans.

So, it was no surprise that when we rolled into the town, the local people we met at a small coffee shop were suspicious about the two outsiders inquiring about the Rooney farm and the spinster sisters. They asked questions about who we were. We told them we were from America and wanted to pay our respects and such. A few calls were placed, and within a few minutes we were provided directions to the Rooney farm. We were told that we had to see "Gallagher" first, however. He lived on the farm located just below the Rooney farm and he was unofficially the guy in town who had the job of "looking out for" the Rooney sisters.

When we pulled up to his home, Gallagher was waiting for us. He welcomed us and led us into his small home. He set out a few glasses on a table and offered us a drink. We accepted and he pulled out his best brandy. He poured us each a full ten-ounce glass of brandy, even though it was ten in the morning. I looked over at my brother. He was already halfway through his glass and I thought, Okay . . . *when in Rome. . . .*

Gallagher pointed to some pictures on his bookshelf. There on the shelf were photos of many of my cousins who'd already made the trip. We drank the brandy. Not knowing what we know now, we did not consider the brandy might have been Gallagher's way of preparing us for the trip up to the Rooney family farm. We should have been alerted, however, as he kept referring to the farm by saying things like, "It's not what you might be expecting." But we remained blissfully unaware. As we drank, he brought us up to date on the *farm situation* as he called it. There were my two grandaunts, still living on the property. These were my grandfather's sisters. One of the sisters, Josie, had just recently been admitted to the local hospital. She was not doing well. In fact, she passed a few months later. Only Agnes, the younger of the two sisters, was still living on the farm.

The Rooney farm had been passed down through the family for generations. It was a small dairy farm at the top of a hill. In that part of Ireland there's little arable land. Cows and their milk are about the only source of income. It's a hard place to make a living. That was likely the reason my grandfather purchased a one-way ticket to America in 1920, and had only returned to the farm once a few years before his death.

I asked Gallagher whether we should give Agnes a call so as not to surprise her. There's no phone service up there, he told us. This should have been another clue about the farm and Agnes. We then loaded into Gallagher's little car and drove up the hill to the farm. My brother and I were excited to meet our Irish relative and spend a little time with her. We drove up a rutted road for about fifteen minutes until we came to an open metal gate, swinging in the breeze at the bottom of a cow pie–covered grass driveway. To describe what we saw as *resembling* a scene from the Third World doesn't really begin to paint a true picture. It *was* the Third World. It looked like poverty. Not the garbage-strewn-street poverty of Caracas or someplace like that (I've been there), but the *"lack of any modern convenience"* kind of poverty. There was a low-slung white stone farmhouse with a thatched roof with open windows and doors.

There was no running water or electricity. The day was hot, and cows wandered lazily in and out of the farmhouse, seeking shade.

We were not expecting this. We looked at Gallagher, and he returned a look that said, "I told you this might not be what you expected!" He'd been trying to tell us what we now could plainly see . . . that the farm had been falling apart for years and that the sisters—now Agnes alone—could no longer manage it. The reason for this, as we learned, was that she was stubborn and refused to leave her home. In truth, the only reason she was able to remain in her home was because Gallagher made it possible. He checked on her and kept her stocked with supplies.

It was evident that this wasn't going to be one of those sit-in-the-living-room-and-look-at-pictures-and-chat visits to reminisce about our grandfather, her brother. We waited there at the driveway gate with Gallagher. Agnes was nowhere in sight. Gallagher called out to her. We waited a few minutes before she appeared. She was eighty-six years old. She came walking down the dirt driveway toward us. She was tiny—maybe four feet ten inches tall—and dressed like any homeless person you'd see on the streets of New York. She possessed that layer of dirt and grit that colors the skin when you haven't bathed for a long while. Her hair was gray-blond, loose and matted. She wore some kind of sandals whose soles looked like they'd been made from actual car tire treads. Her skirt appeared to be an old bathroom throw rug. It was cinched around her waist by some kind of hemp rope. She wore a T-shirt and a dirty blue sweater over that. She was lean. She was as hard as steel, and her hands were gnarled from age and years of farm work. She had piercing blue eyes that contrasted with her dirty brown skin.

It was her eyes that held you, though. They were clear and sharp. They bored into you. I remember thinking to myself, "What the heck is going on here?" Gallagher *had* warned us. But nothing he could have said would have prepared us for what we were actually experiencing. It was so unexpected. But there she was, my grandfather's sister. I looked over at my brother—a few feet away—to see what was going through his head. He was as speechless as I was. I didn't know what to say or do at that moment. But Gallagher took charge and said simply, "Hi, Agnes, you have some visitors from America. These are Maurice's grandkids."

Maurice was my grandfather's given name, but everyone called him Morris. Agnes looked at my brother and me, saying nothing for what seemed like an eternity. I was thinking that this woman is not even aware of what is happening, and she is certainly not all there. I think Gallagher was getting ready to leave when Agnes finally looked over at me and said, "You're Helen's boys, aren't you? You look like her. You know Helen was always Maurice's favorite. He loved her the most."

The story my mother and her sisters told us cousins, over the years, was that my grandmother was tough on my mother. She doted on her firstborn, my godmother and aunt, Kathleen. Because of that, Helen became my grandfather's favorite. So much so, that he would take her away from home for the day, and ride the subway from Queens to the Harlem neighborhood where he walked his beat.

I could hardly believe what I'd heard. I wanted to say something, but before I could say a word, Agnes just turned and walked away back up the grass and cow pie–covered driveway to her home, as if there was work to be done, and time was being wasted. And that was it, the end of our visit. We lingered for a few minutes more, taking in the beautiful scenery before we drove back down the hill. We'd come all the way to Ireland to see our glorious past, and we'd met Agnes living out her Third World life on a farm that a few years later was left to Gallagher when she passed away.

We didn't find what we expected to find in Ireland. Instead, we found something much better and maybe even more important. We discovered that underneath the First World Americans we'd become in just one generation, we were the grandsons of tough, stubborn, and gritty salt-of-the- earth farmers like Agnes. The phrase *salt of the earth* has its origins in ancient times when salt was a valuable commodity. Salt was so valuable, it was often used as currency. And the phrase *salt of the earth* comes from the Sermon on the Mount, where Jesus said, "You are the salt of the earth" (Matthew 5:13). He was trying to communicate to his followers that the common people— the fishermen, shepherds, laborers, and farmers—were as worthy and as virtuous as any of the wealthy and privileged.

Mufasa in *The Lion King* had it right when he told his wastrel son, "Remember who you are. You are my son and the one true king." Because of those few moments with Agnes, I got a look into who I was and where I had come from. I am the son, of the sons and daughters, of more sons and daughters of gritty, tough, salt-of-the-earth farmers. I take a quiet pride in knowing this. It grounds me. And now it makes sense to me why I loved watching *The Modern Farmer* on Saturday mornings. Somewhere, deep in my DNA, I *knew* something about farming, I knew what I was watching because I had come from those people and places. That short visit with Agnes reminded me of my roots, and who I am. . . . she gave me my humble moorings. If I could make a wish and add it to this story, it would be that I'd be able to introduce Agnes to my mother, Helen, my grandfather's favorite. I think the two would recognize each other instantly, peas in a pod, and two apples from the same tree . . . proud, hardworking, and gritty salt-of-the-earth people. It's so important to know where you come from, so you never forget who you are.

Final Note: Here are some facts about Kiltyclogher:

Location—GPS coordinates: 54.3562° N, 8.0369° W; Elevation: 249 ft.

Kiltyclogher means "stony woods" (*Coillte Clochair* in Celtic). The Internet says it is a small village in North Leitrim close to the Fermanagh border and the hamlet of Cashelnadrea. Seán Mac Diarmada's family home is there and open to visitors just off the Manor Hamilton road. You can sign up for a tour at the Heritage Centre in the village. You might also want to attend the annual Kiltyclogher Traditional Music and Set Dancing Weekend that takes place in mid-August, where you can enjoy concerts, classes, and a door-dancing competition.

CHAPTER 8

Friends Forever

*"For everything you've missed, you've
gained something else, and for everything
you gain, you lose something else."*
—Ralph Waldo Emerson

I've worked with enough people in business over the years to reach the conclusion that some people never really "graduated" from high school. What I mean, and without making any judgments, is that some people still act like teenagers when they should be living adult lives. Their need for drama and gamesmanship makes me feel like I'm right back in high school again. Don't believe me? Just log on to a phone app called "Next Door" and see what passes for dialog amongst so called adults. And none of this is good, because when I was in high school, I couldn't wait for it to be over. And when I think back on some of those days, the posing, the worry, and drama high school created for everyone, I wonder why anyone would ever want to keep on living that way. When I graduated, I put high school and all that in my rearview mirror for good.

Don't get me wrong. I didn't hate the school or the people in it. I wasn't bullied or an outcast. I knew lots of good people in high school. But I avoided the cliques and tended to go my own way, as I found those kids tedious, even back then. So, on graduation day, at a ceremony held under gray skies for one thousand of my senior classmates, I silently swore that I'd never return to that place. It's a vow I've kept, with the single exception of my twentieth class reunion, when, two decades after graduation, I flew back to New York from California to attend the get-together.

So, for the first time in twenty years, I drove back onto my high school campus. The place seemed so much smaller than I remembered. I think we all have this experience with the past at some time in our lives when we revisit a place we haven't seen for years that was central in our lives. We're surprised at how small it looks in comparison to the way it was when we were there. For example, take the time I returned to my childhood home in Farmingdale thirty years after we had moved away. The place looked so tiny that I had a hard time believing seven people actually lived in that house at one time. And again I had the same experience when I moved to Dallas for graduate school and traveled to Dealey Plaza where JFK was assassinated. I was surprised by how small the place actually was. The distances appeared so much greater on TV. I could see that those fateful shots didn't have to travel very far to their target.

In many ways high school today is very different from what it was in 1973. My classmates and I didn't have smartphones, social media, or the Internet. We used pay phones to call friends or the rotary home phone that was patrolled by our parents. Without texting and social media, we congregated in hallways and hung out in the quad. We went to the library to do research, using a card catalog to locate the books we needed in the stacks. When we found what we needed, we made notes as we had no access to copy machines. And we were lucky if we had a friend with a typewriter; otherwise, we wrote our papers by hand. In spite of all these obvious differences, not much has really changed in the way high school works. There are still jocks, brains, mean girls, popular guys, criminals, greasers, nerds, and stoners. And there are still the loners and outsiders who don't fit into any of these categories and simply refuse to join any clique.

Returning for my reunion brought back many of these memories. So much so, that from the safe remove of twenty years, I was looking forward to going there and seeing how my classmates were doing in the world. I was hoping to see some of my friends from those days. Friends whom I hadn't seen in two decades, as I hadn't been in touch with anyone from the class in at least fifteen years. I didn't know what to expect, but I assumed some classmates would be the same . . . and I was not disappointed in that. But I hoped some would be different . . . and I was not disappointed in that, either. When I arrived and surveyed the room, it appeared that at least several hundred had decided to come to the party.

When I first entered, a tall beautiful woman walked up to me and introduced herself. I read her name tag, but I wasn't able to connect the name to her face. Who was she? I was scrambling for a memory, but it was evident she knew who I was.

She saw the look on my face, I guess, and she said, "We were in homeroom together with Mr. Clarke. Remember? I sat a few seats in front of you for two years."

I tried to picture the homeroom seating chart in my mind's eye and . . . then it clicked. Helen! But this woman in front of me could not possibly be that girl! That girl, twenty years ago, was a nerdy, gangly, brainy kid who wasn't in any of the popular cliques.

This woman was stunning, confident, and, yeah . . . gorgeous. The last twenty years had been good to her. We chatted for a while. She was funny and charming. She had stayed in New York. She worked in Manhattan for a publishing company. She'd been married and divorced. We were having a good time talking as we scanned the room, pointing out different classmates. She had stayed in touch with several of our classmates and was able to tell me about many of them. Finally, she pointed to a tall woman at a table.

"Do you remember her?" she asked.

There was something about the woman I recognized, but I could not come up with a name. "No, who's that?"

"You don't remember?' she said, smiling.

"I can't place the face," I said.

That's Kelly, the girl you had a crush on during senior year."

"How did you know I had a crush on her?"

"Everyone knew, Kevin."

Kelly looked very different but not in the way Helen did. The once-willowy redhead had become heavier and, well, less willowy. All around the room, swans seemed to have become ducks and ducks had become swans. Helen continued to point out people until she landed on another tall women.

"Oh, there's Judy."

I immediately recognized Judy. She, too, looked different, but I knew her in an instant, despite the fact that we hadn't seen each other in twenty years. She saw me at about the same moment and she smiled, too.

"Will you excuse me for a moment, Helen? I'm going to say hello to Judy. It's been nice to see you again." I meant it. And I walked across the room to Judy.

I don't recall today what was said or who said it first, but I do know that we spent the next few hours catching up and laughing like the old days. During my senior year, Judy and I were best friends. We were never boyfriend-girlfriend friends. We'd just sit together in the cafeteria every day and talk. And we sat together at almost every basketball game. We would spend the entire time making wisecracks about everyone and everything around us. We talked. It felt like we had picked up the same conversation that we'd left off in midsentence twenty years earlier. We were right back in high school in 1973. We were the same people to each other. Time disappeared, and it was 1 a.m. before we realized it. We parted with promises to "keep in touch."

Today, almost thirty years have passed since that evening. I've not spoken to Judy since. That is a real tragedy, in a way. In another way, maybe it is as it should be. She has her life and I have mine. We graduated from our old lives long ago and left high school and all its dramas and relationships behind. Still, I regret not keeping in touch. I guess it's true: *for everything we gain, we lose something else.* Sad. Yet I feel certain that if she and I were to meet yet again, we'd pick up the conversation again right from where we left off that night . . . friends forever from high school.

That evening made me reflect on another friend, from another time. After high school I went right off to college. I was the same person entering college as I had been in high school. I avoided drama and gamesmanship by running in my own small circle. That was until I met Lorraine in my junior year. She was a senior, one year from graduation. I was a shy junior. She just sort of showed up in my life one day—just like Judy had in high school. I do not even recall the circumstances of our first meeting.

At the time, Lorraine was like the mayor of the dormitory. She was the Managerial Assistant to whom all the Residential Assistants reported. She knew everyone and everything that went on. She was large and in charge. She could talk. She was funny and generous.

And for some reason, she fixed her eye on me and ended up re-
cruiting me as an RA. We became the closest of friends. We talked
every day—just like Judy and I had. The difference, however, is that
Lorraine and I remained in touch over the years. In fact, she was
the "best man" at my second wedding. Although we were never
boyfriend-girlfriend, we did everything together that year. She took
me under her wing at a time when I needed more confidence. As a result, I did grow in confidence that year—and those lessons "taught"
by Lorraine have lasted me a lifetime. I could tell you about the
conversations or things we did together but that would digress from
the point of the chapter . . . and that is that some friends are forever
even when you see them infrequently or not at all.

"Losing" her was one of the saddest days of my life. I watched
her senior class graduate, as I sat with her family, who had traveled to New York to bring her back home to Washington DC. The
ceremony finally ended and we had to say good-bye. I remember
feeling the loneliest I have ever felt, watching her drive off with her
family on that sunny day in May as she left Stony Brook for good.
That next autumn, my senior year, I subconsciously looked for her
everywhere half expecting that she would appear through a door or
from around a corner, and we'd pick up exactly where we'd left off.
Of course, that never happened. My senior year wasn't the same
without her, and by graduation day, I was as ready to leave college
as I had been ready to leave high school. And at my graduation ceremony, I made the same vow I had made four years earlier at that
other graduation. I vowed that I'd never come back.

Three decades went by before I returned to my college campus
for a homecoming game and football team reunion. That experience
was as good as my twentieth high-school reunion experience had
been. It was nice to see all those people again. But this time I knew
that we'd never keep in touch. We had all moved on with our lives.

There may be an analogy here to house cleaning. Every year, I engage in a thorough house cleaning. I usually start in the garage, the place where things accumulate . . . all those things I've kept, thinking I might need them someday. I sort through them all, and make a decision: sell it, donate it, or keep it. I guess I am the antithesis of a hoarder. I don't accumulate things and let them clutter my garage. I do the same in my personal life, I clean out the old and make space for the new. I've known more people—who have come and gone in my life—than I can properly recall these days. It's a bit sad, but I suppose that holding on to too much of the past, creates too much clutter, and can weigh one down and leave little room for the new. This makes it harder to move lightly and easily into the future. I guess it's true, as Mr. Emerson said, that in order to move forward in life, we have to lose some things to gain some things. Yet I never throw out *all* of the old stuff when I clean out the garage. I keep a few things to remind me of what once was. And you never know, you *may* need some of those things! I think this helps me connect the past with the present and the future—and ensure a level of permanence in a world full of change. Like Judy and Lorraine, some things are permanent . . . friends forever, no matter what.

in New York. This was New York, the place where I was born and raised. These were the very buildings in which I attended meetings when I worked in Manhattan. What the hell was happening?

While the magnitude of what was going on was overwhelming, there were also practical matters to consider at that moment. And every road warrior like me knew what those were. We knew that we were not going anywhere soon. We all made for the exits to catch a cab and get to any hotel ahead of the crowd that might not yet have realized that we were all going to be in Omaha for at least a little while. By the time I made it to a hotel downtown, with a few other guys in a cab, we knew the airspace had been shut down. Every flight was cancelled at least for that day. By the afternoon of that day, there were no rooms to be had anywhere in the city, just as we road warriors had anticipated. Everything was booked up. In some rooms, hotels were even doubling up people who knew each other, just to make space.

I've stayed in hotel rooms, as best I can count, for more than eight thousand nights over the years. And since I'm outgoing, I've met many interesting people while at these hotels. That's mainly because I'm not a fan of room service. For me, solo in-room dining is one of life's lonelier experiences. I made it a practice to dine at the lobby bar, as I never could get accustomed to sitting alone at a table in a dining room. There was always more action at the bar. I'd grab a seat, and I'd strike up conversations with other road warriors like myself. And we'd shoot the breeze while we all watched a hockey game or something. It was fun.

This camaraderie among road warriors was never better than in those days right after 9/11. We were all together, sharing the same national tragedy in Omaha. We grieved for the poor people who had died, and we shared the same anger at those who had destroyed their lives. There was a powerful feeling that we were all in

CHAPTER 9

No Place Like Home

"There's no place like home."
—Dorothy in The Wizard of Oz

I think all of us of a certain age remember where we were when JFK was shot in 1963. I was in fourth grade class with Miss Puff (really that was her name), when the announcement came over the PA and we were sent home to our parents. Likewise many of us recall exactly where we were when those planes slammed into the towers in downtown New York on September 11, 2001. At least I do. On that September day, I was in line with a crowd of passengers, preparing to board a plane, when someone on the concourse said something about a breaking news story playing on the airport TV monitors. On September 11, 2001, I was in Omaha, Nebraska, waiting to board a flight home to California. A few hundred of us watched TV as the second plane slammed into the South Tower "this thing together" as Americans. In fact, that feeling of camaraderie is my most enduring memory of those terrible days, and it stands in stark contrast to the fearmongering and finger-pointing associated with the COVID pandemic.

I spent part of that first day, Tuesday, in the hotel lobby bar. The place was packed from early in the afternoon until it closed later than usual that night, simply because people didn't want to go back to their rooms. We were glued to the TV as the day's events played out. None of us really wanted to be alone, I guess. We were amped up, and missing home. So it didn't take long before everyone was scheming on how to get home since the airspace was going to be shut down, at least for a few days. In fact, the only thing we saw in the air on that first day was Air Force One landing and taking off from the Strategic Air Command base in Omaha. All else was clear blue and silent.

Necessity, as they say, is the mother of invention. And if nothing else, Americans are endlessly creative and innovative. We are quick to respond to adversity. Breakfast on Wednesday morning was crowded with people discussing and organizing trips home. Those of us who lived far away on the coasts decided to sit out another day in hopes that the airspace would reopen so we could get a flight home. But those who lived within an eight-hour drive were busy making arrangements. They were so busy that by the end of the day on Wednesday, every rental car in Omaha and the surrounding area was taken. I was going nowhere. And since I was staying put, I decided to take a walk and explore the downtown area. With all due respect to Omaha—and it's a fine town—I was finished with my walking tour by lunchtime. It's not that Omaha isn't interesting; it's just that it's not that big. I spent the rest of the day catching up on work before heading back down to the bar for more of what we'd done the night before. But I was itching to get home, like everyone else. I called the airlines several times, but it was the same story every time: there were no flights scheduled that day or the next day, Thursday.

With that news circulating through the bar, the people who lived within a sixteen-hour drive of Omaha began to get busy. Since there were no more rentals available, they were now purchasing used cars, driving them home in a group, and then selling the car when they arrived at their destination. I heard that this actually happened more than a few times. I thought the idea was brilliant. And it demonstrates how much people want to get home. Then I had an idea. And just so you know, I don't have all my best ideas or make all my decisions while talking to strangers in a bar, but I was chatting with a few people when I floated my idea. I suggested that if there were no flights scheduled for California the next day, Friday, I'd go to a local motorcycle dealership, buy a motorcycle, and ride it home. The weather was still warm. And the route home went through some beautiful parts of the west that I'd never seen before. I'd ship my luggage home, buy a helmet, boots, and jacket at the dealership and make the cross-country ride. My friends thought it was a great idea. I called my wife and explained the plan. I could hear her rolling her eyes. I actually heard them roll. But then she said that staying in Omaha didn't make any sense, either. It was all set. I returned to the bar— spousal authorization in hand — and shared the news.

Before I turned in for the night, I made one final call to the airline. I managed to get through after a fifteen-minute wait to a tired-sounding agent. "What's going on with the flights to the coast?" I asked her. She said that the airspace was slowly being reopened, but that flights were scarce.

"Anything heading to Los Angeles from Omaha?" I wondered.

She typed on her keyboard and about a minute later she came back on the line and said, "It looks like there is a flight scheduled for tomorrow to Los Angeles."

"Seriously?" I asked her.

"There's a flight scheduled to depart at 6:30 a.m."

"Can you book me on it?"

And that's what she did. "I'd get to the airport early," she advised me. "Everything is still in a fluid state, and if that flight doesn't go, something else might. Just be prepared for that."

I called my wife and told her the news and the potential arrival time. I packed and went to bed, setting the alarm for 4:30 a.m.

I arrived at the airport at 5:15 a.m. on Friday morning. When I tell you there was nobody at the airport, I mean not one soul! There were no police, security, janitors, or gate agents anywhere. If there had been tumbleweed in Omaha, it would have been rolling through the concourses and ticketing areas. It was eerie but really exciting. I might be going home! I lined up alone in front of the airline ticketing desk . . . and waited. If this didn't work out, I thought, I still had the motorcycle plan to fall back on. But one way or another, I was starting my trip home *that* day.

I waited alone for about twenty minutes before other passengers began arriving and lining up behind me. Their arrival seemed like a good omen to me. Maybe there'd be a flight home after all! We were all waiting for a ticketing agent to appear. And by 6:30 a.m., when no gate agent had appeared yet, we were all getting a little worried. While we were waiting, I'd been observing some activity at another ticketing counter at the other end of the concourse. There were people lined up there, too, but there was an agent working the line. I could see people walking away with paper tickets in hand.

I decided to check it out. I asked the guy behind me to save my spot. In return, I told him that I'd bring back the latest information from that line. When I got there, I asked the people in line what was happening. Were they getting ticketed to fly today, and to where? I learned that there were two flights scheduled with that airline. One was going to Philadelphia and the other to Los Angeles.

"Los Angeles?" I asked. "Do you know if they have seats available?" They did. I couldn't believe it. I went back to my line to report the news, and then I made tracks back to that other line with about twenty other people in tow.

When I finally got to the front of the line, I presented my ticket from the other airline to the agent. I was prepared to negotiate some value for my ticket and pay any difference. I just wanted to get home. The agent looked at my ticket and told me to keep it. She started typing on her keyboard, pushed a button, and handed me a boarding pass.

"That's it?" I asked.

"That's it," she said. "Go to gate twenty-three."

On the flight to LA, I sat next to a group of guys who looked as if they'd been traveling together for some time. They were seated across the aisle from me. We started chatting as the flight took off. They told me the following story. On Tuesday morning, September 11, they had been in downtown New York, giving a presentation in a conference room that faced the Twin Towers. They witnessed in real time the second plane exploding in a ball of fire. They were in shock. They looked at their client, offered apologies, said it might be best to go, and they left. They grabbed a cab to get them to the closest airport, LaGuardia. When they got into the cab, the driver informed them that all the New York City area airports were already shut down. They asked the driver if he'd be willing to drive them to an airport upstate that might still be open. They drove past White Plains and all the way to Albany, only to discover when they arrived there that all airports nationally were closed with no schedule for reopening. They paid the cab driver $2,000 and thanked him for his trouble.

They were now in Albany and a long way from home in California. They were able to rent a car and stayed in Albany for the night. The next day, they started driving west. Their plan was to drive until they found an open airport that had a flight that would take them home to Los Angeles. They spent the second night in Chicago. They arrived in Omaha on Thursday, and just as I had, they booked themselves on the same flight I did, and they were in the group that followed me to the other airline line. That's how they came to be sitting across from me. We talked for the entire trip home, flying halfway across the country in empty skies.

We landed in Los Angeles, one of the busiest airports in the world, and it looked like one of those old and abandoned gas stations you might see on a lonely and closed stretch of the old Route 66. It was eerie. There was hardly a soul in the place. But we were home. We lingered a bit at the gate, chatting, before we said our good-byes. We all felt like we'd survived something and faced an uncertain future . . . like "what's going to happen next?" But we were home. My wife was standing curbside, as there was no one there to "move her along." "You okay?" she asked me.

"I am now," I told her. It is true: there really is no place like home. It's just funny that it took a week in Omaha to remind me of that simple truth. And the older I get, the truer it feels.

Final Note: That week, more than three thousand Americans never got to go home. They died in those buildings and on those planes in New York, Washington, DC, and in a lonely field in Pennsylvania. This chapter is dedicated to the memory of those people and their families. May we never forget.

CHAPTER 10

Welcome to My Universe

*"It is well to remember that the entire universe,
with one trifling exception, is composed of others."*
—John Holmes

I may wander between topics in this chapter, but I promise I'll tie
them all together by the end. My parents were strong solid people
and were central and instrumental in shaping the people that my
brothers, sister, and I became. I will start with my dad. My dad,
like a lot of dads, would often wear the same outfit all weekend
long. We, the older brothers, would tease him about this. He'd come
down to breakfast on Sunday morning, wearing the same outfit he'd
worn on Saturday.

"You're not gonna wear that again, are ya? How can you wear the
same thing every day?"

We were preteen wise guys. Heck, we changed outfits a few times
a day. We also took an hour in the bathroom. My dad, on the other

hand, was in and out in ten minutes. We'd never think of wearing the same outfit twice on successive days. How could it be that he didn't seem to care how he looked, while we were obsessed with it?

Now that I am the age he was back then, I understand the man's choices. He simply liked what he liked. He felt little need to impress anyone inside his home, so why bother dressing up? What was all the fuss about? I understand now that as time marches on, sons become their fathers. My mother, on the other hand, was careful about her dress. Today, she is more than ninety years old, and she is just as careful, and dresses just as elegantly, as she always has. My sister is the same way. And so, daughters, too, become their mothers.

This is not to say that sons have nothing of their mothers in them. They do, as I very much have. And this doesn't mean that daughters don't take on some of their fathers. They do. I know, I raised a daughter, and she is in many ways like me. But, even if she didn't want it to be so, she will always have much of her mother in her. Let me be clear: My daughter is not her mother. I am not my father. Each of us has a unique personality. But deep down, we both have absorbed much of our parents. And this can be a helpful thing to understand, especially when it comes to something as serious as making a marriage work.

In my experience, and this is not based on anything other than my own observations of my brothers and my friends, a man marries the bride's mother. And the same seems to be true with women, in that the bride marries the groom's father. I am not qualified to explain why this is. But the knowledge is enough for me to suggest to any young man, wanting to marry the girl he loves, that he spend some time with her mother. If he likes her mother, and can live with what he sees (the future), then by all means marry the daughter.

It's the same with fathers. The apple usually falls pretty close to the tree. My father has been gone for almost a quarter century now, yet we still talk about him—even his weekend choice of attire. But my brother, Tim, said something at his wake that reinforces what I'm saying here. We were in the viewing room at the funeral home. It was packed with family and friends when my brother stood up and delivered a short speech, the gist of which was . . .

As I have become an adult, I notice that I act and talk very much like my father. I have become like him in many ways that I once thought I never would . . . and I am very proud to say that, and proud that I have become the man he was."

That's about as clear as it gets. I rest my case . . . for now.

If you will allow me, I want to change the topic as I said I would and delve just a little deeper into the idea that children become their parents. We all become what we are because of who we were. Let me explain this tongue twister. I attended a seminar presented by a business consultant named Morris Massey. He was in front of a room filled with executives, making the case that if you really wanted to understand someone, you needed to know who they were with, and what they learned from them, *before* they reached the age of ten. His research suggested that in the first ten years of life, we all learn and adopt our core values from those closest to us—usually, but not always, our parents. He went on to say that even though we all continue to grow intellectually after the age of ten, our core values are imprinted by that time. Who we are, at our core, in our gut, is imprinted in those years, and those lessons last us a life time. The only way they might change, he said, was the occurrence of some significant emotional event, which might turn all that upside down. But for most people, most of the time, this was an exception. We are, today, who we were, then.

I found this idea fascinating, and inserted it into this chapter because it's relevant to my story. Dr. Massey's research shows that the value systems of entire age groups were amazingly consistent. For example, people born and raised in the 1930s, during the Great Depression, valued thrift and were careful with money. And people born and raised in the 1940s, during World War II, valued duty and were joiners of causes . . . and so on. In other words, at a very deep and subconscious level, we are the products of our childhood.

What has this to do with my father's choice of weekend wear? I'm getting to that. My mom was a stay-at-home mother as was every other mother in our neighborhood. But she was ahead of her time, too, or so she says. She believed she was a wife and mother first and a housekeeper and maid, a far distant second. My father's role—as he worked every day—was to provide the money. That was his primary job aside from being a present father, which he was. He took an LIRR train into Manhattan for thirty-six years. He'd catch the 5:40 a.m. train each morning to get to his office on Madison and Twenty-Third Street, and then he'd return home at 6:10 p.m. each evening for dinner.

Both of my parents were busy doing their "jobs." My father worked long days, and my mother was at home caring for six kids. Even though we were the "oh so precious" children, we were not the center of the universe. My parents made it clear that the family was the center of the universe. Practically, this meant that the house-keeping duties had to be the *first and foremost* job for somebody, and so that fell to us boys—primarily the first four. The last two kids escaped these duties for the most part, and I think they missed some important lessons as a result.

From the time I was seven years old until the time I left home for college, there was "the List." The List was a yellow legal sheet of paper posted on the refrigerator door, where no hungry boy could fail to see it and claim ignorance of his responsibilities. Each week, your name was assigned to a task for the week. Your assignment rotated among the other brothers on a weekly basis. This is what the List looked like:

	FEBRUARY			
	Week 1	Week 2	Week 3	Week 4
Laundry	Kevin	Tim	Brian	Michael
Kitchen	Michael	Kevin	Tim	Brian
Cooking	Brian	Michael	Kevin	Tim
Yard	Tim	Brian	Michael	Kevin

The chart was written in my dad's precise cursive penmanship. You knew your job for the week. On the occasions when you *were* unclear, my father made sure that you were clear on your responsibilities. Shirking was not tolerated. There were no excuses. Just do your job! And because we each had to do every job on the list, we all learned how to cook, iron, sew, wash, and clean. And some of these tasks were considered "universal" – like each of us did our own sewing for example. We grew up in this system. And if you were smart about your job, you'd get your chore done quickly and then disappear before more work could be assigned. My dad had an inexhaustible supply of chores he'd assign if were you close by.

After I finished my chores, I took off and stayed far away from home almost all day until the bell rang. When the bell rang, it was time to come home. My father installed a bell outside the garage so he wouldn't have to chase all over the neighborhood, looking for each of us when he wanted us home. That bell hangs there to this day, more than a half century later, above the garage in the same home where my mother still resides. It doesn't get used anymore. It's been quiet for decades. But it's a reminder of a time when we were all kids. The bell had about a quarter-mile audible range. Once you heard it, you knew you had about twenty minutes to get home before dinner was served. So, you started for home when it rang.

If you didn't get home on time, no one made a big deal about it. You simply ate what was left over. We all made for home when it rang because one could ever count on leftovers. In fact, for many years, we didn't even own any Tupperware. There wasn't any need. There were never any leftovers. I only learned about leftovers from a friend. We were having lunch at his home one afternoon and deciding what to have. My friend suggested that we "just heat up some leftovers" and have those.

"Leftovers?" I asked. "What's a leftover?"

"You know, the stuff left over from dinner last night."

I told him that we didn't have any of those at our home. If it got cooked, it got eaten, all of it, that day.

The List was our way of life. We grew up in that system before we were ten years old. It was the way things were. We thought everyone did it. But not everyone did— as we later learned. And we never really grew out of it, either. My wife, who's been married before, also, says that she has never met a man who could cook, sew, iron, clean, and do all the things I just naturally do. I don't know any other way. That system is a core value!

The system was good for my mother in another way, too. It provided her with the opportunity to do something she had wanted to do for the family, and for herself, for a long time. That was to get a real job and to go back to the working world. The List made it possible. Because we had the list, she didn't need to worry about running the home and keeping house. When I was sixteen, she took a full-time position in the New York State civil service. She started as a secretary to the police commissioner, at the lowest "job" rating. She retired twenty years later with the second-highest civil service "job" rating, as a director in the social services department in Suffolk County, New York.

The List was only part of my parent's method for raising their children. Proper behavior with other people was the other core value. My mother, especially, trained us in proper manners and etiquette. Included in this training was the importance of proper dress. She'd say things like: Make sure you wear your best underwear today because we're going to see the doctor. Tuck in your shirt. Comb your hair. Shine your shoes. She told us that we should dress in consideration of the family's reputation as well as in consideration of other people. Slobs were offensive to others and the height of impoliteness. I dress with this in mind to this day. I dress simply, and so consistently that everyone knows how I will come into the office on any given day— just like my father. I wear navy, charcoal, or black wool dress slacks, creased, cuffed, and pleated. I wear a long-sleeved button-down shirt in solid white or pastel yellow or blue, with polished black dress shoes and a matching black belt. I dressed that way when I was in the boys' choir. It was what I knew and valued.

Of course, the world has changed dramatically since those days when it comes to dress codes. And I understand that some relaxation around office dress rules is a good thing, but it may have gone too far, judging by what some wear—or forget to wear. I blame the slippery slope that was introduced by the generally good idea of "casual Friday." I, for one, don't miss the days of suits and ties in the office. But casual has morphed into careless, judging by what I observe in some offices, and especially at the airport. I won't go on a rant here, but I have a few suggestions for airport dress codes at the end of this chapter that might just bring back some of what's been lost as we've slid down the slippery slope of personal appearance.

Manners were so important to my mother that before "company" arrived for a visit, she'd assemble her boys in the living room.

She made us practice rising to our feet, greeting the women first, then greeting the men, before making some small talk and finally taking everybody's coats and drink orders. We practiced it! My mother would be in complete agreement with Miss Manners who wrote in her book, *Star-Spangled Manners*, about such trainings.

> *"Since the mid-twentieth century, this country has been ruled by the idea that manners are bad for children because they inhibit them from being themselves. Well of course they do. That's the point. Uninhibited children are barbarians requiring some civilizing. If you think I am incorrect in this, consider your last restaurant experience where the children ran rampant. I bet that you did not consider it "adorable." I bet you wanted to punch the parents who allowed it.*
>
> *Children must be trained in etiquette. The principle behind etiquette is to think from the other person's point of view. You have to train for that in childhood. Etiquette is designed to inhibit the instinct to act on one's worst impulses. That's what civilization is all about; formal and proper boundaries among people that respect "space."* (Judith Martin)

What's my father's weekend dress have to do with any of this? What I did not tell you, and we did not know then, was that my father was a lot like me when it came to his choice of outfits, later in his life. He did wear the same thing. But he did not wear the *same exact* clothes every day. He just owned several versions of the same outfit, and he wore those all the time. I am certain my mother had something to say about this as proper manners and dress were so important to her. They were part of the system of living with others designed to respect other's "space." And since space must be shared, no one person can be at the center of it.

Welcome to my universe. I learned early that I was not the center of the universe but simply a part of space. I learned that I had to be responsible for my part and play it. These were and still are core values. And it seems today that it's a core value so old-fashioned as to be completely dismissed, if only judging by the number of people I meet who act as if they *are* at the center of the universe, and that everything revolves around their needs and whims. You don't believe me? Just take a trip to the grocery store, shop, and check out . . . and experience the too-many people who act as if you are invisible and in fact in their way. They have their rights you know. Whatever happened to manners in public? Or visit the airport and observe what people wear—in public. Whatever happened to dressing in nice clothes when traveling?

Not one of us is the center of the universe. We have a responsibility to be aware of other people and their space. I just wish more people would know this and realize they would be happier if they obsessed about something other than their own needs. Okay, end of rant. Thanks for listening.

Suggested Airport Dress Code Guidelines

MEN

- No shorts and sandals. We don't want to see your hairy legs, and don't get me started on your feet. . . .

- If you must wear jeans, then wear ones without big gaping holes. They look awful. And put on some socks.

- No tracksuits, please. I know the New Jersey mob guys on *The Sopranos* like that stuff, but did Don Corleone ever wear a tracksuit? No!

WOMEN

- No tracksuits, either.

- No pajamas and slippers, either.

- Run a brush through your hair before you get to the airport.

- No yoga pants unless you look like Mary Lou Retton. And if you have to ask whether you do, then you don't qualify.

FOR ALL

- No dogs, cats, llamas, or peacocks on board. If you need support and comfort on your flight, buy a seat for your shrink.

- In general, think about others and dress with *them* in mind.

Final Note: I considered using another quote to begin this chapter, but after some thought it seemed like it was a little too dry... though still very funny to me. So I provide that quote for you here for your enjoyment...

"In the beginning the Universe was created. This has made a lot of people very angry and been widely regarded as a bad move."

—*Douglas Adams*

CHAPTER 11

Listen to Your Mother

"Red sky at night, sailors delight.
Red sky in the morning, sailor take warning."
—*Old adage with roots in the Bible (Matthew 16:2–3)*

There is actually some scientific evidence that backs up this old adage. I can vouch for that personally. I worked on the water, running a clamming operation for two summers on the Great South Bay of Long Island. If the sun was red at night, we made sure we got to the dock early the next day, and if the sun was red when we got there in the morning, we usually turned around and went home. The adage proved to be amazingly accurate. Trust me, it's no fun being on the water in a small craft in stormy weather, so we heeded the adage. In other words, it might just pay to listen to and heed the warnings, however unscientific, of people "in the know."

Some years ago, my family was planning a surprise fiftieth birthday party for my brother, Brian. Brian is number three in the birth order and a classic middle child. As part of the celebration, my wife and I decided to create a music video and scrapbook of his fifty years . . . in pictures. I went to New York to visit my mother to find some of the older pictures. She directed me to the back of a closet where there were boxes of Kodak slides and old photographs from our youth. As I was going through the boxes, looking for photos and slides of Brian, that's when I found the picture.

It was a picture from 1955 of my mother and me. We are in our apartment in Queens, New York. I am looking at the camera, and I assume it's my father who is taking the picture. I am happy and smiling. My mother is holding me in her arms. She is dressed in that elegant way they dressed at home in the 1950s. She is wearing a classic blue housedress that looks perfect on her. She, too, is happy and smiling. But she is not looking at the camera. She is looking at me. She looks so happy to be a mother with her firstborn. She looks like she'd do anything to keep me and protect me. She looks like the picture of love.

My mother and I have traveled a lifetime since that picture was taken. She went on to give birth to, and raise, five more kids. As they came on board, and I grew older, she and I fought more, especially when I was a teenager. We disagreed, as teenagers and parents do, about priorities, responsibilities, and behaviors. One time she was so upset with me that she packed all my belongings in two suitcases and placed them out on the front lawn, suggesting that I just go somewhere else to live. I did not make her life easy during those years. I'm not even certain why—maybe I just missed being the center of her attention like I was in that picture. Or, more likely, it's simply nature's way. Children must grow up and leave home, and that process can be hard on both parties. I left home for good by age twenty. And as the years passed, we both grew older and closer.

During those years my second brother, Michael, got married and had kids. He was the first to deliver grandchildren. Then Brian got married and did the same. Yet I remained single. I'd had a few serious girlfriends and relationships. In fact, one that should have, but never did, end up at the altar. Everyone liked her and thought she was the one. Instead, I married someone else, on the rebound from the breakup of that relationship. As it turned out, my family was right. I married the wrong girl. But you can't tell a guy who's in love . . . anything. You can only warn him about the impending storm and hope he'll heed the warning. I was warned, just like "red sky in the morning."

Even though the marriage failed early, the funny thing was, I really liked my first wife, the one I should not have married. She was fun, smart, and pretty. Of course, those things aren't nearly enough good reasons to make a marriage work. And from the very beginning, there were signs and warnings of the approaching storm. I just ignored them . . . all of them. One warning was obvious: she, too, was on the rebound, having recently divorced. And if history is a guide, rebound marriages often don't last. Then there was the episode several months before we were to be married when she got "busted" at work, snorting coke in the women's room with her girlfriend. It wasn't clear that she had actually "done the coke." In her account of the incident, she just happened to be there with the others who *were* doing it. She said all the right things. All the things I wanted to hear, to confirm my feelings that she was "the one." There were no arrests made, but she was put on notice by the company, and in my mind, by me, too.

We planned for a late December wedding in New York. In advance of the wedding, my fiancée and I traveled to New York that August to meet my parents. The plan was for her parents to make the trip, too, so we all could get to know one another. We went and met, and if something was not going well, I was oblivious to it. It appeared to be nothing but green lights on the way to the altar.

That was until about a month before the wedding day. That's when I found a bag of coke she had carelessly left out on a table in our apartment. I confronted her with the evidence. I was not happy.

"What the heck is this?" I wanted to know, without really wanting to know.

"It's not mine." That answer deflated me almost completely. She could not even take ownership of what was obviously hers.

She said something about holding it for her girlfriend because her girlfriend was in hot water with her boyfriend about *her* drug use. Now I felt there was a real problem. We were so close to the wedding date, and now I was having second thoughts. What should I do? I called a few of my friends who knew us both to discuss their views on the situation. They all concurred that the bathroom bust earlier that year was not a "one time" thing. Most everyone knew she was partying, *some*. When I shared this with her, she insisted it wasn't true. Maybe it had been true at one time, but now that had all changed and she was a different person. She wanted to get married. I called my mother.

I remember the phone call. I told my mother what was going on. She listened and asked a few questions. She never came right out and said, "Don't marry that girl." She would never do something like that. She was only concerned for my happiness. And she also knew how bullheaded I could be when backed into a corner on any subject. She knew that if she said, "Don't marry that girl," I would have become defensive, and less likely to listen to what she had to say.

But, unbeknownst to me, my mother had already established her own opinion about my bride, without the coke incident I was now describing to her. She'd met the girl's parents that summer, and based on that, and her mother's intuition, *she* was having second thoughts about this marriage. But instead of telling me to run for the hills, she said something like: "If you are unsure about this, maybe you should just wait. And if you're worried about canceling the ceremony and putting us out, don't worry about that; no one will think badly of you for waiting and rescheduling." She was telling me indirectly, "Don't marry that girl," at least until I could see things more clearly.

My mother saw from the very beginning—after watching us together and spending time with her parents—what I would not or could not see. We were not a good match. She never said my fiancée was a bad person. To this day, even after all the pain my ex put me through in the divorce and custody proceedings, she has never said a bad word about my ex-wife. She was simply focused on what was good for me. Obviously, I did not take my mother's advice . . . red sky in the morning, sailor take warning.

We flew to New York from California for the December wedding. Even on the day of the wedding, God felt it necessary to show up and attempt to halt the proceedings. The weather on our wedding day was so awful—snow, ice, and sleet—that we were afraid that most of our guests would be unable to attend. The roads were terrible, the sky was dark, and the clouds were low. It was the worst winter storm in over twenty years. But even God could not stop that wedding from taking place. We got married. It was a nice wedding, and maybe even one of the last truly happy days we had together. Though we both tried, we failed. We were not a good match, just as my mother had clearly seen. She knew.

Mothers know things about their children that their children don't know about themselves. And when I found that picture of a young mother with her firstborn son, and the way she looked at him, it became very clear that they do. They can see storms coming, like the red sun in the morning. And they can raise the storm flag, but it's up to their children to heed it. I should have listened to my mother. It's a wonder we all don't do that more often.

CHAPTER 12

One-Hit Wonder

*"In the future, everyone will be
world-famous for fifteen minutes."*
—Andy Warhol

When I typed "one-hit wonder" into a web browser, the very first result I got was a Wikipedia list of the music industry's biggest one-hit wonders. It's a long list, and it makes for great reading. It's a walk down memory lane and has the side benefit of sharpening your car-radio trivia skills, assuming you don't have Shazam. My name isn't on that list. Maybe yours is. If so, congratulations. I guess that means I'm a no-hit wonder.

The phrase "one-hit wonder" connotes a certain sense of failure or the sadness of being just a flash in the pan. This, I think, is a little harsh and certainly an unfair assessment of someone's music career. For most of us toiling in obscurity, we'd love to be a one-hit wonder—if just to be able to say: look at what I did! What we forget, when we wisecrack about being a one-hit wonder, is the reality that the artists, whoever they were, left a lasting legacy. They are remembered long after they departed the scene. In other words, they were only famous once, but, now, they are famous forever.

I am a bit of a one-hit wonder. The story starts with a poster that has hung in my office for almost forty years. It's titled "21 Suggestions for Life" by H. Jackson Brown, Jr. I don't recall how I came to own it, but I liked it when I first saw it, and I refer to it still. I have used the list to focus on becoming better at one or two of the suggestions, and working on them exclusively for a year, so that ultimately, over many years, I might become good at all of them. I am still working on the list today. The second "suggestion" on the list is "Work at something you enjoy and that's worthy of your time and talent."

I used this suggestion to decide to become an independent consultant and work in an industry with the kind of people I enjoyed being with. I was fortunate enough—*to do what I loved*—and to do it for thirty years. I made good money, but the most valuable thing I derived from those years were lasting relationships. It was these relationships, developed over the years, that provided me with the opportunity that made me a bit of a one-hit wonder—as the founder of an industry's leading software company. These relationships were instrumental in helping raise the capital we needed to hire the people we needed, to create the first version of our software product, and to get our first customers.

Starting a software company from scratch is a hugely risky venture. But it never really felt that way to me. I trusted not only myself and our people, I trusted that all our relationships would make it happen. How could we fail with all the support I had, I thought? On top of all that, I was so focused on making it happen, and dealing with cancer treatments, that I never considered the very real possibility of failure. We just came to work every day, trying to make something great, and, step-by-step, we grew. We started working out of a small business park where we leased one small office cubicle. And as we grew, we had to add more cubicles to house our growing staff. In a short time, we had a lot of these small offices with our people spread out all over the business park. The arrangement was not optimal for getting work done. We had to travel around the park when we wanted to talk to someone else on the team, heading past the offices of other people, in other small companies, just to have a meeting.

We realized we needed a better arrangement. As it happened, we weren't the only ones thinking we needed to go someplace else. The landlord of the office park came to us, at about that time, and informed us that it was time for us to leave. We were too big and taking up too much space. He reminded us that we should be happy about this because we'd outgrown them. Their business model was designed to incubate small start-ups by providing flexible and inexpensive office space, before sending them out into the world as functioning companies. We'd been successful becoming self-sufficient and getting off the launch pad, and now it was time for us to go. We leased and moved into our first set of new offices.

Move-in day arrived, and we planned to celebrate the grand opening. I flew to St. Louis, where we were located, to christen the new offices with all the members of our team. There were about ten of us at the time. When I arrived and walked into the new building, I had to pinch myself. This is really ours? We did this? These are our offices? Wow! The plan for the day included a lunch and our first meeting in our new conference room. As the founder, I felt like the new place was a big step for us, and I needed to say something about where we'd come from, and where we were going as a company. I prepared notes, but I wasn't happy with what I'd put together.

It was good stuff, it all made sense, but I felt it lacked the emotion of a compelling vision.

We ordered lunch and set up in the conference room. The plan was to eat first, then I'd make my short speech, and then we'd review our business plans. We turned on the big screen TV to project the presentation. But first we had to figure out how to get the computer to connect to the TV. We, a high-tech company, were having trouble doing this. While we were fiddling with the computer, an Internet radio station was playing through the TV. A song I recognized was playing, but I couldn't remember the artist who'd written it. So I asked nobody in particular, "Who wrote this song?"

That's when someone said, "Oh, that's so-and-so. They were a real one-hit wonder."

I don't remember the song or the artist now. But I do remember saying something in response like: "One-hit wonder, huh? So, how many hits do you have?"

My colleague looked at me like I was pulling his leg. I know I can be intimidating, but I wasn't challenging him. I was teasing. So, when he laughed off my question, I pressed on: "Seriously, how many hits do you have? Because I know I've got none. I'd kill to be a one-hit wonder. I'd kill to be remembered as the guy who wrote something that people would remember years later." I thought I was on to something, so I just kept talking:

"Did you ever wonder how that guy, and that song, got to be a hit? I bet it wasn't by mistake or luck. I bet he worked on that song for a long time, perfecting it. And I am willing to bet that he tried writing a lot of other songs that never made it at all."

My coworker looked at me and he was still wondering if I wasn't pulling his leg. I decided that *this* was the speech I wanted to make. The song and conversation had managed to crystallize in my mind the message I wanted to share: "What do you want to bet that wherever the guy who wrote that song is today, that he looks back and recalls those days and the success he had. I bet he's still proud of that one hit."

By now, everyone was listening. "You know what I'd love to see happen with us? I'd love to see us make this thing we are doing a big success. I'd like to be gathered together in some place like Hawaii ten years from now, looking back at these days, and toasting our success and the memories of what we did. I'd kill to have that moment with you guys. I think someone will do it in this industry. Why not us? Why don't we write our own hit?"

That lunch meeting took place five years ago. Since then, we did write the best software. And we also sold part of the company to a big investment management firm who wanted to turn our company into an even bigger company. We did put money in our own pockets. But most memorably, we produced *our hit*. I still own shares in the company, and I still work there. But it's not the same. I miss the days working with the original ten people because today we employ ten times that number. But it's those people, that little band, that produced the original hit. I am proud of them.

I am also very happy that we were able to reward all the people involved—my staff and the people who trusted and gave us the capital to start our company. We created a lot of jobs, jobs that many people rely on today to support and raise their families today. And I was able to be part of something that very few people can claim—doing something you love and building something lasting and good.

It's a fact that we fail more often than we ever succeed in life. And even if I had never had this particular experience, I can look back today with satisfaction at the entirety of my career. But it's nice to hit a home run once in a while, instead of just grinding out base hits. It's nice to have one hit and to know that it will last and be remembered. It also reminds us of a basic truth: that any one of us, with dedication and a willingness to throw the dice, is just one step away from being a one-hit wonder.

Final Note: If you're interested, here are the rest of the "21 Suggestions for Life," which were written by H. Jackson Brown Jr.

21 Suggestions for Life

1. Marry the right person. This one decision will determine 90 percent of your happiness or misery.

2. Work at something you enjoy and that's worthy of your time and talent.

3. Give people more than they expect and do it cheerfully.

4. Become the most positive and enthusiastic person you know.

5. Be forgiving of yourself and others.

6. Be generous.

7. Have a grateful heart.

8. Persistence, persistence, persistence.

9. Discipline yourself to save money on even a modest salary.

10. Treat everyone you meet like you want to be treated.

11. Commit yourself to constant improvement.

12. Commit yourself to quality.

13. Understand that happiness is not based on possessions, power, or prestige but on the relationships with people you love and respect.

14. Be loyal.

15. Be honest.

16. Be a self-starter.

17. Be decisive even if it means you'll sometimes be wrong.

18. Stop blaming others. Take responsibility for every area of your life.

19. Be bold and courageous. When you look back on your life, you'll regret the things you didn't do more than the ones you did.

20. Take good care of those you love.

21. Don't do anything that wouldn't make your mom proud.

Postscript: As the final edits were being made to this manuscript, we sold the rest of our little company ensuring that what we built will now last for a very long time. This makes me both a little sad and a little happy.

CHAPTER 13

Best Day Ever

"From this day to the ending of the world . . .
we in it shall be remembered—we few,
we happy few, we band of brothers."
—Shakespeare, *Henry V, Act 4, Scene 3*

There are days— times and places – you will remember forever. You might even be thinking of one of them now that I've mentioned this. They can't be planned. They just happen. In fact, *your best day ever* often starts out like any normal *run of the mill* day, until circumstances and decisions make it anything but. One of my best days ever involved a round of golf. This is so out of character for me because I don't connect playing golf with anything good at all. What I do in regards to golf cannot accurately be called "playing golf." It's true I do own a set of clubs. It's true that I do go to the golf course and visit the pro shop and pay my green's fees. It's also true that I walk onto the first tee. But after that, what happens is not what most people who play golf would call "playing golf." Despite investing thousands of dollars and untold hours attempting to "play golf," I still cannot play golf very well. It's odd, then, that one of my best days ever took place on a golf course.

Here's how it happened. My friend Scott was a golfer. One of his bucket list items was to play as many of the top one hundred courses in the world as he could. And as any golfer knows, not a small number of these courses are in Ireland and Scotland. Scott was planning to go to both those countries, and asked if I wanted to go along with him. As a rule, I am up for almost anything, anytime. But what he was asking me to do was to sign up for two weeks of mental anguish and the expense of hundreds of lost golf balls. I had to think about it, I told him. I wanted to keep him company, so I tried to talk him out of going to Ireland and Scotland. Why travel so far? We can be miserable much closer to home for far less money, right? Scott dismissed it out of hand. He was going. And as they say, a friend in need . . . I signed on and we went.

We were scheduled to play ten rounds in twelve days. We played a week in Ireland, then we traveled to Scotland in the last week in August. As we were driving from the airport to our hotel in Scotland, there was a weather forecast flashing on a large electric sign over the highway—warning: heavy rain tomorrow all day. I thought at the time, that's saying something when a sign like this was posted on a highway in *Scotland*, a place where heavy rain is the default setting for the weather forecast.

I looked at Scott and he said, "What the heck do you think that means?"

"It always rains here, doesn't it?"

"Wonder why they are making such a big deal about it?" I said.

"Well, it doesn't matter. We're here, and I'm playing rain or shine . . . heavy or un-heavy rain."

And so went the conversation until we got to the hotel, unloaded our stuff, and headed out for dinner. We didn't give the forecast another thought.

The next morning, we had a nine a.m. tee time at the historic Crail Golfing club, which is located not too far south of the Old Course in St Andrews. The sky was gray and threatening, but we'd played in worse weather. Even when it began to rain lightly as we were unloading our clubs with the caddies, we thought little of it. We looked at the sky and decided that a little rain wouldn't keep us from playing golf. After all, we had traveled a long way to get here, and there were no "do-overs." If we bailed out now, we'd never get to play the course.

I'll save you some suspense: we teed off in a drizzle, but we finished not in heavy rain but in a full-on North Sea gale. So, here now, are the details of a "best day ever." It rained steadily while we played the front nine holes. But by the time we arrived on the tenth hole, the "heavy rain" had arrived. I thought back to the highway sign we'd seen the day before, but I did not recall it saying hurricane force winds. You'd think they'd have mentioned that small detail. It was raining sideways and . . . and hard.

Most of the golfers who were on the course were making for the dry confines of the members' clubhouse. The weather was so bad that even lifetime Crail members, whom I assumed were accustomed to this weather, had long since retired to the clubhouse. They were tucked in with a whiskey and entertaining themselves watching the Americans slopping around in what can properly be described as Bill Murray caddying for the bishop in *Caddy Shack* conditions. So by the time we arrived on the fourteenth tee, there were only two foursomes out on the course, us, and since it's a links course with no trees, the other guys two holes ahead were easy to see. They, too, turned out to be Americans. Like us, they'd come a long way to play, and they were going to play come hell or high water.

We played on. We'd hit, and then we'd splash and wade after every shot. The weather had turned par-4 holes into par-6 survival exercises. And you could forget about any par-5 that was playing into the wind. Ten was a good score. And I thought I'd properly prepared for the Scottish weather. I had purchased a top-of-the-line "Scotland-rated" set of rain gear in preparation for the trip. I was, in theory, dressed for, and protected from, the weather. But I was soaked to the skin. That rain and wind would have penetrated anything we might have worn that day.

By the time we reached the sixteenth tee box, with the rain pelting our faces like we were being hit by bullets, one of the guys in our foursome asked, "Do you think we should go in?"

I looked at the other guys and said, "Are you actually thinking of going in? You can, but I'm staying out and finishing." He looked at me like I was a madman.

"Hell," I said. "I can't remember the last time I've had so much fun. If nothing else, think of the stories we can tell later at the bar. I'm staying." And we all stayed.

The final hole, oddly enough, was a par-3. This is unusual for a golf course. The hole was playing directly into the teeth of the North Sea gale. The tee box was located just about twenty feet below the level of the clubhouse where there was a massive viewing window that looked down on the final hole. The lights were shining out of that window, penetrating the gloom. We could clearly see that there were forty or fifty club members watching us. A par-3, 180-yard hole usually calls for something like a 7 iron.

I pulled out my driver and looked up at the club members and waved it. They just watched. Maybe they were discussing whether it would be enough club. My tee shot landed a few yards *short* of the green, using a club that in normal circumstances should go 100 yards further. The members watched us putt out to finish the round. That too was an exercise in futility, as there was so much water on the course by this time that it was actually coming up out of the hole. Every putt skittered over the top of the hole. We waited for the last guy to putt, took off our rain caps, shook hands all around, and headed for the locker room. It was a moment and a memory for the ages.

In the locker room we just sat there, looking exactly like wet cats. We could not have been colder or wetter, had we actually been in a boat on the North Sea that day. We were so cold and wet that we tried using the hair dryers to warm ourselves up. "What do you think? Should we get some drinks?" I finally suggested. We all looked at each other, and not saying anything, walked dripping to the barroom. We looked like men who had just emerged from, and survived, combat or a bar fight or some other like event. We were all zonked and reeling from the experience.

When we walked into the barroom, the members smiled and made jokes with us about the weather. We smiled and ordered. That first sip was, as you'd imagine . . . life-reaffirming. We were quiet, and while we sipped, I watched the members talking among themselves at their tables. They were likely discussing small things like their golf game or what they had to do the rest of the day or tomorrow's plans. But once in a while, I'd see one or two look over at us and then continue their conversation. They may have been chatting a bit about us. I am a student of history. I read a lot about people, wars, and history. Looking back now, and thinking about the conversations they were having that day, I like to think that some of those men were shaking their heads and saying, "Those bloody crazy Yanks! You have to admire their tenacity and courage." And, perhaps, even some of the oldest members were recalling a time when we Yanks came to their island in the millions, preparing to embark on that great crusade (D-day), a crusade where, in the most horrific of conditions possible, Americans gave their lives to save their island from Nazi tyranny.

Scott caught my eye and we looked at each other as the gale howled just outside that big window and we sipped some fine Scottish whiskey. He asked me, "You okay?" I said, "Yeah, that was the best day ever, wasn't it?"

Final Note: In hindsight, I now know why Scott was so insistent on going to Ireland and Scotland instead of staying closer to home like I wanted to. He knew he was very sick and dying. He knew this was the only and the last time he could go. There would be no other time for him. This was it. He passed away four years after the events described here.

CHAPTER 14

Obsessed

"I'm not saying you're wrong, I just know I'm right."
—Hal Greenberg (I found the quote and liked it.
But I don't know much about the author.)

Once I get something in my head . . . watch out. I will laser focus on it to the exclusion of almost everything else. Sometimes I'm like a rocket launch that quickly hits the target. Other times, I'm like a glacier remorselessly grinding down everything in its path. I am all about completing the mission—and sometimes there is collateral damage. This is especially true when I feel I am right about something, or I feel I have been wronged and justice has not been properly meted out to the wrongdoers. Even as I write this now, I realize how scary this sounds. I can only look back with empathy for those who had to experience this because of their proximity to me. I can become a man obsessed.

Obsession: (äb-'se-shən) noun. A persistent disturbing preoccupation with an unreasonable idea or feeling.

Obsessions are not all bad, though. Many of the most successful people in any field—business, politics, and especially sports—are obsessive. There are stories of players staying for hours after practice, after everyone else has gone home, shooting jump shots even when these people are already—by consensus—the best players in the league. Are these people obsessed? I think they are. Is that bad? Sure, to some extent. Every obsession produces collateral damage. The lives of many of these successful people, are full of personal drama—divorce, bankruptcy, and, yes, even crime. There is a cost to every obsession.

Knowing that I can become obsessive about things, I've developed a mechanism to alert me to the possibility that what I'm doing at any moment might be approaching an *unhealthy* preoccupation. I do one of two things. First, I ask myself, what would an old friend Larry (whom you will learn about shortly), say to me right now? And second, I reflect on a scene from the movie *The Hunt for Red October*. In this movie Sean Connery is the captain of a Soviet submarine, the *Red October*. He is seeking to defect with his submarine to the United States. The USSR wants to stop him. They send another boat to hunt him down and bring him and the boat back. And if the captain of that chase boat is unable to bring back the *Red October*, his mission is to then destroy it before Sean Connery and his crew have a chance to defect.

The captain in the chase boat becomes obsessed with this mission. He's obsessed because he's appalled that a comrade would even consider doing such a thing as defecting. He's sure he's in the right, and he wants to exact proper and swift justice. When he finally locates the *Red October*, he orders the torpedoes ready for firing. He is so intent on sinking the submarine that he ignores the standard weapon-arming and launch-safety protocols, despite the pleas from his subordinate officers about the imminent dangers. These protocols were put in place, in fact, to prevent a heat-seeking torpedo from honing in on and sinking a captain's own boat once the torpedo was set loose in the water. The captain ignores his men's warnings. He is so intent on meting out justice and payback that he launches the torpedo, anyway. Sean Connery, captain of the *Red October*, is familiar with all the protocols, and he pulls a U-turn around the chase boat—in essence hiding behind it. The torpedo, of course, "turns back" on the chase boat captain's own ship, destroying him and his crew. In the final transmission from the stricken boat, one of the officers is heard saying to the captain, "You ass, you've killed us." Yes, I worry about being an ass because of my obsessions.

I actually think of that scene, but what I do mostly when I'm becoming unreasonably obsessed is what my friend Larry once told me to do. First some background: Larry and I worked in the same company for a few years. We became friends. He has rescued me from myself more than once. He took me into his home when I got divorced and had no place to go. He gave me a room and one for my two-year-old daughter. The invitation he extended was intended to be a temporary arrangement. But my daughter and I were at his home for almost three years. Those three years allowed me to get back on my feet financially, and more important, allowed me to call someplace home. He is that kind of guy—generous and gracious. He asked me to make a toast at his wedding, and I reciprocated when I remarried. And one of the comments I made in my toast to him and his bride was "When you look up the word 'prince' in the dictionary, there should be a picture of Larry . . . it would provide you all the definition you needed."

Larry and I worked for the same boss, and he was already at the company when I joined it. He already had a relationship developed with the boss. I had to build one. And over time it became obvious that our respective relationships with our boss were very different. Larry's was workmanlike. Mine was contentious. You may be remembering my track record with some of my other bosses as you read this. Suffice it to say, this was not something new for me and, for now, it doesn't really matter why it became contentious, but it did. The simple explanation of why it was contentious would be that my boss and I were alike in some ways, and we competed for "space in the room." We both were naturally comfortable when we were the center of attention and uncomfortable when we were not. Larry never had the need to be the center of attention. In fact, quite the opposite. And when it comes to who wins the center-of-attention battle, it's always clear that the boss wins. Unfortunately for all, he and I never developed a good working relationship. I think had we been able to do that, what did happen might never *have* happened.

What happened started with my decision to divorce my first wife. I was counseled by my lawyer that if I wanted a reasonable amount of custody, which I did, then I had to demonstrate to the court an ability to be "at home," and not "at work" all the time, especially because my daughter was so young. That convinced me to make the decision to resign my current position and "go out" and start my own consulting practice. I wanted to be a parent first, but I also needed income. To achieve both these goals, I approached several of "my clients" at the time, and ultimately arranged to take a couple of with me as my first clients and my source of income. This arrangement, I felt, would guarantee me enough money for at least a year while allowing me to work from home often. I was frank with these clients about my situation, and as far as they were concerned, I was "the company" to them, as I was the guy who did all the work. They were open to the arrangement as long as it was done professionally.

With these clients "in hand," I approached my boss and explained my reasons for leaving and informed him that I'd be taking these clients with me. I also proposed compensation. I'd pay him a commission for the first year on any fees I generated from those clients. I thought this was a fair offer. I admit that I left him little wiggle room to disagree or have much say in the matter. I presented him with everything as a fait accompli. This may have been impolite and unfair, but I saw no other way. I was in a tough spot as far as I was concerned, and I needed to think about my daughter. Had my boss and I had a better working relationship, and could talk, things may have transpired differently. At least that is what I tell myself.

My boss wasn't happy, and said so. He thought it was unprofessional. I can't actually remember his words, but it was clear he felt like I was stealing his clients and that I was ungrateful for all that he'd done for me. I entered the meeting, hoping we might be able to work out a subcontracting relationship, but those hopes were quickly dashed. I felt my boss could have handled the situation better, and he certainly felt the same about me.

I left with the clients and survived my first year on my own. Being on my own eventually did get harder, but that is another story. Over the course of the following few years, whenever I spoke with one of my friends, like Larry, who still worked at the company, all I talked about was the way my ex-boss had treated me. I yammered endlessly about how unfair he was, what a jerk he was, and how I was so much better off now without him and his company. I was obsessed with the feeling that I was right and he was wrong. Larry just listened. That is what Larry does so well. But my guess is that he was not only tired of me talking about this, he was thinking that I was becoming a little bit "crazy" with my obsession. And so he looked at me one day after one of my rants and said, "You talk about him a lot. You know he isn't going to change. And you haven't even seen him in years, anyway. Why not talk about something else?"

"What do you mean, 'stop talking about him'? Do you mean like stop talking about him right now, or forever?"

Larry said, "Forever."

I was a little shocked. "How am I supposed to do that?"

"Well, you just talk about something else and avoid ever mentioning him."

"When should I do this?"

Larry suggested that the present would be a good time to start.

"Try this," he said: "For the next month, simply never say his name. And when you feel like you want to, talk about something else."

Larry never said that he and everyone else were tired of hearing about my obsession with Richard. That's our boss's name. But clearly they were. They were all just too nice to say something like that in hopes of shutting me up. But it was clear to me that Larry was tired of my obsession.

I thought about what he said for a long time. I asked myself why, indeed, was I still talking about this guy after all these years? I made a commitment right then to do what Larry suggested. I stopped uttering my ex-boss's name for the next month. One month turned into two. Then, a year passed, and I still hadn't mentioned his name. The obsession was gone. I even felt better, too. I hadn't realized how much bad energy my Richard obsession had created, and how much it affected my relationships. I've come a long way on this particular experience. I can say my boss's name now without spiraling into a dark place of self-righteousness. After a few months of following Larry's advice, I felt like some clouds had parted and the sun had peeked out. I felt better. Seriously!

Obsession can lead to blindness and insanity. Obsessions sap energy. Obsessions ruin relationships. Really, what did I care about being right or seeing my former boss punished? After all, he wasn't a bad guy. We were just two guys caught up in our own sense of self-righteousness. There was likely never going to be a positive conclusion that would be satisfactory for either of us. And all I was doing was keeping an open wound . . . open. It was time to let it close, heal, and scar over.

Thank God for Larry. His advice was wise and simple. It was as simple as the punch line to the old doctor–patient joke, in which the patient complains, "Doc, it hurts when I do this," and the doctor replies, "Okay, then stop doing it!" An obsession starts with an unhealthy *"I'm not saying you're wrong, I just know I'm right"* sense of righteousness. That level of obsession can lead to a kind of insanity. And the problem with that is, when you're that crazy, you're often the last to know. Everyone around you can plainly see that you are a little crazy and obsessed, but they won't tell it to you.

And because many friends are too nice to mention that you're crazy, your righteous obsession is confirmed and you get even crazier. So, you can't always rely on your friends to whack you on the head. You have to be wise enough to check in and self-diagnose your craziness. That's why today, when I start getting obsessive about something, I think of Larry or I think of the captain in *Hunt for the Red October*, and I try to put things into their proper perspective. Maybe if we all did this more often, there'd be less insanity, and life would be easier and happier. After all, what goes around does eventually come around. Obsession is like a boomerang. You throw it out there, targeting one thing, and then it can loops back and hits you in the back of the head when you least expect it. And that can really hurt!

CHAPTER 15

No Good Deed

"No good deed goes unpunished or unrewarded."
—At various times credited to Clare Booth Luce, Noel
Coward, Oscar Wilde, and even St. Thomas Aquinas

It's been said nice guys finish last. Believe me, if you live long enough and you're nice enough, you actually begin to believe this because that's the way it seems. Maybe this explains why we get crabbier and more cantankerous as we get older, and why we lose our shiny-eyed optimism and become more clear-eyed realists. We've simply had a longer time to deal with enough people to know that the world can be a pretty selfish and ungrateful place. How's that for an opening line? They don't not call me Mr. Sunshine for nothing. We like to think that people appreciate and love heroes, but that's not human nature. Too often, at least if history is any guide, people find a way to bring heroes and good guys back down to earth if not outright destroy them. I warned you. You may now want to move on to the next chapter to avoid what follows. It might make you happier. But if you are like most of us, and if it's true that "misery loves company," this chapter is for you.

I related earlier how I got married to the wrong girl. But I never said how it ended, how it started, and of course what happened between *those* two dates. I will only share some of the relevant highlights so as not to bore you with all of them . . . and believe me, there were many. So, here they are. As anyone who has been through a divorce with children involved, you know there is no such thing as *amicable*. So it was with my ex and I, as at the time we began the divorce proceedings, we had a daughter who was soon to be two years old. We both loved our daughter and wanted to be with her. In fact, soon after we began the divorce process, my ex snapped a picture of my daughter and me on her second birthday that says all you need to know about how much a dad loves his little girl. That picture is still in my office. The words on the frame say, "I (heart) Daddy." That little girl, and the way my ex and I felt about her, as well as the way we felt about each other, was at the heart of everything that happened from that day to the day of our daughter's high school graduation. This is that story in reverse chronology.

The drama and the connection between my ex and me finally *ended* on the football field of Dana Hills High School on the day of our daughter's high school graduation. On that day, sixteen years after I wrote the very first child support and alimony checks, I wrote the last child support check. I'd thought a lot about how to handle this final court-ordered payment. I felt that it marked an important passage that needed to be, well, marked, requiring me to do something special to celebrate it. I even thought of delivering my ex-wife the final payment in a bag of 175,400 shiny pennies, but the logistics of doing that were just too much, and in the end, I simply didn't have the energy to send her a pointless message. I was just ready to move on. I handed her the check and said something like good luck and "this is the last one." My ex-wife, of course, disagreed and insisted that it wasn't the last payment. She maintained that as our daughter wouldn't turn eighteen for another five months, in October, that I wasn't done paying her yet. Then my ex-wife suggested I read the sixteen-year-old divorce agreement more carefully. I just looked at her with an expression that said "really?" I did not tell her to "pound sand." Instead, I simply said, "Yeah, we're done here, and if you think different then you reread the agreement and take it up with *your* lawyer." My ex-wife said she would. But I wasn't worried—I knew I was right. This *was* the last payment. I *had* read the fine print of the divorce agreement. I wasn't legally obligated to pay her another cent. I guess she spoke with her lawyer, and he told her the same thing, because I haven't heard from her since that afternoon a dozen years ago.

When there are kids involved, divorce isn't the end of a relationship with your ex—it is simply the beginning of a new relationship. For better and for worse, the two of you are in it together for the duration. Looking back on that graduation day, I think it's funny that when the day actually came to hand over that last check, the day I'd been dreaming about for years, I actually felt very little joy. The highly anticipated moment of completion and release was a zero. My anger at feeling done poorly by her had either been spent, or I had overrated how good the moment would feel. What had started all those years before with such high hopes ended with a whimper on a sunny football field with one last parting shot from my ex. It's not that I expected any thanks from her that day. But it would have been nice, as I had been a stand-up guy throughout. In fact, I was more of a parent than she ever was. I never missed my custody days or a payment. You'd think that, after sixteen years, she might have been a little generous and said thanks. Nope. Instead, I got "you still owe me." No good deed . . .

What do I mean I was a better parent? During our divorce proceedings, my lawyer hired a Private Investigator to do some detective work into my wife's background since one of the reasons I was divorcing her was her substance addictions. The PI found a history of DUIs. This was important in California because the father is normally treated as a second-class citizen, and the mother is assumed to be the better parent. No, the law is not written that way, but that is the way it plays out in court. I've watched it happen a dozen times while sitting in a courtroom, waiting for my turn in front of the judge. It was these facts about my wife's DUIs that ultimately led the court to grant me primary custodial custody of my daughter, with an agreement to a 50/50 time split in custody days. And that 50/50 time split was all I ever wanted from the very beginning, but I had to spend a lot of money on lawyers and on a PI to get that one simple thing. What took place in that court never needed to happen. It happened because that's what *she* wanted. From the very beginning, I proposed the 50/50 co-parenting split and a monetary support plan that I thought fair. My ex-wife told me to "pound sand." She told me to get a good lawyer, as she knew her rights. She told me she was going to get what she had coming to her. That conversation took place on the steps of the court building after I made what I felt were reasonable offers. And instead of working out something with her, on the very next day, I heard from her lawyer. He was good, and he made my life miserable for two years. But in the end, the court ruled, and she wound up with much less than what I had first offered her in both money *and* custody time. And I was $30,000 poorer in lawyer fees—paying for hers and mine. No good deed . . .

Later, when my daughter was twelve years old, my ex got another DUI. This time the judge had little wiggle room and had to sentence her to a mandatory one hundred twenty days in jail. At that moment, I had to scramble. I was now a truly full-time single parent, one with lots of expenses, and a job to hold down, while she was now absent from *her* responsibilities, sitting in jail. My ex needless to say was not enjoying her situation. She decided to write me a letter from jail begging my forgiveness, for everything. She described how lonely and awful it was in lock-up. And she promised to make changes when she got out. I felt badly for her, so I visited her there, hoping to bury the hatchet and work out a better future plan once she was released. I suggested that I would take care of our daughter for a while after her release so she could handle what she needed to do and get back on her feet with work and such. And of course, during her incarceration, I didn't remit my monthly support checks to her. After all, she was *in jail*. Our daughter was with me full-time. Three weeks after her release, I heard from her lawyer again. She was suing me for the four months of back child support that I had not paid while she was in the lockup. I went to court, thinking, "This is a no-brainer. . . ." I'll win this one, and they won't make me pay her. But the judge awarded her the back payments—with interest. No good deed . . .

All this drama did have a beginning. It all started on a sunny August morning when I woke up and looked over at her lying next to me in our bed, and it hit me. No more! Just like that I was done trying to live with her. Almost three years of sleeping with an addict had finally come to this moment. I knew I had to leave for my sanity and my daughter's safety. That's when I offered to move out of our home while we worked out a final agreement. I believed that upsetting a two-year-old's environment was not in my daughter's best interest, and thus I suggested that she and my daughter stay in the home while I temporarily moved out during the divorce negotiations. But my then wife refused to negotiate in good faith, and later when we did go to court, the act of moving out of our home somehow demonstrated abandonment of the family, according to her lawyer. I got hammered for it by the court. No good deed . . .

It got worse during those first months of separation while we were operating without any court order. I sent my ex-wife money so she could run the household. The year of our divorce just happened to coincide with the first year I'd made some really good money. So, when I filled out the court paper work, instead of entering what I typically made in a year, I entered my new—higher—number. That seemed honest to me. But I didn't then know how things worked in that twilight zone called divorce court. Both of those actions—sending my ex-wife money and the amount I reported as income— turned out to work not for me but against me. Those acts established, in the mind and wisdom of the court and her lawyer, that I was wealthy and that, as she was accustomed to being a stay-at-home mom at a certain income level, she deserved more. Of course, I wasn't wealthy, as I lived the next three years in Larry's extra bedroom while my ex-wife lived in our marriage home. No good deed . . .

Before we had a final court ordered custody plan, I had agreed to sharing less than 50 percent custody with my wife, simply to make my daughter's life less crazy as she went back and forth between the two of us. But instead of being generous with me about time, my ex would simply disappear with our daughter, sometimes for weeks in a row, without providing a forwarding address or returning my calls. And when I complained to her, she told me to call my lawyer. Again, no good deed . . .

The truth is I never cared about the money. I cared about the custody. Okay, Kevin, you're a saint. What do you want? A pat on the back? A proclamation saying *"good job. Kevin"*? Actually, yeah, that would be nice. Sure, and maybe just a thank you note for trying to do the right thing. But that's something that will never come from the place where it would be most meaningful. So, I don't expect gratitude from my ex-wife and, by extension, I rarely expect it from anyone else anymore. Is this cynical? I don't think so. As I said in the chapter introduction, it seems to be reality. Even knowing this, I guess deep down I believe good intentions and deeds do eventually get rewarded... at some point.

I'm not the shiny-eyed optimist I once was. I'm more of a realist, simply because I've dealt with enough people to know that the world can be a pretty selfish and ungrateful place. Others just say that I'm a grouch. And maybe they're right. However, it's not all clouds and rain with me. Sometimes nice guys *do* finish first, and good deeds *do* get rewarded! It's true. Here it is three decades later and my daughter thinks I'm a stand-up guy. She is happy and successful, and we are close these days. That feels like reward enough for me.

In the end, everything I experienced confirmed that my decision to divorce my ex *was* the right one. And though it brings me no great joy, my daughter knows now that her mother, my ex-wife, is not a real stand-up person. There's some reward in knowing that, isn't there?

So, what's my advice for the good-deed doers and nice guys of the world?

- Be careful for whom you do good deeds.

- When doing a good deed, don't expect any gratitude.

- In fact, know that your good deed may not even be appreciated.

- And lastly, whatever happens, never involve a lawyer in anything.

I've decided that after all the crap with my ex, I'd just be a good guy, anyway, and let the chips fall where they might. It's just easier to do the right thing. There's great karma in that! Now, don't you feel better that you read the whole chapter?

CHAPTER 16

Under the Bus

"You don't throw friends under the bus..."
—Herman Cain (American Businessman)

We all eventually get thrown under a bus. And, at least in business, you can almost anticipate the arrival of the bus when someone starts a conversation with the words, "This isn't personal—it's just business." The moment you hear those words, you should get your head on a swivel and start looking for the bus . . . because it's coming. I've been thrown under the bus more than a few times. It's never fun, but it happens, especially in partnerships. However, it's still a surprise when the bus arrives because you feel it's coming from the direction that you'd be the least likely to expect. Alas, not true, and that is the subject of this chapter. It took place in the business at the center of my one-hit wonder story. You already know a little about how that business started. Well, this is how it ended.

I started the company with a business associate, one whom I considered a friend. We'd worked together on common clients for a few years, so when he approached me one day seeking my advice, I was happy to help out. He told me about his two current partners. They were having serious issues working together, and the partnership was becoming dysfunctional. There were claims and counterclaims of bad faith and dishonest dealings. My friend was unhappy. And the battles were becoming a case of the two of them, against my friend. He'd reached the conclusion that he wanted out and needed help figuring out how best to do that.

It became obvious in short order that what he really wanted to do was purchase a part of the company from the other two partners, and he wanted to know how to value it fairly. The part he wanted to buy was based on a single software product the company had developed under his leadership. He felt that it could be cleanly separated and evaluated. I thought the idea had merit and an evaluation fairly made. We reviewed the company's financials, and ultimately landed on what appeared to be a fair and supportable proposal. The valuation involved a not insignificant amount of money. So, I asked my friend, "Where are you going to get the kind of money needed to buy this?" It suddenly got quiet on the call, and it then occurred to me that there might be another reason why he had reached out for my help. The next thing my friend wanted to know was, "Would I be interested in joining him in the buyout?"

I thought the software had long-term potential, and that the price was fair, and that I could help raise the cash. I made a quick decision and said, "I do have some interest. But only under certain conditions." I went on: "I'll come up with the money, but I want to be a full partner and own fifty percent of the company."

My friend thought about it for a moment, and agreed to those terms. We figuratively shook hands on it and began the legal process of putting together an offer to present to his partners. I became the "silent partner" in the deal, as I did not want his two partners to know I was involved. I didn't know those two guys, but the less information they knew about how the deal was going to funded, the fewer complications we would face in trying to get it closed. I was now committed, but I had concerns about the success of the buyout. Would his partners actually sell to him? I knew enough about them to know they were cagey, and that they'd likely react emotionally and negatively to any offer.

"So, what happens if your partners say no to our offer? What are you going to do then?" I wanted to know.

"They won't say no to this kind of money," my friend replied.

"Yeah," I said, "but what if they do?" What's your Plan B?"

I asked this because I was pretty certain there wasn't a Plan B. There was only a Plan A, and that's what I was signing up for— Plan A!

"Well, if they say no, then we'll just start a new company and build our own software," my friend said.

I may be stating the obvious here. But buying into something that already exists, has customers, and is producing money is a very different proposition from starting something new from scratch. Creating and bringing a software application to market is an enormously expensive process requiring a big up-front investment. I know this because we ultimately did it, and at the time I did not have the personal funds to be investing that kind of money.

"Building a new software application," I said, "is a totally different thing. I've never done anything like that before, and it's a lot more money than I have to invest. And, come to think of it, those same two things apply to you."

My friend was certain his partners would take the money, and that we'd own it within two months. And because he was so certain they'd accept the offer, I assumed it would happen, too. So, imagine my surprise when I received a call from him after he presented our offer to his partners.

"I've been walked out the door," he told me.

"What do you mean, 'walked out the door'?"

"I've been fired. They had their lawyers there. They ambushed me. They handed me a piece of paper invoking a clause in our buy-sell agreement that allowed them to buy me out for the same amount of money we offered. They gave me a check for what we offered, and walked me out of the office in front of all the staff." His partners had thrown him under the bus.

You have to hand it to his partners: they *were* cagey and emotionally mean-spirited, and they got the best of him that day. But in the end, his partners turned out *not* to be the smartest guys in the room. That day this happened was the twenty-eighth of June 2013. I marked it on my calendar, and it's still marked there today. I refer to it as the anniversary day of the founding of our new company—what would come to be known as Plan B. As I listened to him relate the events of the day, I felt badly for him. I could imagine how awful that scene must have been for him and the shock he felt. He'd been so certain the deal would go through that day, and now here he was unemployed. The people with whom he'd started that company, the people with whom he'd been friends and partners, had thrown *him* under the bus! I knew how that felt. It had happened to me before!

During the entire process, I'd never fully committed to doing anything other than the Plan A buy-out. I never said I'd actually do anything like a Plan B. It had always been a faint possibility for me. And that's where things stood when I flew out to St. Louis to meet with him a week later. He still looked in shock about how he'd been handled by his partners. How could he not be? He was angry, and felt betrayed and like he'd been thrown under the bus. The conversation quickly turned to Plan B—starting a new company and building a new software application. At that time, I had a great and profitable consulting business going. I didn't need to do Plan B. I hadn't really signed up for it. It wasn't only the money that would be necessary to launch Plan B, the real problem was there was no actual Plan B. We'd never fleshed out any of the details. And we were personally in very different places. My friend needed Plan B or he'd have to go find a job somewhere. I had a great business going. And although I hadn't promised I'd start a new business, I felt I had implied that I would, so in short order I said, "Okay, I'm in." And that's how we started out, a journey that a few short years later led to that conference room story I shared earlier about the one-hit wonder.

Now here's how our story ended. By the time we entered our third year in business, we began to get emails from investment bankers. We just ignored them initially. We thought, who the hell would want to buy our little company? On top of that we weren't really that interested in selling it, anyway. But the emails kept coming. There were so many of them that I started to save them in a separate email folder. Within a few months the folder was filled with a hundred emails from more than three dozen bankers, each requesting that we get in touch with them. These people were very persistent. So, we responded to one of the emails. I just picked one of the companies because they'd sent so many emails and returned one. And that opened the floodgates. We were soon interviewing lots of investment bankers.

When an investment banker wants your company, the process is a no expenses-spared courtship dance. They tell you how great you are and how proud you should be of what you've built. They wine you, and they dine you. We went to a lot of expensive dinners with these guys over the course of six months. And for those who've ever

127

been involved in this process, they'd be lying if they told you that all the wining and dining and the attention didn't go to their heads a little. After several months of this, we finally narrowed the field down to two firms. Both were willing to offer us a very good deal in exchange for a controlling equity interest in our company.

It may help to provide some personal background here to help clarify our decision. I am about fifteen years older than my partner and past the age of Medicare enrollment. I tell you this simply because age difference provides a very different lens and point of reference when it comes to selling a business. At the outset, my friend wasn't convinced that we should sell a controlling share of the company. But any other deal structure or setup was not an option, as that is how these guys do their deals. If you want the money, they want control. We understood that was fair, but my friend was still hesitant. I was much less so.

"Why should we sell now?" he wanted to know.

I told him, "We don't have to sell. But I'm older, and cashing in some of my chips makes sense for me. And I think it does for you, too. We have an offer in hand with money that will guarantee your family's financial future. I think you have to consider that. And it's the kind of money that may never come our way again. So, I'm in favor of doing the deal."

I don't know what my partner thought of my position, but a week later he called me back and green-lighted the deal. "Let's do it," he said. I can't say exactly what happened behind the scenes with the investment bankers and my partner, but it's evident a separate verbal deal was made. Maybe it was because I was sixty-five years old and closer to retirement. Maybe it was because of my cancer, and the risk my health had on the management of the company. Or maybe my partner was just more their kind of guy. But he was offered a different management and leadership role than I was. I was not aware of this at the time. I found out about it about a week later when we were discussing the final details.

"So, what percentage of your shares are *you* going to sell to them?" My partner asked me at dinner.

"What do you mean?" I asked. I was a little perplexed by the question, because in my mind, we'd been in this together from the beginning, and we'd be going forward together to write "chapter two" of our business partnership, and that meant we'd be selling exactly the same amount of shares.

"I think that we sell the same amount, of course," I replied. He just nodded and said okay. But I knew right then that something had changed. I knew he had his own plan, and he was moving forward with it apart from me. What I did not know then is what that meant for my future in practical terms. I left the meeting feeling depressed. I felt sucker punched and, I bet, not a little unlike the way he might have felt when his partners showed him the door four years earlier. I could feel the bus coming. And it showed up soon after the deal was consummated when I found out that I would be relegated to a figurehead role, and my partner would run the company. He actually said to me a few weeks later, "Kevin, it's nothing personal—it's just business. Take the money and be happy with that."

Two years removed from those days, I hurt less about it. I've accepted my role, and I'm okay with it because I have to be. I'm more upset with myself than I am with him. I wonder, did I miss something about him? How did I not see it coming? Why was I so trusting? I guess, having been run over before, I should have known better and been wiser.

Let me tell you something: business is *always* personal. After all, that's what businesses are—a collection of people working together where trust is the essential glue holding them together. I understand there are limits to loyalty, and that there are good business reasons why hard decisions must be made about people as companies grow. But trust demands that those hard decisions be made out in the open, above board, and with all due consideration. I may be old-fashioned, but I believe in the old maxim *"you dance with the one that brung ya."* Loyalty demands at least that much. I had *brung* my friend to the dance in large measure, starting back in those days when *he* was unemployed, and he needed *me* to make Plan B a reality.

The bus has left the scene now. However, I occasionally share my sad story with others who knew us both. It happened that I shared it with a close friend several months after these events took place when my feelings were still raw. He listened to me and was sympathetic. We hung up the phone, and about an hour later he did something unexpected. He sent me an email, and in it were the words of Rudyard Kipling's famous poem. I share these words, written so long ago, as they are wonderful. At the end of his email my friend added: "These are the words I read as part of my eulogy at my father's funeral. I want you to know I feel the same way about you, as I felt about him. He was a good man. I hope these words help you heal a little bit."

IF

If you can keep your head when all about you
   Are losing theirs and blaming it on you,
If you can trust yourself when all men doubt you, But make
   allowance for their doubting too;
If you can wait and not be tired by waiting, Or being lied
   about, don't deal in lies,

Or being hated, don't give way to hating,
    And yet don't look too good, nor talk too wise:
If you can dream—and not make dreams your master;
    If you can think—and not make thoughts your aim;
If you can meet with Triumph and Disaster
    And treat those two impostors just the same;
If you can bear to hear the truth you've spoken
    Twisted by knaves to make a trap for fools,
Or watch the things you gave your life to, broken,
    And stoop and build 'em up with worn-out tools:
If you can make one heap of all your winnings
    And risk it on one turn of pitch-and-toss,
And lose, and start again at your beginnings
    And never breathe a word about your loss;
If you can force your heart and nerve and sinew
    To serve your turn long after they are gone,
And so hold on when there is nothing in you
    Except the Will which says to them: 'Hold on!'
If you can talk with crowds and keep your virtue,
    Or walk with Kings—nor lose the common touch,
If neither foes nor loving friends can hurt you,
    If all men count with you, but none too much;
If you can fill the unforgiving minute
    With sixty seconds' worth of distance run,
Yours is the Earth and everything that's in it,
    And—which is more—you'll be a Man, my son!

Kipling's words did help. I liked them so much that they now hang on a plaque in my office. Time heals all wounds and wounds all heels, as the satire goes.

But time doesn't heal all wounds, *completely*. That's the way it is with some pain. But we have a choice. We can dwell on things like this, or we can commit them to the past. When the past lives on in the present, it's easy to get trapped in it. I want no part of that. Sometimes it's better to forget, even when you can't forgive. It's unfortunate that a friend will throw you under the bus. But that need not paralyze you or mire you in bitterness. Besides, there's the hard truth that must be considered and that is that *it takes two to tango*. I must share some responsibility for the way these events unfolded. Which raises the question, was my partner a bad guy? For me the question is irrelevant. The damage is done. The only thing to do in such a scenario is pick yourself up, dust yourself off, and move on down the road . . . and remember: there are still people who love you and that they can sustain you and be at your side to fight for you in life's future battles.

Final Note: Kipling wrote "If" as if he were giving advice to his son. He wanted to help him find his place in the world and to live with integrity by developing the qualities that he considered made a "good" man: self-worth, compassion, a strong work ethic, the ability to interact with others from all walks of life while not stooping to the pettiness of others, and the capacity to care about others while maintaining self-dignity.

CHAPTER 17

Somewhere Over the Rainbow

"Somewhere over the rainbow, way up high,
there's a land that I heard of once in a lullaby."
—Written by Harold Arlen and Yip Harburg;
from the movie The Wizard of Oz

Dear Reader: You will be happy to know that this is an uplifting chapter. Let me start then by telling you that I am a goal-oriented person, and the key to achieving almost any goal is perseverance. Perseverance is essential because some things take a long time to achieve, and because there are often so many obstacles thrown in the way that the urge to quit is powerful. But I'm lucky that, by breeding or birth, I'm just thickheaded and stubborn enough not to give up very easily. It seems that I've been programmed to operate like a tank that has only forward gears. I don't have a reverse gear. This, of course, is a blessing and a curse. I choose to focus on the blessings, but I've certainly experienced the curses, as you, by now, know.

I've always been a good, or at least capable, athlete. I excelled in many sports when I was young. During the summers when I was a boy, I played baseball all day long. By the time I got to college, and it was clear that my baseball skills were unexceptional, all I wanted to do was play football. And after playing football throughout college, and failing in a pro football tryout, I had to come to terms with the fact that I was at the end of my time in organized sports. There were no more teams on which I could play, except for a few softball leagues, and I did do that. But that level of play was a far cry from what I had once been involved in—serious competitive sports. So, I quit, and I got lazy. I tried to stay in some kind of shape, but I did nothing too challenging. At most, I'd run one or two miles, for one or two days a week, on the roads near my home.

And that's all I did until a coworker saw me running and approached me the next day at work. "I didn't realize you were a runner," he said.

"I'm not a runner," I told him. "I occasionally go out for a run."

"Oh, it looked like you were keeping up a pretty good pace."

I just nodded.

"Have you entered the Fort Lauderdale Annual Spring 10K race?" My fellow worker wanted to know.

"No. And what's a 10K race?" I asked.

"You know, 10K," he said.

"No, I don't know. What's a "K," and how far are ten of them to run?"

He said, "A 10K race is a little longer than six miles."

"Six miles? All in a row, and on the same day?" I thought the idea was ludicrous. "Are you serious? Do people actually do that?" I asked.

My colleague assured me that people actually did, and that this 10K race was a highlight of the year in the city. He saw me running and, based on that alone, he thought I might want to consider entering it. I like a challenge and I signed up for the race because it gave me a goal. My goal was just to finish six miles without dying. The race was just forty-five days away, so I started training the very next day. I ran a mile the first day. Within a week I was up to two miles every day. That's right—I was running every day. A week before the race, I completed a five-mile run, and by then I'd run out of training time, and I had to do the 10K with the level of training I had. There was no "not showing up," despite my fear at that point. I was nervous on race day, as I didn't know how races actually worked. I pictured a few really dedicated athletes showing up, and that I'd be watching them disappear into the distance as the race progressed, with me chasing them down.

But when race day arrived, there were thousands of people at the start line. It was a circus. I was astounded. Judging by what I saw, I could hardly believe that some of those people could run two miles, much less six. But they did, and so did I. I finished the race with a fairly competitive time for my age group. And knowing I could have a goal for a faster time in the future, I suppose I got hooked on road racing that day. I decided that I would run another race and do it faster. I trained every day that summer, in the Florida heat and humidity. I ran until my feet squished in my shoes from all the perspiration that collected there. By that fall, I was convinced I could run a marathon.

That October, just six months after my first 10K race in Fort Lauderdale, I ran the 26.2-mile New York City Marathon. The details of that marathon are the subject of another story in another chapter. But it's enough to say here that my first marathon experience was life-changing. After that race, I felt like I could walk through walls, that I could do anything. With those beginnings, I ran nine more marathons over the course of the next few years, before injuries, schedule conflicts, and my running obsession ran its course. In fact, it was the train wreck experience in my last marathon that convinced me that I never wanted to do another.

Yet I kept running for years after that last marathon, though I never again logged the sixty to seventy miles I once had every week. I'd train a little bit, and I'd enter the occasional Thanksgiving Turkey Trot or a Fourth of July event. But age and bodily wear and tear took their toll, and I turned more and more to hiking with my now wife, Lorraine, and my daughter. At that time, we lived at the top of the coastal range of mountains in Laguna, California. This range is full of hiking trails. We would hike along the rim trails or down to the beach, where we'd swim, and then hike back up the hill home. The hikes were challenging, but we were able to complete them without too much drama, so I thought we might want to consider doing some *bigger* hikes. I decided that since I'd graduated to marathons from 10Ks, my family might do the same with hiking trails.

When I mentioned this idea to my wife and daughter, they didn't exactly share my enthusiasm about the bigger hikes. But they didn't rule them out, either. And when I suggested a Grand Canyon hiking trip, the silence was deafening. I wasn't proposing anything crazy like a top to bottom and back to the top hike, I said. I'd done that hike years before, and *that* is an aggressive hike. But I did know the trail and I thought I knew their capabilities, so I suggested not going all the way to the Colorado River but only to Plateau Point, before returning to the rim via Bright Angel Trail. The two of them agreed, thinking it would be at most a five-hour round-trip, but one with incredible scenery that would take their minds off the actual physical exertion.

For those who have hiked the canyon, you know the Bright Angel Trail is the main thoroughfare into the canyon. And since we were making the long trip to the canyon from Southern California,

I thought why just stop at the top and look down into it? Why not walk in and really experience it? We made it to the canyon with plans to do the Plateau Point hike. The Bright Angel Trail descends 4,400 feet over 9.5 miles all the way down to the river. It's important to know that the trail actually descends through two canyons—the outer one and the inner one closest to the river. We planned to hike just the outer canyon, turning around at Plateau Point, the place where the trail then descends all the way down to the river through the inner canyon. The inner canyon hike is longer and more difficult. We set out early in the morning on the trail. The sun was shining and the temperatures were pleasant. I felt confident that it would be a good day. What could possibly go wrong with a hike that "old women and children" routinely do?

The short answer is . . . a lot. For the sake of brevity, let me state that my wife, Lorraine's experience was bad enough that day that she considered initiating divorce proceedings before we even emerged back on top of the canyon rim. Yes, I am exaggerating about the divorce proceedings, but the hike back up the Bright Angel trail from Plateau Point was so awful for her that at one point I actually considered calling a helicopter to airlift her out of there. Let's just say that she did not enjoy the hike. It's true the hiking was tougher than I'd thought it would be. I had underestimated its difficulty. Thank God my eleven-year-old daughter, Julia, found a friend on the way up, and the two of them walked together and danced out of the canyon like happy little girls do. It took two days before my wife cooled off enough to resume speaking to me. When she did, I apologized and said, "In the future, honey, I'll be more circumspect before suggesting another hike like that one."

A year later, I was online, reading about Utah outdoor destinations. It's a spectacularly pretty state, and of all the places I've toured on my motorcycle, it is my favorite because the roads and the scenery are great, and because it has so many national parks. Utah has lots of outdoor activities, too, including hikes. We were looking to do a road trip somewhere, and Utah looked like a good place for a weeklong vacation. I suggested that we make the trip, mentioning we could do some sightseeing and *maybe* even do some hiking. We drove up to Moab and the Arches Park National Park area, traveling in the springtime, but when we arrived, the temperatures were much warmer than normal. During the daytime, the mercury hovered near one hundred degrees. The first morning we went to the arches area, did a short hike, and took a lot of pictures. It was fun, but the hike was easy and a bit tame. The girls were happy. I need to mention here that I get bored easily, especially on vacations. I always want to be doing something, and the more challenging it is, the better. In fact, my perfect vacation day is a day full of activities so physically demanding that by the day's end all I want is some beer and tacos, before collapsing and falling asleep.

The next morning, I was in the hotel lobby, thumbing through one of the local guidebooks when I ran across a potential activity I thought we all might want to do. This is verbatim what I read in the guidebook: "The Negro Bill Canyon Trail is a pleasant five-mile roundtrip hike four miles from Moab, Utah. At the turnaround of the hike is the Morning Glory Arch, which with a span of 243 feet is the sixth-longest natural rock arch in the United States." I thought, this sounds "doable." After all, I had not forgotten the Grand Canyon hike just twelve months earlier. And I did not want my wife having that experience again. I told my wife and daughter about the trail. They were less excited about doing it than I was. I could see that they were having a "here we go again" reaction. "But," I persisted, "look at what it says here . . . a pleasant five-mile roundtrip hike." What could possibly go wrong?

It was already hot when we started out on the hike that morning. There weren't many clouds in the sky to relieve the glare of the sun or to temper the heat. And after about a half hour, the mutiny began. My wife and daughter started out with some lower-level griping. You know, saying passive-aggressive things like, "It's really hot out here," and "It looks like no one else is out hiking today but us." It was true—we hadn't seen another soul on the trail. I thought, maybe it's true that "only mad dogs and Englishmen and Kevin venture out in the noonday sun." But, heck, it wasn't even ten o'clock in the morning yet. To be fair, it *was* hot. I tried to ignore the gathering mutiny and ploughed ahead on our family hike to the sixth-longest arch in the world.

We'd never hiked in the area before, and since I rarely read the details of anything before setting out, we had no real idea what still lay ahead of us on the trail. It was also hard to judge how far we'd walked. It wasn't just the temperature fanning the flames of their growing dissatisfaction, it was also *not knowing* how much farther we had to go. We finally stopped as I wanted to check in with them before their concerns about our hike blossomed into a full scale—*we're turning back*—mutiny.

"What's going on with you two? Are you okay?"

"It's hot out here, and it's getting hotter. And there's no one else out here. Doesn't that tell you something?" my wife said.

I was hot. And a cold beer did sound pretty good. But I countered, "We've come this far. It's probably not too much farther. Why not just keep going? We can see that arch, and then we can turn back and get lunch."

"It's hot out here, and there's no one else here. Why not go back now?!"

"I know you just mentioned that. But we're really close, I think. If we turn back now, we might miss something really great. It's like life.

You start out, you get tired and dejected, and all you want to do is quit. What you can't know is how close you may be to the prize, and if you quit because the going is tough, you might miss out on that prize."

My daughter rolled her eyes. She was accustomed to my sharing these life lesson talks. She wasn't buying this one, but she agreed to go on "for a little longer." "Okay, let's go ten more minutes, and then we'll go back."

Five minutes further on, we crested a hill on the trail and there it was . . . the sixth-longest natural stone arch bridge in the United States. But that's not all there was at the end of the trail. No, it's what was *under* the bridge that caught our attention. Under this big stone arch lay a pool of crystal-clear water about the size of a backyard swimming pool. It was right there, blue and wet at the end of the trail. It seems that the arches in Utah are comprised primarily of sandstone. Sandstone is porous and very good at trapping water and moisture. And I guess that when temperatures reach a certain point during the day, the arch essentially "sweats out" this water, and gravity does the rest, causing the water to drip into pools in the shade under the arch.

I ran to the pool of water, kicked off my hiking boots, stripped down to my underwear, and plunged in. The pool was about four feet deep in the middle, and the water was perfectly cool. My wife and daughter stood there, watching. "You're coming in, right? This is the prize I was just talking about back there on the trail. C'mon. Get in. You will feel *so* much better." It took a little persuading, but they jumped in, too. The water was perfect. We were the only ones out there on the trail, enjoying that pool. It was a wonderful moment. And best of all, I'd been right about continuing on with the hike. I love it when I'm occasionally right about one of my life's lessons talks. But I didn't rub it in. Instead, I just grinned like I was about to rub it in. My wife looked at me and said, "Don't even think about saying what you're thinking!"

"What would I be saying?" I asked in mock seriousness.

"You know . . . your little lesson a few minutes ago about pushing on and the prize at the end?"

"I'm not saying anything." I really didn't have to. She had just said it all.

"This is pretty cool, though, you must admit? Think what we would have missed if we had turned back?"

My wife glared a little in mock anger, but she was having fun, too.

We spent a half hour out there, on a hot day in Utah, floating in perfectly clear cold water before we headed back to the car, where somewhere along the way the griping about the heat and the hike resumed. But we were headed home, and nothing could burst my little bubble, so I said nothing. I just let them talk, as I know that as long as the two of them are talking, everything is well. It's the moment they stop and it gets silent that I have to worry. I wasn't worried. Heck, the day was already perfect. I was happy the whole way back, thanking God for that pool of water, and for saving my ass.

And that was our Utah hiking trip. I didn't press my luck any further on that trip by suggesting another hike. When I think back, I wonder what might have happened had that pool of water not been there. The truth is, we would have simply walked back, maybe in silence, and within a day the hike and the heat would have been forgotten. But because the water *was* there, the hike will never be forgotten. It has become the stuff of family legend. I believe there *are* good things at the end of the rainbow if you push on, just like that pool of water was at the end of the trail that day. Of course, there's no guarantee that there's anything at all at the end of the trail when you chase a rainbow. But there's always the promise that there might be, and for me, that means if one keeps the faith and believes, that there just might be the work a pot of gold at the end of the rainbow.

CHAPTER 18

The Zone

"It's a dimension as vast as space and as timeless as infinity. It is the middle ground between light and shadow, between science and superstition. It is an area which we call the Twilight Zone."
—Rod Serling, narrator of the introduction to the TV show - The Twilight Zone

What happens in the "Kehoe Zone" was the original idea that gave birth to this book. I thought I could write an entire book on all the little stupid, frustrating, and meaningless things that have conspired to drive me crazy in life. I'd had so many experiences where if something could go wrong, it did go wrong. I thought I'd write about all those mind-numbing experiences where, for example, contractors disappeared in the middle of a job, or they installed something backward, or water leaked in some inaccessible place in our home and required an army of plumbers to find it, or a package that was absolutely promised for delivery on a certain day never showed up, or my computers did whatever they damn well pleased whenever they wanted, or I had to deal with anyone in government on anything. But, as I began writing that book, I found that all those stories became a bit tedious. Even though each disaster was different, the common plotline was some version of someone saying, *I've never seen this before, Mr. Kehoe.* That's why I decided instead on sharing a single story in this chapter to convey the message about all the little and large annoyances that drive us crazy.

In our home, we call this place, where *if it can go wrong, it will go wrong*: the Kehoe Zone. It's like the Twilight Zone. You know you are in the zone when the people you hire to repair your problem say something like, "Mr. Kehoe, I've never seen anything like this before." We've heard the words so many times that we created "the Code." The purpose of the Code is to warn and inform any contractor and vendor, *before* they do anything, that they can never utter those words. Yes, I actually tell people this before we engage with them. I nicely let them know, "I've hired you to fix this problem because I'm assuming you're the expert. And if it does turn out that you've never encountered my problem before, my hope is that you will not say those words and simply find the solution." That seemed like a fair request to me.

Here's an example of the Zone. I was on my computer attempting to play an Amazon Prime yoga class. The virus had shut down the health club we went to, so I wanted to do some kind of workout. This seemed like a simple idea, until the "Unsupported Plug-in" message popped up on my computer screen. I immediately felt deflated. All I wanted to do was to take the yoga class and now the Zone shows up? This should be a simple thing to do, right? But it never is in the Zone. I took a breath and, wanting a quick solution, I called my computer-expert friend, Larry. You've already met Larry—he's the "prince," and also an expert on all things related to Apple computers. I was hoping he wasn't busy, as when he's available, he's usually willing to help me find a quick solution in such situations. In fact, he's been bailing me out of my Apple computer problems—as well as some other problems—for decades. I was hoping for a quick solution so I could just do the darn class.

I was irritated for sure. Because, for crying out loud, why couldn't my computer work for this one little thing? Was that asking a lot of a $2,000 device? How many years have the engineers and programmers had to bulletproof these things, anyway? What if cars had the same track record for reliability? Am I expecting too much? Yet here we are in the twenty-first century still needing expert "geek squads" to make them work. I don't see any auto service squads roaming my neighborhood. This is what the Zone does to me. It reduces me to a babbler of rhetorical and existential questions.

I got Larry on the phone. We started working on the "Unsupported Plug-in" problem. Ten minutes into the call, Larry got quiet. Then he said, "I know I'm not supposed to say this, but I have never seen this before, Kevin." Larry knew the Code. He'd been read in. He knew better than to say the words. I reminded him of this. He laughed and apologized. This could only mean that the problem was bad, and there'd be no quick fix and no yoga class. I would have turned the computer off right then and gone out and taken a walk instead, but it was one hundred degrees outside. Now what?

The Kehoe Zone has been around for as long as I can remember. My friends joke with me, saying, "Kehoe, if you didn't have bad luck, you'd have no luck at all." I know this is not really the case, and these little annoyances are not unique to me, but it feels like this kind of thing happens way too often. In fact, it sometimes feels like I'm living in a bubble where the laws of physics and simple common sense are suspended, for no good reason at all. I'm not being paranoid. It actually does feel like the Zone is out to get me. That's why Larry and everyone who knows us understands the code, and knows never to say, "I've never seen this before." The Code is like the first rule of Fight Club: you don't talk about Fight Club. We try not to talk about the Zone.

The Zone is not limited to computers. It includes everything and everyone: home improvement contractors, customer service departments, equipment and vehicle manufacturers, car dealers, and, yes, even the world of health care and medicine. The Zone rarely takes a day off. In the middle of a perfectly good day, the Zone will roll in like a dark cloud and wreak its havoc with microproblems that occupy hours of my life, and can at times come close to reducing me to a babbling lunatic. And it can happen anywhere, not just at home. There was the time when my wife Lorraine and I were driving to my doctor's appointment, and we heard what sounded like a beeping noise coming from under the dashboard of our car. My wife was driving so I dialed up and asked to speak to a technician at our car dealership. The tech wanted to hear the beeping noise, so I pressed my cell phone onto the dashboard so he could listen and hopefully diagnose the problem for us. He almost immediately said, "Sir, I have never heard that noise before."

My wife was listening to the call on the speaker. She looked at me in mock horror and mouthed, "Has he not been read into the Code?" I looked at her and shook my head, "Probably not, he's too new." I explained the Code to the tech. I was attempting to be humorous to relieve the tension, but he didn't get my joke. He was one of those millennial tech guys. You know the type: two dogs, no kids, drinks the right beer, and has a beard. For a guy like him, baby-boomer humor barely registers, so my joke fell dead or went completely over his head.

I changed the subject and asked him, "What should we do? It sounds like the beeping noise is getting louder." And, in fact, it was getting louder and more regular. My wife was very concerned and wanted to know if we should stop and turn off the car or keep on going. She was already stressed out, as we were on the way to my weekly chemo-infusion appointment. These appointments weren't fun. We spent six to seven hours hooked up to multiple tubes that look like spaghetti, all of which pumped poison into my veins through a port device buried under my skin. On top of that, we knew that for the following forty-eight hours, I'd feel like hell, vomiting and praying for relief. That is hard for anyone to watch, but it was especially tough for my spouse.

If you are not familiar with chemo treatments, you show up at the hospital, check in, and you're assigned a nurse. She shows you to your chair and hooks you up to an IV. You're in a big room with a lot of other people all going through the same routine. The treatment begins with a dose of steroids and anti-nausea medicine. This infusion can take an hour or longer. Then you get the real poison. It's usually a cocktail of several anti-cancer drugs. The stuff is designed to kill cancer cells. And these drugs are nondiscriminatory— they kill healthy cells, too. That's why you lose hair and the feeling in your hands and feet due to neuropathy. Like I said, it's not a fun day. It was always stressful for my wife to watch, and the beeping noise was adding to her stress level.

For those like me who survive and beat the cancer back, returning to an infusion center after treatments are complete is often enough to induce the same nausea I felt when I was actually receiving the treatments. Even to this day, I can't go into one without feeling a little like that. I guess I know what those poor people there are experiencing. However, I make it a point to return there on occasion, usually following my quarterly PET/CT scans, to visit the nurses who helped me get through those days. They're always happy to see me, and I'm happy to see them again. They tell me that they are always glad to see former patients alive and looking like humans again. It makes them feel like what they do matters. And it does.

Thanks for allowing me that digression. I continued talking to the technician while my wife drove on to the hospital. She was getting frustrated with the technician. He was trying anything by this point, asking things like, "Have you checked this? How about that? What indicator lights are on?" My wife kept saying that nothing looked out of the norm. And while she was talking to the tech, I did something out of character. I opened the glove compartment and began leafing through the oh-so-easy-to-use, 1,200-page owner's manual. My wife was nearly in shock. "What are you doing?" she asked. "You're reading the manual at a time like this?"

"Yeah, I thought it might help."

"I've never seen you read any manual before."

"I usually don't," I said, "but I think the tech could use some help."

It's true. I never read manuals or instructions. Manuals are too long and the people who write them assume I have some prior knowledge of the subject—which I don't. Also, I don't bother reading them because an 800-number is usually provided, and I just call the number right off the bat. I'd rather wait fifteen minutes than try to decipher the written instructions of some engineer. And I use those fifteen minutes, before someone joins the call, to push buttons on whatever device I'm calling about to see what happens. My wife was still talking to the technician when he suggested we pull over and turn off the car.

"We are not turning off the car," my wife yelled. "We're already late, and if we turn the car off, it might never start again. I'm not pulling over! What if something is really wrong and turning off the car causes more damage?" My wife can be a panic-button pusher. She imagines every possible awful ending. The tech was frustrated now, too. I could hear it in his voice. My guess was he'd thought that he'd have solved the problem by now. It was right about then that I discovered the source of the noise.

But first, an important digression. When I was getting chemo, it was delivered over three days. Day one was at the infusion center, where the initial dose was delivered. Day two was at home, as I was still attached to an infusion device and pump, which delivered a continuous but slower flow of the poison. Then day three was the return to the infusion center to have the entire apparatus disconnected, until the next time. We were in the car on the third day of that cycle. We were returning to the infusion center to have the device and the pump removed. And in all the excitement of the call, and with the warming temperature inside the car, I decided to take off the sweatshirt I'd been wearing. And that's when the beeping noise got really loud. I found myself looking at the pump which until then had been hidden under my sweatshirt.

"Hey, honey," I said. "I think I figured out where the noise is coming from."

"You found something in the owner's manual?" my wife asked.

"Not exactly," I said. "I think that beeping noise is coming from my chemo pump." And so it was. That day, we were running late. We had, until then, always arrived at the infusion center *before* the pump ran empty. We had been told, but never experienced that when the pump ran dry, it would beep and flash a warning light. We'd heard the beeping, but we hadn't seen the flashing light because the pump was underneath my sweatshirt. The noise wasn't coming from the car—it was coming from the pump.

I looked at my wife. We burst out laughing. The tech had no idea what was going on. "I think we found the problem," I said. And I told him about the pump, and that things like this only happened to us inside the Kehoe Zone, and thanked him for all his help. And that was that. Or was it? I now think that God gave my wife and me that moment in the middle of those terrible days of chemo to remind us to laugh, because as bad as things can seem at times, even in the Kehoe Zone, good things could still happen.

I was thinking about that day in the car with the chemo pump as Larry worked on my "Unsupported Plug-in" problem.

"Try this," he finally said.

I tried his suggested fix, and it made the problem go away. I got to take my yoga class after all, with Dean, the millennial yoga instructor with a beard. Maybe you too have a "zone" with unsupported plug-ins and beeping noises. I think the zone is God's way of reminding us that even when things go wrong, things still go right . . . and that the little things really are just the little things. If after considering all this, you still feel like drop-kicking your computer, you might just want to "walk away" from the problem and start Happy Hour earlier that day. And while you're having that martini and looking up to heaven, wondering "why me?," you might want to thank whomever you pray to that *you* never have to visit an infusion center.

Postscript: During the process of final manuscript review, Kevin's cancer returned, and he is back in the dreaded infusion center.

CHAPTER 19

Good Men

"Two roads diverged in a wood, and I took the one less traveled by, and that has made all the difference."
—Robert Frost

The one constant in life is that we have to make choices and be responsible for those choices. It's not something that can be delegated or ignored. At least, that's my experience. And if you're like me, you've made both good and bad choices and had to live with the consequences. I've thought it would have been nice not to have made so many dumb choices and had to learn so many lessons the hard way. And I've also wished, on occasion, that life came with a handbook and instructions. It took me some time to realize that life does come with a handbook and instructions: it's called your grandparents. If you have good grandparents, and not all of us do, they can show you how to avoid at least a few of life's harshest lessons—if only because they've made those mistakes themselves. And though my grandfathers were not big on giving me advice, I learned a lot just by observing them.

Those two men were similar in temperament but very different in the choices they made about how to live. You've already met my maternal grandfather. His name was Maurice Rooney. He was born in Ireland. He was an immigrant. He passed away at age seventy-five of colon cancer, which was the same disease that almost took my life. He was a police officer with the NYPD and walked a beat in Harlem in the 1930's, and the people there called him Red. He, like my mother and I, had red hair. He fathered four daughters and a son. His only son died of cancer in 1966 at the age of thirty-four. Other than his love for his children and his adopted country, America, the great love of his life was his wife, Nellie.

Nellie wasn't an easy woman to live with, as her daughters will tell you. But I know she loved me. I think that's because she preferred boys to girls. And I *was* her first male grandchild of the twenty-three she had. The great love of her life was her son, Tommy. After he passed away, she survived him by less than two months. They say she died of a broken heart. I was young at the time, but I remember both of their deaths. It was a terribly sad time. My grandfather mourned them both to the end of his days. And since I was older when he finally passed away, I recall his funeral in detail.

Irish wakes and funerals are traditionally three-day affairs concluding with a Mass, a funeral procession that drives past the decedent's residence on the way to the cemetery, and a burial ceremony. All this is capped off with a big gathering at someone's home where there's food, whiskey, toasts, and remembrances. My grandfather's funeral followed this tradition. What I most remember about his passing, however, were the number of people who came to pay their respects. There were so many people at the funeral home and the Mass that both were filled to overflow. The size of the crowds made

ONE HIT WONDER

a lasting impression on me. And I thought then that I'd like to have as many people mourning my passing.

Why had so many people come out to say good-bye to my grandfather? The simple answer is that he was a good guy. He was extroverted, funny, kind, helpful, and *happy*. He wasn't rich or famous. He didn't change the world in any spectacular way. He was simply a good and dependable man whom everyone seemed to like.

My father's father, Edwin Kehoe, was my other grandfather. He was born in Brooklyn, New York. I don't know much about his early life but he, too, was of Irish descent. His father owned and operated a trucking company, so the family had money. But he didn't follow his father into the family business and instead sold it, banked the money, and took several midlevel management jobs throughout his life. He fathered four children—two boys and two girls—and he had thirteen grandchildren. My father was his oldest. Like my mother's father, my father's father also buried one of his sons. His second son, his namesake, was murdered in Manhattan one night inside his restaurant on West Twenty-Third Street. Both my grandfathers experienced the pain of burying a child.

Other than his love for his children, my Edwin Kehoe's great love, or at least where he spent much of his time, were his fish aquariums. He had four or five very large tanks filled with all kinds of fish, which I loved to look at when we visited him. Just like my other grandfather's wife, his wife also was not an easy person to live with. She was a difficult woman. But unlike my mother's mother, who was all heat and passion, my grandmother Dorothy Kehoe, was all ice and hard edges. She wasn't evil, as my mother firmly believed, but she had a cold personality. Their marriage was very much the opposite of that of my mother's parents. What I most remember was the difference between the funerals of the two men. Where Maurice's funeral was packed with mourners, Edwin's had almost

153

no one. He was introverted, quiet, kind, helpful, and I think, *un-happy*. He was richer, but he wasn't famous, either. He didn't change the world. But he was a good and dependable man whom very few seemed to know.

There was no Irish wake for Edwin like there had been for Mau-rice. Why this happened is a sad story. It was an unhappy ending for a man who deserved better. The few people who did come to his wake—well, *almost* attended his wake—were primarily close and immediate family, not the crowds that attended the service of my mother's father. I say *almost* attended his wake because my fam-ily tried to but were prohibited from attending. Here's how that happened. When my father and his sister, Mary, and their children arrived at the funeral home, a fight broke out between one of my cousins and the husband of my father's sister, Patricia. I wasn't in-side the funeral home when it happened so I can't say exactly what precipitated the brawl, but the incident was rooted in the circum-stances that led up to my grandfather's death.

Just days before my grandfather passed, my father, who wasn't getting good information from his mother and sister, Patricia, re-garding his father's health, made a trip into New York City to his parents' home, uninvited. What he found there was . . . very trou-bling and disturbing to him. His father was lying alone in bed, and it appeared he'd been left unattended for some period of time. His condition reflected this lack of attention . . . and I will leave it at that. My father was greatly upset by this and with the way his own mother and sister had neglected him. He shared the details of what he'd found with his other sister, Mary.

So, when Mary arrived at the funeral home with her family, she was seething with anger over the way she felt her mother and sister had neglected her father near the end. My Aunt Mary is not one to sugarcoat things. She isn't bashful. Immediately upon entering the funeral home, she said something to her mother and sister, accusing them of poor behavior. My Aunt Pat's husband was there at the door when that conversation took place. He was a lawyer and, by agreement of all, not a good guy. He stuck his nose into the conversation, telling Mary that he was a lawyer and that he was now barring them from entering the funeral home and paying their respects. Of course, Mary told him where he could go with his lawyer talk. And that's when he physically stepped in her way to bar her entry. He was a much larger person than my aunt. A few more words were exchanged, and Mary's son, my cousin, took exception to his words and actions, and the lawyer wound up on the floor, the result of a right cross delivered to his jaw. Ironically, all of this happened in the very same place where just a few years earlier my other grandfather's wake had been held.

As a result, my father and his sister, Mary, were barred from the funeral home, and a day later served with papers banning them from the funeral services and suing them for assault. The case ended up in a courtroom a few months later, but they were both acquitted. How's that for a send-off for my grandfather? My father's father was not a bad man. In fact, he was a nice guy. I liked him. But he, unlike my other grandfather, didn't marry the love of his life, and in many ways lived in unhappy circumstances. . . . that left him alone in death. One guy left the world with lots of people mourning him, and the other left with hardly a soul to see him off. His own son, my father, never got to attend his father's wake, mass, and burial. I loved both men, as much as I could love people who were only a small part of my life growing up. But even though I lacked close contact with them, they both taught me a valuable lesson . . . at least their funerals did. Choose wisely those with whom you spend your time!

The *choice* to be happy is the most important one we make, and it is mainly the result of our relationships with the people with

whom we surround ourselves. If we get that choice wrong, we pay
for it. Just as Maurice Rooney never talked about hiring lawyers to
solve his problems, Edwin Kehoe always did. It was like he didn't
trust the people around him, so he needed the lawyers to protect
him. My mother's father trusted the people around him because
he knew they'd do right by him. Just that knowledge, I am certain,
brought him joy and contributed greatly to his happiness. And in
the end, my father's father was proved right. His own family could
not be trusted to care for him when he needed them the most. Our
happiness seems to be tied up in the people we choose to be with.

If it were possible to grant you a vision of your own funeral
right now, would you want to see it? What if we could like Charles
Dickens's character, Scrooge, and get a glimpse of the future? I
wonder how many of us would not want to have that opportunity, perhaps frightened of what we might see. I got to experience
my grandfathers' funerals. Each man—for better and worse—was
a reflection of the choices he made in life about *how* to live. They
were two good men, from similar backgrounds, in similar times.
But they were two men who made a fundamentally different choice
about people. And those choices colored everything that happened
in their lives: their marriages, their families, their work, and, in the
end, their deaths. Maurice's funeral provided me with one vision
of a future. And I decided the day we buried him that I wanted a
funeral like his.

I've tried to emulate his choices over the years, especially in the
types of people with whom I choose to associate. I may have had
a head start with this, and been gifted with some of who he was
simply through genetics. My mother has told me, on more than
one occasion, that I am a lot like him. He may not have provided
me with many direct verbal lessons, but the way he lived and died
gave me with enough of a life handbook and instruction manual to

make some important choices about people and trust. We all make mistakes. That's the way we learn. But it is nice to know that when we arrive where a path diverges in the wood, we know enough to choose the right one—with the right people. It does make all the difference.

CHAPTER 20

Nine Lives

"A cat has nine lives. For three he plays, for three he strays, and for the last three he stays."
—*An old English proverb*

There's something powerful about the number nine. The Beatles wrote a song about it. For Christians and Hindus, nine symbolizes completeness. In China, nine is a lucky number. In Norse mythology, the universe is divided into nine worlds, and for some reason, the Greeks had nine muses. They say a cat has nine lives, and if that is also true of humans, then I am running out of lives. The reason for running through all these lives, according to my wife, is that I am rough on things and like a "bull in a china shop." This is the story of how I ran through almost all nine of mine and am now left with one, at least according to the old cat proverb. Am I worried? Well, yes I am, a little. Then again, maybe my count is off by one or two lives, so why change the way I do anything? And who knows, maybe the universe will grant me a few extra ones.

I started using up my lives at an early age, or at least I developed the behaviors that would use them up later. Though it may be family myth, it's been said that our local emergency room had a coffee cup labeled "Kehoe" on hand, just so my mother could have a something to drink while she waited for me or one of my brothers to be treated and released. I was then—and still am now—accident-prone. My mother and I have been to the ER more than a few times. The last time she accompanied me there, I was fifty-eight years old. She was visiting us in California for Thanksgiving weekend. My mother, my wife, and my daughter and her friend went to the beach that Wednesday evening to watch the sun set and enjoy the seventy-degree weather. I brought along my surfboard, thinking I'd "get wet." The surf was rough, windblown, and the waves were "walled up," but I paddled out, anyway. I was on a wave when I crashed as the lip closed out over the end on the board. As I tumbled, the edge of the surfboard caught the side of my head while I was in the spin-and-rinse cycle and opened a gash on my face. I was a bleeding mess as I walked up onto the beach. My daughter screamed and the life-guards came. People gathered, and I was rushed to the hospital and admitted to the ER to repair a broken nose and have seven stiches to close the gash the fin made when the board hit me.

My wife, my daughter, and my mother, all of whom were at the beach when the accident occurred, accompanied me to the ER. There was a long wait, and by the time I was released a few hours later, only my mother was still there in the waiting room. My wife and daughter both had prior commitments that evening, and I'd told them to go on ahead, assuring them that I'd be all right. That left only my mother alone in the ER, waiting for me, just like the old days—though she was without her coffee cup.

Hospitals never allow you to walk out under your own power. There's always a wheelchair. And when I came out in that wheelchair and the nurse asked me, "Do you have someone to drive you home?" I looked into the now empty waiting room and pointed to my mother and said, "Yeah, my mommy's going to take me home." The nurse didn't get the joke. God knows I try to light up the world with dry humor, but sometimes you're only as good as your audience. We went home. My mother drove, and I, who by now had two black eyes and a big bandage on my head, only looked forward to a shot of tequila.

My wife swears that I bleed almost every weekend. When she's not worried about my safety or my latest injury, she thinks I'm cute. You know, cute the way twelve-year-old boys are cute, despite the carnage they create and trail of broken things they leave in their wake . . . and for which they are *really sorry*. I can be like that. For example, when my wife and I hike in the hills, I toss stones over the edge of cliffs, just to watch them roll and crash. Or when we walk along the shore, I skip stones to see how many jumps I can make. I run when I should walk. I get cuts and scrapes all the time. That's why our medicine cabinet is well stocked with Band-Aids and ice bags.

The truth is, I've been hard on my body since I was a boy, sometimes so hard that I've had to pay with one of my nine lives. I actually used the first life up when I was twelve years old. It wasn't my fault. I was just there. In fact, I was asleep when the accident happened. We were returning home from a visit to our grandparents, Dorothy and Edwin. My dad was driving, and my mom, who was eight months pregnant with her sixth and last child, was sitting next to him in the passenger seat. It was raining hard on the Grand Central Parkway. We were headed eastbound when our Oldsmobile Vista Cruiser hydroplaned and was launched over the center divider into oncoming westbound traffic. By some miracle, we missed every car coming the opposite way, but we leveled a light post before spinning to a halt upside down in the outside lane. The car was totaled. Miraculously, my mother and I were the only family members who were admitted to the hospital. She, for obvious reasons, as she was in her eighth month, and I, for a brain concussion—my first of five. My dad and three other brothers and my sister were treated and released, suffering only cuts and bruises. It was a miracle. Pictures of the car confirm that it was almost completely flattened.

I used up my second life about twelve years later, again in a car. I had graduated from college and was playing semi-pro football, hoping to land a shot at a pro tryout. I had my bell rung in a game, on a hard tackle, and I had likely sustained a concussion. There were no concussion protocols in semi-pro ball in New York in those days. If you could identify the number of fingers someone flashed in your face, you were cleared. After the game, I was driving home, and my best guess is that I blacked out while driving, veered across traffic, and rammed a telephone pole in my 1968 Dodge Dart. My head created a bubble-shaped imprint on the windshield, which likely caused my second concussion in the space of a few hours. The telephone pole that stopped me was conveniently located in the driveway of a firehouse. At least convenient for the EMT crew who simply had to open the firehouse garage door and walk to the curb to respond. At least I had made the first responders' job easy. The dent I made in that telephone pole is still visible today.

However, I was not yet finished expending lives in auto accidents. A few years after the telephone pole incident, I fell asleep at the wheel of my 1973 Lincoln while I was driving home from my night manager's job. It happened early in the morning on the Southern State Parkway on Long Island. I was headed home when I nodded off for just a few seconds. That's all it took to have the car exit the highway and enter the wooded center divider. By the time

I was fully alert, there was a tree branch coming through the open driver-side window, almost poking me in the eye. The car was moving fast when I grabbed the wheel to stop the spinning and forward motion, just twenty feet short of the stone bridge abutment of an overpass. I looked around and looked up to God and thought, Jesus in heaven! It was completely quiet. There was no one around. After I composed myself and assessed the damage, I determined I could drive the car, so I headed home . . . wide awake! I was able to get the car home that night, and I didn't suffer any injuries, but that 1973 Lincoln never went anywhere again. It remained where I had parked it in front of my parents' home that night for the next two years, with grass growing under it during the summer. It was just too expensive to fix or tow away.

But there was a happy ending of sorts to the story. After two years of sitting out front in the street, my father finally issued an order: "Get that thing out of here tomorrow." That very evening, the neighborhood stoner, Kevin C., was out in his car partying when *he* fell asleep at the wheel and crashed his little VW into my Lincoln, wrecking his car and denting mine. Since I had been paying the insurance premiums on the car, I called the insurance company the following morning, and they sent out the claims adjuster. He looked the car over and said something like the best he could do was $500 for the damages. "Okay," I said. "It's not much, but I'll take it." I was trying not to grin too much. This was manna from heaven. By the way, Kevin C. was uninjured, but he had a big headache the next morning. In the end, I got $500 when in just a few short hours I was going to have to come out of pocket for the $150 towing fee to take it away. Oh, yeah, the insurance company paid the towing fee, too.

My fourth life was far more costly but continued the pattern of luck I had with vehicle accidents. I crashed my Suzuki 750 motorcycle, the one I rode to Florida and back to New York, on the entrance ramp to a parkway in Connecticut. I was late to a wedding reception, and I was in a hurry. I was going too fast when I crashed. I had entered a declining-radius turn onto the parkway, and I ran the bike wide and hit the guardrail. I hit it so hard that that the front wheel sheared completely off, and the rest of the bike was twisted into a funny shape. I was able to get to my feet and walk back to what remained of my once pretty bike. I remember walking over to the front wheel, picking it up, and trying to put it back on the rest of the bike. I was thinking that I could fix it. At some point, I gave up and walked back down the ramp to find a phone. I wanted to call my girlfriend at the time and tell her that I would be late to her brother's wedding reception.

The nearest phone was located back down the entrance ramp inside a Howard Johnson's restaurant. Later, on the way to the ER, the EMTs told me that when I walked in and asked for a phone, the receptionist almost fainted, seeing my condition. I was covered in dirt, I had road rash, and I was bleeding everywhere. I don't recall much of this. My first clear memory is waking up in the ER at Yale Memorial Hospital, the place where I would spend the next seven days of my life. I was admitted with a fractured spine and other assorted injuries, but the real concern for the doctors was a ruptured pancreas. The doctors believed I would require surgery to repair that damage. So, I never did make it to the reception that day.

When the pancreas is ruptured, it goes into high gear, producing too many of the enzymes that assist in normal digestion. According to the doctors, my pancreas was producing so many of these enzymes that there was a real risk they'd essentially digest my stomach. Because of my other injuries, any surgery had to wait until I was more stabilized. Until such time, and in order to save my stomach from being digested from the inside out, a tube attached to a pump was inserted into my stomach. The tube is first inserted through the nose and down the throat. If you've never had a tube inserted like this, count yourself lucky. I rate the tube through the nose into the stomach as my top five all-time awful things that can happen to a human. In addition, I was immobilized by sandbags to stabilize my spine. I was not permitted tranquilizing or pain-killing drugs because those might mask potential unseen nervous-system problems.

I was installed on the surgical ward in a room with two other guys. I was in such pain the entire time that by the third day I was in complete misery and couldn't bear the thought of another sleepless night. I was desperate for some relief. That night, in the early morning hours, I buzzed the nurse. I begged her for drugs, but she was firm, telling me that the doctor had forbidden them. I insisted that I needed them. She answered that we could discuss that in the morning when the doctor made his rounds. It was two a.m., and that was the wrong answer. I vaguely remember grabbing her by her collar: "You call the doctor right now and get me the drugs, and then I will let go. You decide." The other nurses on the station attempted to reason with me, but in the end, they woke the doctor and I got my drugs. I never saw that poor nurse again. Wherever you are, dear, I apologize. I was a desperate man that night.

One of the two other patients in the hospital room with me was a blacksmith. He looked pretty healthy compared to the rest of us, so I asked him why he was in the hospital. He explained that he'd been shoeing a horse when the animal reared back and kicked him. When that happened, he swallowed a nail that had been clenched between his teeth. He'd been admitted to the hospital so the doctors could monitor the nail's progress through his system and be ready to rush him into surgery at any moment to extract it. The doctors were hoping he might simply "pass the nail" without the need for surgery, but they didn't know. Thinking about this today, it's still hard for me to imagine that was a good plan. But there he was, in the same room with me. There's not much to do to entertain oneself in a hospital. Almost any diversion becomes exciting. In our bored state, we decided to start a wagering pool, betting whether the blacksmith would pass the nail or not. The early action, I recall, was on surgery, but as the days went by, the action turned to the "passing the nail." I'd bet on "passing the nail" right from the start, and in the end that's what happened. He passed it and three of us split $20.

I never had my surgery, either. The doctors weren't able to explain why or how, but by the fifth day at Yale Memorial, my pancreas showed signs of healing and turning off its furious production of stomach-digesting enzymes. And by the seventh day, the best day, that tube came out. While the procedure was unpleasant, I'll take the memory of relief I felt to my grave.

My fifth life involved a car, again. Except in this instance, there was no wreck. In fact, it was the absence of a crash that makes it feel like another miracle. My buddy John is a force of nature. And when he decides to do something, he does it. We were at school together at SUNY Stony Brook. One evening, John decided to go home to Ossining in upstate New York and wanted company for the drive. It was a bad night. It was cold and the roads were icy. I suggested we wait for morning to make the drive but, in the end, I got in the car with him and off we went. We'd had a few drinks that evening, and when we hopped in the car, we also realized we were flat broke. What I mean is that we had no money at all in our pockets, and there were at least two cash-collecting tollbooths between us and his apartment.

I recall two things about that ride. The first was about one half hour into the trip. I had fallen asleep. I was the passenger. John, too, had fallen asleep, though, and we found ourselves parked in a snowdrift on the side of the road. That should have ended the trip. But it did not. My next memory is waking up in John's apartment the next morning. I could hear him yelling from outside the apartment. It turned out, he'd gotten up, walked to a nearby deli, and purchased a "scratcher" lottery ticket. He'd won five thousand dollars. Go figure. When I asked him how we got home the night before and passed through the toll booths, he just shrugged his shoulders. I don't think he knew either. What I do know is there was no crash that night. That's a mystery I can't explain to this day. God gave me a "pass," and deducted one life from my ledger.

I left my sixth life out on Ortega Highway in Orange County, California. Ortega Highway, Route 74, starts in San Juan Capistrano and goes clear across Southern California through places like Lake Elsinore. The section of road from San Juan Capistrano to Lake Elsinore is forty miles of twisting turns, and, for motorcyclists, there's no better place to ride early on a weekend morning if you want to have some fun before the road fills with traffic. I made it a routine to ride that section of road almost every week. There's a big curve on the westbound return that is a long and open-throttle, full-lean left-hander that I loved to do at speed. I'd done the turn a hundred times before without incident. But on this particular morning, maybe because there was moisture on the road from the night before, or because a vehicle had deposited some oil I could not see, the tiny patch of tire that keeps a bike on the road let go its grip.

Whatever the cause, I low-sided off the road into the underbrush and trees and somehow landed on a small patch of grass fifteen feet below road surface. Had I been knocked unconscious, I might have lain there for a long time, as where I landed was invisible to passing motorists above. After I recovered my senses, I looked back to where I'd left the road. I saw that I had flown between two trees, splitting them like a football would slice the goal posts on a field goal try. The bike was a wreck, and there was no way to get it back up to the road on my own. I climbed up by myself and dialed my wife on my cell phone. There was no coverage, as I was pretty far from civilization. I wasn't too upset about not being able to reach her at that moment, as I wasn't looking forward to telling her what had happened. As I stood by the roadside in full bike gear, a couple of other bikers riding by saw me with no bike in sight. They stopped to investigate and helped me haul my bike back up the slope and call for a tow truck. They gave me a ride home, where I explained the morning's events to my very upset, but very relieved, wife. Only God knows how I bisected those trees and landed in the only patch of grass in a field full of rocks and boulders.

I was able to resurrect that bike, though, and give it renewed life. The frame and engine suffered minimal damage, and the bones of the bike were solid. I had that street bike transformed into a competitive race bike for the race track. And that's where I spent my seventh life—at a racetrack—specifically at Willow Springs Raceway. I loved to race that Suzuki GSXR 600 motorcycle at that track. We'd go there at least one weekend every month. I had recently obtained my racing license with a bike racing organization called WERA. The week before my very first race, we went to the Willow Springs Raceway to tune up the bike, practice, and hang out with other racers. The racing circuit is like any other hobby organization, whether it be fishing, boating, bowling, or surfing. There's a group of people where the track is part of their lifestyle, and you see the same people all the time, and you get to know them—a community of people with a shared passion.

I'd circled that track hundreds of times before then. I knew everything about it, just not enough to avoid what happened at Turn Nine that day. I don't remember anything about my crash. But the people at trackside who saw the crash said that I entered the turn hot, apexed a little too early, got back on the throttle, and simply ran out of track before I could pick the bike up. I exited the track at about 100 mph, entered the dirt infield, and cartwheeled. I and the bike rag-dolled about one hundred yards before coming to rest. It was what bikers refer to as a classic "yard sale." That phrase comes from what you usually see when you drive up on a garage sale—items are strewn everywhere around the place with little discernable organization. That's what my crash scene looked like. Pieces of my bike and my gear were strewn everywhere. My wife, who did not see the crash, told me I was conscious when she first saw me, but I was "not there" for at least thirty minutes before I started remembering anything.

We loaded the wrecked bike and drove home, dropping the bike at my mechanic's shop before I headed for the couch to lick my wounds. I refused to go to the ER that day. I relented the following morning when I awoke in such intense pain that I could not move and could hardly breathe. I should have gone to the ER the day of the crash. Why didn't I? I think the brain has a way of shutting out trauma as it's happening and in the immediate aftermath. Maybe it does this as a survival mechanism to give the body a head start on fixing itself before you realize how badly off you are. But I can assure you that twenty-four hours later, when that process was completed, all hell broke loose and my body said—take me to the hospital.

We went to the ER early the next morning. I was admitted with injuries that included ten broken ribs, a collapsed lung, and damaged knee. This time I stayed in the hospital for five days, where once again I made the acquaintance of my roommate. I don't recall his exact ailment, but it was a recurring condition that had over time required him to be hospitalized on many occasions. He was a good guy, and we spent a lot of time talking between morphine pump injections. He related how he'd smuggled in food and other items that were against hospital policy. Nothing dangerous, just things. I thought that was interesting, so before dinner arrived on the second day, I asked him, "Red or white?" He gave me a funny look, so I clarified: "If you had a wine preference with dinner tonight, what would it be? Red or white?"

"White," he said.

I texted my wife one word: "white." She arrived just before dinner smuggling in a bottle of white wine.

"Is this what you mean by smuggling?" I asked him.

"Exactly," he replied.

And this became our dinner tradition for the remainder of my stay. I'd ask: red or white? Then I'd text my wife, who'd arrive with a bottle of wine. I was on so many painkillers that the wine wasn't going to make any difference in my mind. And my roommate thought it was great fun.

As we got to talking more, I shared my impatience with hospital stays and my desire to leave as soon as possible. He wondered why I felt that way. He felt that staying in the hospital was preferable to going home.

He said, "You're better off here, you know."

When I asked him why, he simply said, "Better beds and better meds, dude."

He was so right about that! I soon discovered exactly what he meant after I was released. The quality of the beds, and the quantity and quality of the meds you have access to at home, are far inferior to what a hospital provides. With ten broken ribs, I should have stayed longer. It took another six weeks at home in bed before I could function again, and then only gingerly. We had to rent a hospital bed because I was unable to rise to a seated position from a regular bed. I needed the assistance of an electric-powered bed just to move. I never heard from my roommate again, nor have I been back to the racetrack since. That was a very near call.

Colorectal cancer still consumes my eighth life. And that experience is the story of another chapter. I can provide a brief summary here, however, starting with the fact that I am a survivor seven years after having been first diagnosed. I was stage 4 with a 30 percent three-year survival prognosis. Yet I am still here. When I asked Dr. Tara Seery, my oncologist, why I had thus far beaten the odds, she said, "It's hard to say exactly. But you're a bit of a freak of nature. Everyone's cancer behaves differently. Your cancer seems to be a *good actor*, not a bad actor like others I deal with. You're lucky, and that's my best guess."

Maybe what Tara said explains everything that's happened in my life. All I know is I'm on life number nine right now, and that I *am* lucky. I'm also grateful, and a little worried, too. Yet despite all my experiences and close calls, I'm still the same guy I've always been. I haven't changed much. My wife's right. I am like a twelve-year-old. I'm a little too reckless with my body and my choices. But I am older now, too. And I can't help rethinking the way I do things, especially in light of my brushes with mortality. I'm old enough to know that I'm not immortal and bulletproof like I was when I was twelve years old. I do take fewer risks these days, and I am more circumspect in what I choose to do. But I have to be honest: because if you offered me a bike and a free day to join you at the racetrack, I'd think about it, and I'd probably say—yes.

Final Note: That bike, my Suzuki GSXR 600, the one crashed twice and dropped off at my mechanic the day of my crash . . . still lives on. I ended up selling the bike to my mechanic. And about a year later, he texted me a picture of it from the track. He'd fully restored it and was racing and winning on it. Damn, if that bike doesn't have nine lives, too.

CHAPTER 21

That Guy

"I used to be somebody,
but now I am somebody else."
—Crazy Heart, *the movie*

You've probably watched a movie or TV show where one of the characters is sitting in a doctor's office with his spouse and a grim-looking doctor enters the exam room, holding the test results and diagnosis, and says something like, "I'm afraid it's cancer, Mr. Smith." And if you have any kind of heart, you can't help but feel your stomach drop, looking at those people as they register the news . . . and you think, I'm glad I'm not *that guy*, and I'm glad that will never happen to me. I've watched that movie. I've thought those things. I was glad I wasn't that guy until, one day, I was. But let me go back to the beginning.

About two years before I was diagnosed with cancer, I noticed some signs. There's no mystery about these signs as you can read about them on any medical website by typing in "colorectal signs and symptoms." I know—I visited those sites and I paid attention to the signs. I saw one of them and I contacted my doctor just like the website suggested. And when I did, my doctor did not seem as worried as I was. Just eight years earlier, I'd undergone my first colonoscopy and was given the ten-year all-clear prognosis. I wasn't due for my next colonoscopy for another two years. Instead of scheduling it earlier than the ten years recommended, he suggested another, less invasive, test, just to make certain. We did this and it came back negative. With now perfect hindsight, this proved to be a false result. The reality was a polyp had made the transition from benign to malignant . . . and it was continuing to grow.

The chief reason my doctor thought the colonoscopy was unnecessary was my lifestyle. I'd been doing everything "right" to minimize my chances of ever getting colon cancer. I watched what I ate. I consumed very little red meat, never touched fatty or fried foods, and avoided most sweets in my daily diet. I exercised and took care of myself. I was the poster boy for the guy who *never* gets colon cancer. That is what my doctor was telling me.

When I look back on it all, the fact that I got cancer despite all the lifestyle sacrifices I'd made to avoid cancer pisses me off a little, especially when I think about all the french fries, donuts, and hot dogs I missed out on. I got cancer despite my best efforts not to. After my false negative result, my symptoms persisted and I finally insisted that my doctor schedule me for another colonoscopy. What makes his resistance seem so surreal is that right up to the day before the test, he kept insisting I had no need to concern: "Don't worry about it. It will turn out to be nothing." I took what he told me as gospel.

On exam day, I came out from the anesthesia in the recovery room and saw my wife standing next to the bed. It took a few moments before my brain fully adjusted, and I could see that she and the attending nurse were there, talking to me and saying something like, "They found something, and the doctor will be in shortly to discuss it." My wife looked like she was going to cry.

"Okay, honey, what did they find? A gerbil? The keys we lost last year? What are we talking about here, sweetie?" The only reason I mentioned the gerbil was that I'd heard somewhere that some Hollywood actor once did something with gerbils in precisely the area of his body that I'd just had examined. Then the doctor came into the exam room.

"It looks like cancer," the doctor said. I think I went into shock. I was *that guy* in the movie, and I was having that out-of-body experience that happens when you get bad news. I felt like I was looking down on the three of us as he delivered the news.

"You're sure it's cancer?" I asked.

"Yes, pretty certain. I sent the sample off to the lab just now, and the results will probably be back in a few days."

A few days? Are you kidding me? I was thinking, I'm supposed to just go home now and somehow function for the next few days, waiting for the results?

"You told me not to worry," I said. "How can this be?" I guess my shock turned into anger at this point. But my wife was crying, so wringing the doctor's neck wasn't going to change a thing right then—it would only make the entire morning far worse. There may be more excruciating experiences in the world, but waiting three days to get confirmation of cancer is certainly somewhere on the list. The only way to avoid going to very dark and scary places in your head during those three days is to tell yourself that the tests will come back negative, and that you've done everything right in your life to avoid this very diagnosis. You tell yourself that it's not possible to have cancer, that you're not *that guy*. But the whole time,

I felt like those parents on the crime shows I watch whose child has disappeared. They have hope, but deep down in some terrible place in their souls, they know their child is gone. I was the same way. It won't be cancer, I kept saying to myself, but deep down, I knew it was.

We left the hospital, and my wife took me to the airport where I boarded a flight for a business trip that had been scheduled months before. I decided to go, as the thought of sitting around at home, with my brain running over the day, over and over again, and what the future might bring, made me almost ill. And three days later, I got the call from the lab. I was standing at Gate 23 at the Sacramento airport when my phone rang. The doctor told me that I had colorectal cancer and it looked bit advanced. He said that we should act immediately.

"Is it that bad?" I wondered.

"It's bad enough," the doctor confirmed. "And you should think about getting your affairs in order." Affairs? What affairs? I wasn't having any affairs. "Are you saying my life affairs?" I asked. I thought he'd said that what I had was treatable. I went into a minor panic. "Are we talking about dying here?" I said. The doctor clarified his words. He said he meant that I should clear my calendar for the near future, in order to get on top of everything as soon as possible. That made me feel a little better. But I was shaken.

In my opinion, there are crueler diseases than cancer, such as ALS, as I have seen what that can do. But cancer is cruel. Despite all the money and time invested in research, there really is no cure for colorectal cancer. This is true for many cancers. Instead, doctors provide treatment in hopes of killing it off for a while or at least halting its spread through the body. The treatments are based on statistically driven protocols tied to survivability percentages. In my case, the treatments could, and did, ultimately include surgery to remove the tumors, radiation to burn those tumors down, and chemo to poison the little cancers cells that had not yet become tumors but might be coursing through my body, looking for other places to grow.

My cancer was active. It *was* coursing through my body, and within a just few months my original stage 2 diagnosis morphed into stage 4 metastatic cancer as the disease spread to my lungs from my colon. Now the situation was serious, and the urgency to address it increased dramatically. I needed help. I was referred to the "best guy" for what I had, and I went to see him about treatment options. The doctor was located in San Diego. As fate would have it, that appointment changed everything that ultimately happened to me, but not in the way you'd think. That doctor actually declined to take me on as a patient because of the low probability of treatment success given where my cancer was at the time. I was shocked. I thought only district attorneys cherry-picked their cases. Doctors did, too? Who knew?

I looked over at the doctor, who'd referred me to this guy, and said, "He doesn't want to take my case? Seriously? Why did we come here? You know what? Screw him. Who even said that I wanted to work with him, anyway?" With that, I got up and walked out of the exam room, ranting the entire way home. I was upset. And when I get that way, I set my teeth. I was frightened, but I decided right there to be one of the three out of ten who survive what I had. That was my statistical prognosis. That's why that doctor had declined my case. Seven out of ten people who had what I had didn't make it past three years after being diagnosed. I understand doctors are busy, especially cancer doctors, unfortunately. But when that doctor declined my case, I changed my attitude about the coming battle, because I thought 30 percent was pretty good odds. Three people make it, statistically. I was going to be one of those three. And that's when and how my wife and I descended into cancer hell and finally met the doctor who saved my life. And her story is the stuff of another book.

It took three years of constant treatment, but we managed to fight the disease to a standstill. I was not in anything like remission, but it had stopped spreading. I was back at work and traveling when I found myself again at Gate 23 at the Sacramento airport. I was in the boarding area, waiting for the flight to be called, when I thought, *Why do I know this place?* And that's when I remembered that phone call from the lab three years earlier. I was where I first learned that I had cancer. I strolled over to the exact spot where I'd stood, taking the call. And I thought about the day in the exam room with my wife and her tears. I thought about the doctor who had declined my case. I thought about how my wife with her constant love, sacrifices, and care had allowed me to stay sane. But, mostly, I thought about being alive and how I could, at least for the moment, consider a future and make plans longer than for a few months. I wasn't cured, but I was no longer dying.

Bad things happen to good people . . . for no reason at all. There is an element of randomness we rarely consider in our day-to-day lives. We assume one day will follow another, as it always has—until in one moment it all changes, and you are *that guy*, maybe even with death staring you in the face. I am conscious of this randomness now. I know that tomorrows can be blown to bits, and you might find that your life is not run by you anymore, but by something else. I am conscious of, and humble about, the way I talk about cancer. I fear and respect the disease. I fear it, because it kills. I've seen people who were diagnosed when I was have their lives painfully cut short.

I respect the disease, because it can blow up like a gale on the ocean out of a clear blue sky. It can "go away" for a time, then come roaring back worse than before. When I'm asked about my battle and my survival to date, I never, ever say, "I beat cancer." That's like poking the bear to me. I don't want to poke the bear and wake it up. I just want to let the bear sleep.

We who survive do so first by the grace of God, and then through good doctors. The bear has a history of waking up just when you think it's hibernating. Then it comes back to claim what it didn't claim the first time around. I know this. I've seen it happen . . . to me. It's come back to me five times, and it resides within me still—like a sleeping bear. When people ask me about my survival, I just say, "I'm still here and fighting."

Bad things happen, not just to other people whom we read about in the news or whom we watch in the movies. It happened to my wife and me. Out of the blue, and into our wonderfully unexciting life, a monster came in the front door. We'll never be the same because of it. But we may be better. We've survived thus far, and because of my wife's love, I was able to keep my head and my hopes. Maybe that is the only way to deal with a monster that comes through the door. It's human to be afraid, but it's not helpful to wallow in fear. It took a while before the shock of the diagnosis wore off and I stopped thinking about dying every day. But from the very beginning, I avoided going down that black hole that starts with the question "why me?" It is not a helpful question as the answer might simply be—

because. . . . Instead of asking, "Why me?" I got into the habit of asking, "What next?" Maybe the old adage is true: "What doesn't kill you makes you stronger." We're stronger now, but what really matters to me is that I'm glad to be alive—today. We'll see what tomorrow brings and deal with it when it happens.

CHAPTER 22

Stupid, Stupid, Stupid

"Stupid is as stupid does."
—Forrest Gump

The stories in this book are the same stories I share with my friends and especially my second wife, Lorraine. She and I married later in life, and so she only knows the Kevin from these last twenty years, not the Kevin from his first forty. And from time to time a story or experience from the first forty years will come into my mind while we're driving or sharing drinks and dinner with our friends. This is one of those stories and I shared one over dinner with Ashleigh, my friend Scott's oldest daughter and her family. Ashleigh liked the story so much, she had a T-shirt made for me that has this chapter's title printed on the front. The events took place at John Wayne Airport in Orange County, California, the place where I lived for three decades of my life. It's an airport I got to know inside and out as I was there almost every week for most of those years. It helps to know, as some background, that *I do not suffer fools easily*, to fully appreciate what happened at that airport one morning. I am impatient with myself, and by extension with others—especially when I think their actions and decisions are, well, just stupid.

For more than thirty years, I traveled forty-plus weeks annually for business. During those years, I've managed to amass more than ten million air miles. That's more frequent flier miles than I know what to do with. But I'll work on that problem, now that I'm semiretired. I'm not boasting about this at all. In fact, I don't recommend the road-warrior lifestyle to anyone. It may sound glamorous for those who only travel infrequently. But, trust me, there's very little glamour in it. And whatever glamour there once was disappeared, for me, after the first two years of doing it. It's a grind and a job like any other. Instead of getting in a car and traveling on the freeway to commute to work, I went to the airport. And whatever small amount of glamour remained for me after the first two years disappeared after the events of September 11, 2001, when air travel became downright grueling.

As an aside, it's hard for me to believe that the TSA was the best possible government response to 9/11. How did they think inconvenience, long lines, and cavity searches replacing a simple walk to the gate was the best solution? And how, in the face of changing realities, like so much stuff getting through their security checkpoints, did they not make some simple adjustments to relieve the tedium of it all? Yet if you have to fly, you have to deal with the TSA and all the little stupidities they've introduced over the years. I'm not putting down the vast majority of people who work for the TSA—they're simply doing their jobs, and most do it with common sense and courtesy. But some of them seem to enjoy the power they possess to make your life miserable . . . a little too much.

My weekly routine involved an early departure from home every week to catch the early Monday morning flight— usually to a connecting flight in Dallas or Chicago—that would take me to my ultimate destination. I'd return home on a Thursday or Friday night, depending on my workload for the week. This was my job. My wife referred to me as her "weekend husband." And who knows, but maybe that in part explains the secret of our twenty years of marriage. We did the same thing every week. She drove me to the airport and she picked me up when I returned . . . always. I've talked to many road warriors over the years about my wife and her insistence on doing this for me, and I've never met anyone else whose spouse was as dedicated and did the same. My wife is a one in ten million.

Since Monday morning departures were my regular routine, it only follows that I crossed paths with other people whose lives and schedules were the same as mine. This included the people who worked for the TSA. They, like everyone else who works, have a regular weekly work schedule. As a result, it should surprise no one that I'd see the same TSA people working at the security checkpoints, doing the same job, every Monday morning. It's not as if I got to "know" any of these agents personally, but there certainly had to be some level of facial recognition going on—*at a minimum*. At least that was my assumption.

The day I'm talking about was one of these Monday mornings. I was in a hurry, running behind schedule, and I was rushing to catch my flight. I'll admit that I was not in a particularly humorous frame of mind, as I wasn't excited about my workload that week. I lined up behind the checkpoint and waited like everyone else. I put my two bags on the belt, took my laptop out (*why?*), and passed through the bag check and the X-ray machine. That was when the TSA agent on station decided to flag my luggage for the extra security protocol.

—·—

183

(*Again, why? Do they have such little faith in all the other screening processes that it's necessary to do this?*) The TSA agent was someone I "knew." She was there every Monday. She saw me, and I saw her, every week. We'd made eye contact almost every week. Of course, that doesn't rate as a major interaction, and she does, I suspect, see thousands of people every week, but I have to assume that there must have been some level of "facial recognition" for her. How could that not have been the case?

Now, I know the TSA is a government program that's for "our own good," so we have little choice but to put up with it. And I had, for the most part, borne all the TSA's inconveniences well enough. In fact, I did not really mind the extra baggage security protocol too much on a return trip when I got flagged for it, because everything in my bag was headed to the laundry, anyway. But on the journey out, after everything has been neatly packed, I wasn't as happy or forgiving about the extra security. So, there I was, late, my clothes neatly packed, looking at an agent who knew me, and now we were going to do the dance?

The woman began, as she was trained to do, by asking me, "Do you mind if I rifle through your newly packed things?" Okay, she didn't actually say that. What she actually said was, "Do you mind if I look inside your bag?" It's not a question. It's a statement of intent, and whether you like it or not, your bags are going to get opened. I sighed. You know that little irritation itch you get when something like this happens and makes you want to be a wiseass? Well, I stifled that urge. But I did look at her with an expression that said, "Really? We're going to do this today? You and me? We see each other every week. You know me. Why would I pack weapons this week?"

I saw no glimmer of recognition on her face. She opened my bag and proceeded to rifle through my neatly packed stuff, asking whether I'd packed anything "sharp." Again, I stifled the urge to be a wiseass. But I was becoming increasingly impatient. There are levels of "baggage searching." For example, there's level one: that's a cursory swipe of the inside of your bag with the bomb detector cloth, and that's it. You're done and free to go. Then, there's everything in between, and up to, level four, where the agents take everything out of your bag, pile it on the counter in public, and when they're done with that, ask you if it's all right if they just ball it all up and jam it back in . . . or would like to do that? This morning, the agent went to level four. And as I watched her, I felt like she was enjoying it a little too much. I was upset and I let my wiseass out. I muttered, "This is stupid."

When I said this, her face turned red. She looked at me as if I had accused her of awful and unnatural acts. She was almost livid. I don't know, maybe she was having a bad day or something and maybe I could have asked about that, but at the moment, from my perspective, her bad day was her problem, and she should have kept her home life out of her work life, just like the rest of us. That's not what she was thinking. She was not happy with my "stupid" comment, and she seemed determined to make whatever her problem was *my* problem. She escalated the situation.

She looked past me, and over my head, to something behind me over at the next checkpoint. When I turned around to take a look, I could see she was trying to get the attention of her supervisor. This man was working the next line over. When she finally got his attention, she pointed at me, indicating my bag using her hands to point to it, and said loudly enough for everyone to hear, "He said this is stupid."

The supervisor apparently couldn't quite make out what she was saying, and he mouthed back, "What?"

The agent repeated herself, "He said this is stupid," pointing at me.

It was like watching a tennis match, with the serve and return between the two of them. And when I next turned to look back to the supervisor, there stood two Orange County sheriffs directly in my line of sight. They were so close that their belt buckles and weapons filled my field of vision. They were big boys. *Wonderful*, I thought. *These guys are going to wrestle me to the ground, haul me off to the back room, and I'm going to miss my flight.*

As I resigned myself to this fate, the agent's supervisor finally digested what she was saying and simply shrugged his shoulders as if to say, "Okay. What do you want me to do about it? It's not illegal, and I'm really busy here." Then he turned his back, and went back to his own work. Now, it was just the agent and I who had to resolve this ourselves. She looked at me and I looked at her and before she could say anything, I said out loud and directly to her, "*This is stupid, stupid, stupid.*" The agent didn't say anything in return, but simply pawed through my bag while everyone in line watched. She was serious about it, too. That day, everyone on that line got to see what a level five search looked like – as everything came out of my bags including lint and old dry-cleaning tags. She seemed to be enjoying it, too.

And it's funny because at that moment, while we all watched her, I no longer cared. I wasn't even angry anymore. And when she was finished, I packed my bag, again. And as I walked to my gate, my mood was lighter and much better than it had been when I first arrived that morning. In wanting to be angry about something that I could not control, I got something else entirely. I got to be in a better mood. I guess it's true that *you can't always get what you want, but instead you might get exactly what you need.*

I needed a better attitude that morning. God knows, she needed a better attitude, too, as only heaven knows what was eating her that morning. Our little dance at the checkpoint snapped me out of my attitude, and I hope it did the same for her. I hoped she felt better later about exacting a little revenge for my comment. I also think it might have made the start of a Monday brighter for a few others. They got some free entertainment, and maybe they felt like my comments were small payback for all the frustrations they wished they could vent to the TSA. That might actually have been the case, because over the following weeks at the airport, I'd see someone in line who'd make eye contact with me, and nod and smile as if in appreciation for what had taken place that day. And I'd smile back, appreciating that they remembered my taking one for the team. The TSA and other small inconveniences are just a reminder that every once in a while it is your turn to take one for the team and deal with stupid … with a smile.

Final Note: Several months later, I ended up in that TSA agent's line again. This time the woman pulled a full-sized tube of toothpaste from my luggage and waved it in my face, pointing out my sin of trying to smuggle it on the flight. She held it in the air, waiting for an admission of guilt or contrition from me, I suppose. I looked at her for a few silent moments, and then I deadpanned, "Yeah, I brush my teeth. . . ." and into the big TSA trash barrel it went.

CHAPTER 23

Banned for Life

*"The Code is more what you call guidelines . . .
than actual rules."*
—*A line of dialog from the movie* Pirates of the Caribbean

I mentioned before that I ride motorcycles. I've done this for over forty years and still do it today, as I own several bikes. In fact, at one point I owned six or seven at the same time. But owning that many bikes was too many, since there simply wasn't enough time to ride them all and still have a job and a family. But I liked to ride as often as I could. Even when I went overseas, I'd rent a motorcycle and ride for a few days . . . Japan, New Zealand, Australia, Great Britain, Germany, Switzerland, Spain, and Italy are a few of those places. Since I enjoyed doing this, I found a company that specialized in operating motorcycle tours outside the United States.

This is how their program works: You sign up and pay one fee for, let's say, a ten-day ride. They provide the motorcycle and book all the hotels and food for you. Everything is included except your bar tab. You just fly into the country, meet up with the tour group, get your bike, and ride every day from one location to the next. The tour company even provides a chase truck that carries your luggage so you don't have to haul it. They recommend a road route for the day, but you could take any route you desire as long as at the end of the day you arrive at the designated hotel.

Why am I telling you all this? The first time I signed up for a tour, we rode for fourteen days in Germany, Switzerland, and Austria. Before the tour company allowed anyone to ride one of their machines, the riders had to participate in a briefing on the first day, acknowledging the rules and signing off on all the lawyer's paperwork. The briefing covered the itinerary, your bike, safety, and of course local traffic laws and enforcement. During the briefing in Germany, we were informed about the laws there, and also told that the German police were sticklers for enforcing the laws. In other words—*follow the rules!*

I had such a good time on that trip that I signed up for another one the following year—in Italy. This time, I knew all about the first-day rider's briefing. And just as they'd done the year before, the tour guide people briefed us on Italy, the roads, the itinerary, and the traffic rules. After the briefing, one of the riders raised a hand and asked about the rules and the police. This was a rider who'd been in the same group the year before. The tour guide said, "This isn't Germany. This is Italy. Here the rules are more like *suggestions and guidelines.* Just don't get too crazy, and you'll be okay."

I thought, "Man, I'm going to like Italy. It's my kind of place. A place where, as *Captain Barbossa, a character in the movie Pirates of the Caribbean,* said, '*The Pirates Code is more what you call guidelines, than actual rules.*'" Don't get me wrong. I do believe in rules,

I'm just not a stickler about following them to the letter. I think of rules more as guidelines.

For those who travel a lot, you know you not only spend a lot of time in airports and on airplanes, you spend lots of time in rental cars. And I did for many years. I'd arrive at my destination and go to the car rental desk. Most of the time, I'd booked the rental in advance, but there were times when weather delayed flights, and I'd neglect to rebook a rental. That's what happened to me one cold winter day in Calgary, Canada. A snowstorm shut down the airport for a day, so we arrived the following day when it reopened. When I got to the arrival and baggage area, I saw that the rental car desks were a madhouse. Hundreds of delayed travelers were trying to get any kind of car. I got in line and waited until I was finally called up to an agent. I walked up to the Avis desk. At the time, I was a member of their "elite" club because I rented a lot of cars from them every year. I asked for a car.

The agent started typing on his keyboard. I watched with a sinking feeling, noticing "This is taking a long time. I wonder why?" Finally, the man looked up from the keyboard and said, "We don't have a car."

"You just told me two minutes ago that you did have cars available," I said.

"Yes, we do have cars," the agent said. "We just can't rent one to *you*."

"Why can't you rent *me* a car?"

"It says here that you are banned from renting with us. I've tried to override it and rent you a car, but it won't allow me to."

"I'm banned from Avis?" I asked.

"Yeah, there's a lock on your account. I've never seen anything like this before."

Here's how I got banned from Avis—for life. Just a few months earlier I had been in New York. I was in an Avis rental car and I was running late to the airport to catch my flight. Traffic on the Van Wyck Expressway was at a standstill. I was getting nervous about making the flight. I still had to return the car to the rental center, board a rental bus for the ride to the terminal, and then make my way to my gate to catch the flight. I looked at my watch and made a quick calculation. It immediately became clear that if I dropped the car off at the return center, there was no way I'd make the flight. Keep in mind that these were the days before 9/11. I decided to drive directly to the terminal, park as close as I could to the entrance (which you could do in those days), lock the keys inside the car, and call my mother and ask *her* to phone Avis and give them the details of the location of their car, while I made a sprint to the gate.

And that's what I did. I knew I didn't have time to argue with an Avis agent about my plan and that's why I called my mother. I knew what I was about to do was "against the rules," but the plan seemed reasonable as, in the end, everyone would get what they needed. I'd get to Colorado, and Avis would get their car back. I parked the car two rows from the terminal under a light post. I wrote down the light-post number, and dashed for the gate, calling my mother on the way (she lived in New York) and asking her to do me this favor. I arrived at the gate just as the agent was closing the door. I'd made the flight by a minute. This all happened on a Friday evening.

On Monday, I was at the top of a ski run when I saw I had a voice mail on my phone. It was a message from Avis. They were wondering when I might be returning the car. I first called my mother and she confirmed that she had spoken with an Avis agent that Friday, explaining what happened and where they could find the car. I felt a little better, but now I was panicking about something else. What if someone saw the keys on the floor of the car, broke in, and stole the car? How would things work in that scenario? Would I have to pay for the Buick I had rented? I called Avis back.

When the agent came on the line, I explained all that had happened and how my mother placed the call. Of course, no one there could recall fielding her call. The man listened and then the phone went silent. "Are you still there," I asked, thinking the line might have gone dead.

"Yes," he said. "This is highly irregular." The agent didn't sound British, but the line struck me as properly British and funny. I'd been expecting a more "New York" response like, "Whaddya, some kind of moron?"

I asked him then, "How long have you worked for Avis?"

"Fifteen years," he said.

"And are you telling me that, in all those fifteen years, you've never had another customer do something like this?"

"Nope."

"Okay, then." I explained exactly where the car was located and suggested that if someone actually went there to retrieve it, they would find it. He was not very happy, and we ended the call with a promise that they would go look and call me back. Two hours later, the Avis agent called me back. They had located the car. This was a great relief. Then the agent proceeded to tell me how much trouble I had caused, and that what I had done was against policy and the rules I had agreed to when I signed the rental contract. I said I knew that, and again I was sorry for causing them all so much trouble. I ended by saying, "But we're good, right?" He said he'd email the receipt in a few days. I felt like I dodged a bullet. And this, you'd think, would be the end of the story. And you'd be wrong.

About one week later, I received the invoice. The charge was about $1,500 for a two-day rental that should have cost me about

$200. I called Avis, and they explained that there had to be extra charges for the extra days.

I said, "That's fine. That should make the total around $400. What's this extra $1,100 for?"

"That's the pickup fee."

"Okay, let me understand this," I said. "You want to charge me $1,100 for someone to drive less than half a mile to pick up the vehicle?"

"Yes."

"Okay . . . that's not happening."

"Well, that's what it is."

"Well, then change it," I said.

"I can't," he said.

"Okay, who can?"

"You can talk to my supervisor."

"Great, put that person on."

I talked to the supervisor and explained the entire situation again.

"Great story," she said. "It's still $1,500."

"Okay. Do you have the contact information for your corporate customer service department?" The woman did and she gave me the department's number and email address. She told me to take it up with them as she could do nothing further at her end. That began a two-month email campaign between me and the Avis corporate people. Back and forth we went. I was relentless, and, as a result, my case finally landed on the desk of some vice president. He called me personally. I stated my case, explaining the situation and my remorse, and concluded by saying that, businessman to businessman, this crazy $1,500 charge made no sense. I said something about being a card-carrying member of the Avis Elite Club and a frequent renter. I spent thousands of dollars with him every year.

Why alienate me? I'm a loyal and paying customer, and I assured him that it would never happen again. He was very nice and reasonable.

"I'll take care of it," he said.

A few days later, he sent me an email with a new invoice stating that I would pay an extra $200 for all the trouble caused and that as far as Avis was concerned—case closed. Now, you'd think *this* would be the end of the story. But . . . it's not.

In every organization, vice presidents delegate things. My case was likely handed off to his manager in charge of such issues. Managers in organizations have procedures and rules to follow. My best guess is that when my case got to the manager's desk, and he read the email from the VP about the charges, he had to complete some kind of case form. And on that form, there might have been a field labeled, *Continue to rent to in the future? Yes, or no.* Guess which box got checked? And this brings me back to the Avis rental counter in Calgary, Canada, where it was announced to me and to everyone else on the line that I was banned from Avis for life.

And that's how I became a lifetime Hertz customer. I thanked the Avis agent for all his efforts, and walked a few yards down to the Hertz counter and got a car. Of course, I simply could not let the lifetime ban from Avis pass without comment. That's why for the next ten Christmases after the events in Calgary, I'd make a copy of my credit card statement with my Hertz rental charges for the year. I'd insert them into a Christmas card and mail it to the vice president, wishing him and his family a wonderful holiday . . . and showing him exactly how much money I had paid to his competitor, Hertz, and asking if he'd uncheck the box on my profile labeled: *Continue to rent to in the future?* That guy is probably long gone by now. But over those years I never got any response from Avis.

They say there are two kinds of people in the world: those who color inside the lines and those who don't. You can probably guess to which group I belong. I'll say it again: rules are important and necessary. Yet life can be messy, and rules cannot possibly address or foresee every possible contingency for which the rules were created. This suggests that it might make more sense to use rules like the police do in Italy, not the way they do in Germany. After all, we're all just human and stuff happens. That's why I think life is not only easier but more livable when we view rules more like guidelines— than gospel.

Final Note: A few years after these events, my wife and I traveled to visit her relatives in Scotland. That's where my second wife was born, before she came to the United States and became a citizen. When we arrived at a train station in Edinburgh, we walked to the rental car desk, looking for the Hertz counter to get a car. There was no Hertz desk. There was only an Avis counter and some other car rental desk open. My wife knew I was banned from Avis. She looked at me and I said, "Damn. Okay, you go rent the car, honey." And I skulked out of the terminal like a criminal, hoping nobody from Avis would see me and recognize me. She got the car.

CHAPTER 24

Sticks and Stones

"Sticks and stones will break my bones,
but words will never harm me."
—Old English adage

You might recall that after I was sacked for the last time, I discovered business consulting and made it my career. It was my career for the three decades before I launched the software company. In both of those businesses, my target customers were the same. They were primarily smaller-sized businesses. There's a reason why I decided to work with smaller businesses instead of larger ones early on in my career. I preferred the way the people communicated and worked in those smaller companies. The people I met were generally easier to work with: more likely to be direct and to implement many of my recommendations with a minimum of politics and a good deal of gratitude for the services I provided. But, even though smaller companies were my target customers, I would, from time to time, work with larger corporations. I did that mainly for the money, as larger companies had bigger budgets, and paid me a better daily rate.

Even though they paid a little less working with smaller businesses paid off for me personally over the years, as I was fortunate enough to develop lasting personal friendships with many of these clients. Who knows, but maybe it was because I was able to be more "honest" with them and thus helpful. That didn't happen as often with my larger clients. To them, I was usually just a "hired hand," and I had to learn how to navigate their internal politics. As a result, they'd employ the recommendations they wanted to hear, which were often not the most critical ones. I was a more effective consultant with smaller clients because I was able to say what needed to be said, when it needed to be said.

An effective consultant has to be willing to deliver the unvarnished truth to a client if any real change is to be effected. I wasn't thoughtless in delivering analysis and advice. In fact, I *did* worry about hurting feelings and bruising egos. But I felt that I was hired, and that they paid me, to get to the root of their problems, and fix them. And though I would not call what a business consultant does the equivalent of tough love, it comes pretty close sometimes. So, I got good at delivering tough news because I delivered it with humor, empathy, and facts. I then gave the client the choice of making the changes . . . or not making them. It's true that I did lose a few clients that way. But I'd tell any fledgling consultant today that they'll lose more clients operating the other way . . . by *not* telling them the truth.

I think for a consultant-client relationship to work over the longer term, both need to develop thicker skins, because the truth can be uncomfortable, and change is hard. Thick skin allows for honest conversations. And if there is any single thing in my career that differentiated my work with the smaller businesses from the larger ones it was that honest conversations were almost impossible in larger companies. As a result, I found it difficult to get to the "truth," and make significant changes because someone's feelings were always getting hurt.

In the end, it was exactly this dynamic that resulted in my final exit from the corporate consulting world. Here's how these events unfolded. I was engaged by a Fortune 500 company to deliver a "problem-solving" training program for an underperforming team. According to the HR people who hired me, the group seemed unable to work effectively resolving problems. As a result, they were failing to deliver products on time and within budget. I usually surveyed my target training audience before designing and conducting a training program. And I did that with this group. I discovered that they were very smart people and in fact had excellent problem-solving skills. The real reason they were underperforming was a lack of honest communications. These professionals were afraid to tell the truth to one another, *if that truth might offend someone else on the team*! They felt that telling a "truth" that might offend someone could jeopardize their careers. Further investigation suggested that it wasn't a lack of skills, but rather an environment that punished this kind of "insensitivity" that was at the heart of the problem.

I mentioned this to the HR people and suggested that a problem-solving training program that failed to address the real cause of the problem would likely produce few tangible results. The responded by saying that I had been engaged to deliver a problem-solving program, and that I should stick to doing just that. And that's what I did.

The day for the first training arrived, and I was ready to go. For many years, I began every program with a few "icebreaker" activities. The goal was to get people to relax and give them a sense of who I was. I've come to believe that for a training program to be successful, the messenger is as important as the message. What I mean is, if the audience doesn't like the messenger, they don't hear the message. So, I employed a few trusted icebreakers that I knew would work. And since this was a new group, I decided to use two of them to start the program that day.

I began with an introduction exercise that always got a laugh. I'd show a PowerPoint slide with four geometric shapes, each a different color: a yellow pentagon, a green triangle, a blue square, and a red circle. Then I'd ask the audience to identify with the one shape they felt was "most like them." I told the audience, "Researchers could tell a lot about a person by the shape they selected." Then I'd relate what the "researchers" had found. Of course, there were no real researchers as this was all a "joke". Then I state that those who chose the yellow pentagon were highly analytical types. Those selecting the green triangle were real team players. The blue squares were outgoing social animal types. The punch line was the red circle – the last shape. Those people, I'd state - with all due seriousness - were crazy, out-of-control sex maniacs. Everyone laughed. Of course, the entire activity was designed to produce a laugh.

Then I'd introduced the agenda and share another set of slides designed to poke fun at the way math was taught in school—to get another laugh. Here's what I did:

(Note: My verbal narration of the slide show is in quotation marks, and the words on the slides are in *italics*.)

Me: "Here's a typical math problem you might be presented with as a student in a 1950s textbook."

Slide: *A logger sells a truckload of lumber for $100. His cost of production is ⅘ of the price. What is his profit?* Note: Again,

I wasn't looking for the audience to really answer the question. This was a spoof on schools.

Me: "Here's that same problem in the new textbooks of the 1960s."

Slide: *A logger sells a truckload of lumber for $100. His cost of production is ⅘ of the price, or $80. What is his profit?* A few people smiled. I waited a moment, then flipped to the next slide.

Me: "Of course, educators changed everything in the 1970s, ushering in the new math. Now that problem looked like this. . . ."

Slide: *A logger exchanges a set "L" of lumber for a set "M" of money. The cardinality of set "M" is 100. Each element is worth one dollar. Make 100 dots representing the elements of the set "M." The set "C," the cost of production, contains 20 fewer dots than set "M." Represent the set "C" as a subset of set "M" and answer the following question: What is the cardinality of the set "P" of profits?* A few more people smiled, as they realized that I was poking fun at our school system.

Me: "Then, in the 1980s, they changed everything again, and that same math problem morphed into this. . . ."

Slide: *A logger sells a truckload of lumber for $100. His cost of production is $80, and his profit is $20. Your assignment: underline the number 20.* That always got a laugh, and I continued on to the next slide.

Me: "The math problem, to meet the needs of the 1990s, changed again and now looked like this in the textbook. . . ."

Slide: *By cutting down beautiful forest trees, the logger makes $20. What do you think of this way of making a living? Topic for class participation after answering the question: How did the forest birds and squirrels feel as the logger cut down the trees? There are no wrong answers.* Most people realized that this was a satire, and they laughed. I had two more slides to show them.

Me: "Then, in the 2000s, we have more changes, and the original problem now looks like this. . . ."

Slide: *A logger sells a truckload of lumber for $100. His cost of production is $120. How does Arthur Andersen determine that his profit margin is $60?* This was a reference to the Enron scandal that sank the accounting firm of Arthur Andersen. I then showed the final slide.

Me: "Now, as we enter a new decade in our school systems, the problem in the 2010s looks like this. . . ."

Slide: *"El hachero vende un camion carga por $100. La cuesta de production es. . . ."*

I didn't say anything else I just let the group look at the slide. Everyone laughed, and then I launched into the material for the training program. That was it.

Three weeks after that session, I got a call from the Human Resources manager. Someone, she said, had filed a complaint about my session. Specifically, about the two icebreakers, and that they had been offended by them.

I asked, "Really? Who?"

"We don't know." She said "The complaint was filed anonymously, as that is in line with our policy about such things."

"Well, that's interesting," I replied, "because you were there in that same session, in the same room, and you participated in those icebreakers, and you thought they were funny. You never approached me about their being offensive to you."

"That's not the point," she responded.

"Okay, what is the point?" I asked.

"We can't have that kind of thing, so we are going to have to discontinue your program."

At that point in the conversation, I knew this was not something they were going to discuss with me. They had already decided. I said, "Fine, I understand."

I could sense that she felt relieved that I wasn't going to argue with her. Then she said, "Of course, we will want you to refund the fees we've paid you to date."

I kept my cool and said, "You hired me to deliver a program, and I did that. And you can cancel the rest of the program going forward if you want. But there's no way I'm refunding any of my fees."

There was silence at her end before she said, "I will have to take this up with Legal."

To which I responded, "Susan, you do that."

I never heard from "Legal" or from Susan again. And that, as they say, was the end of that. I never worked another day with a large corporation.

I can't say I was shocked by the lack of irony of the HR people . . . nor that the company was having a problem with team problem solving. They had hired me to help them solve that problem. But I told them that the problem wasn't a skills problem . . . it was more of a fear problem. Their people were afraid of saying things that might be the truth, but might be construed, anonymously, as offensive, and potentially jeopardize their employment. And now they were sacking me precisely for this very thing. Is that irony, or just obtuseness? In fact, I mentioned this very thing to Susan during our call. It changed nothing. What was important to her was keeping *her* job by making certain that the policy was enforced.

Right now, you may be wondering, "Why is he making such a big deal of this story?" Here's why. You and I will have our feelings hurt in life. Sometimes because what is said is true, and sometimes because it is not. If offense is taken, and "foul" is cried every time that happens, and "justice" and punishment demanded for every such foul, how would we ever hear the truth and get anything done at all? Back in the days when I played a lot of pickup basketball games in the school yard, we dealt with the guys who called every little foul very simply. And trust me when I say that those games could get physically rough. The guys who insisted on calling every foul found themselves sitting on the sidelines, not chosen by any team to play in the next game. Nobody wanted to play with a guy like that because it ruined the flow of the game and raised tensions unnecessarily. We preferred playing with guys who, when fouled, were fair calling a foul, but mainly sucked it up and kept on playing.

Thick skin is a requirement not only for survival but it's a requirement for developing a sense of humor. Thick skin allows us to let go of grudges, allow bygones to be bygones, and keep everyone from being offended by every little thing and calling in the lawyers... or HR. The alternative to this approach is fear, untruth, finger-pointing, and sullen silence. That's what happens when you let the scolds of the world run everything at zero tolerance. And you can count me out on that game. There is always something to be offended by. So it might help to remember what was once taught in grade school: "*Sticks and stones will break my bones, but words will never hurt me."* These words we all know. What many of us may not know is the second sentence that follows afterward: *True courage (and grace) consists in doing what is right, despite the jeers and sneers of our companions.* We all have to be big enough to roll with the punches on occasion. That's part of life. And life is tough enough when you have a spine and thick skin. It's impossible to live a peaceful and honest one without them.

CHAPTER 25

White Lies, Dark Side

"White Lie: an often trivial, diplomatic,
or well-intentioned untruth."
—American Heritage Dictionary

My second wife is a rule follower. As you know by now, I am not. My wife asks for permission. I beg for forgiveness. She has to follow a procedure; I improvise. We approach situations often 180 degrees apart. That, of course, creates disagreements about the best course of action under any given situation, but, surprisingly, over the years it has produced a pretty workable and successful partnership. My wife's approach is perfectly suited to compliance, while I seem to go out of my way not to comply. I don't want to go deeply into my psyche here, but there's a part of me that just hates to be told what do. So, I do just the opposite of policy and procedure just because I can be an idiot.

I will give you an example. I have a hard time dealing with HOAs (homeowner associations). HOAs are in charge of life within their gates. In California, HOAs can, and do, exert tremendous power. So, if you live in a HOA, it helps to be a rule follower because there are so many of them. And if you are not a rule follower, you will eventually run afoul of some HOA rule, if only because you think the rules are too ridiculous to all be followed.

For example, in the HOA in which we once lived, the landscape committee had to approve any changes to the exterior of your home. What that meant, in practical terms, was that if I wanted to add flowers to a flower bed, I'd first have to complete a request form with a project description, submit it, and then wait for an approval. Who has this kind of time and patience? These are flowers, for heaven's sake. I'm not adding a third floor to my home or painting it purple. I therefore simply went to the nursery, picked out some nice flowers, drove home, and planted them all before noon on a Saturday before my wife or the HOA could stop me.

As a result, I was always in a "cold war" with the HOA board. My wife just shook her head and predicted that one day the board would draw a line, send us a letter, and make our lives miserable because they'd finally decided I had crossed some line.

"Why don't you just fill out the form like everyone else?" she'd ask. "You know one day it's going to end up costing us more time and money because you didn't get the proper approvals."

"It'll never happen," I said. "And if it did, what's the worst they could do?"

My wife just shook her head. "Okay, but don't get pissed off when they do." She was, of course, right about this. How is it that the permission askers of the world are always right about stuff like this? It makes me sad, but the reality is that rebels can wear people out, by begging for forgiveness all the time. At least that is what eventually happened with us and the HOA. It started in our backyard one December when I was painting the housing trim.

We had a wooden deck outside our master bedroom. We could walk through a door onto the deck and get a great view of the Pacific Ocean, and at night we could see the city lights spread out below us in the hills and coastal canyons. The deck needed replacing. It was old and rotting. This seemed like a simple job. And in my view, replacing the deck would be cheered by everyone—the neighbors and the HOA—as the improvement would make the home look better. I thought that it would look really good to replace the existing fifteen-by-fifteen deck with a slightly expanded eighteen-by-fifteen version, using nicer materials. I drew up a simple plan and hired a contractor.

We ordered the building materials and scheduled a start date. Early that morning the contractor began the demolition of the old deck. I was home at that time, and looking out the back window at the progress of the demo, I saw a car parked down below on a road that ran behind our home. The car stopped and someone got out, looked at what was going on, went back into the car to retrieve a camera, and started snapping pictures. I thought that was odd, and mentioned it to my wife.

"I'm guessing they're not too happy that you started work without submitting plans," my wife said.

"You really think so?"

"Yes, I really do think so."

"Why would they care?" I asked. "We're improving the neighborhood."

"They care," she said. "That's what they do. Why don't you call them and let them know what we're doing?"

"Let's just ignore them," I said, "We'll be done by Friday, anyway. And by then, it will be too late for them to do anything but protest."

That evening, the HOA called us, informing us that a cease-and-desist order had been filed with the city! My wife gave me the "I told you so" glare. "Now you've created a mess," she said.

"Don't worry," I said. "I'll call the board president and work it out with her. She likes me. We'll be back in business by Wednesday."

I called the board president that evening, to plead my case. She listened, but she was neither charmed nor persuaded. She referred me to the HOA's two-hundred-page manual that outlined the proper submission procedures necessary to obtain approval for projects like mine. The last thing she said was, "Until you submit your plans for review, you cannot continue." I went on to explain that all we wanted to do was make a *like-for-like* replacement that was both safer and prettier. All the board president said was, "Read the manual and submit the forms. Good night."

My wife was listening in on the call, and when I hung up, she said, "Sounds like you had her eating out of your hand. Now what?"

"Very funny," I answered. I hate it when the rule followers win. "Okay, we'll do it your way! Where's that HOA book?"

The first thing we had to do was locate the HOA rules-and-regs book. That was no easy thing, as I had no memory of ever seeing it. My wife knew where it was, of course. She brushed off the dust, read the instructions, and downloaded the appropriate forms from the HOA website. I'm not good at reading instructions as I have a short attention span. Here's what my wife gleaned from the instructions. In order to get all of the proper approvals and lift the cease-and-desist order, we were required to submit—in triplicate, to both the HOA and the city—a package that included:

- a page-long summary of the project

- a list and description of all materials

- a top-down dimensional drawing of the deck within the property lines with exact measurements

- a top-down blueprint of the deck with exact dimensions in three dimensions

- a front-on drawing with dimensions and descriptions of the structure and ground-attachment points

- a weight-bearing load analysis

- a side-view drawing of the underside, calling out all joists and attachment hardware

How hard could this be, I thought? It took us two weeks to gather all the information to complete the "project plan" documents. We then submitted everything in triplicate to the HOA and the city. Then we waited. We waited for a month. Finally, I called the HOA to find out what was going on and get an update on our submission. The HOA informed us that the city first had to complete their review before the HOA could even commence theirs. And they had not yet received anything from the city. This would have been good information to know when we submitted the documents over a month before. I was about to call the city when my wife suggested we just go there in person instead—*to get things moving.*

"You know how they are down there in City Hall," she said.

"Actually, I don't know *how they are*. How are they?"

"Why don't we just go down and see, okay?"

So, we went. We arrived late in the morning midweek. There were more than a few people in the waiting room, and there seemed to be no one working the counter. We took a number and sat down. Two hours later, our number was called. We explained our situation and submission to the person behind the counter. The man asked for our address and disappeared behind into a warren of cubicles. A few minutes later, he emerged and laid our folder on the countertop.

"It appears that this is an incomplete submission."

"Okay, how is it incomplete, and why did we not get a call from the city to that effect?"

"We did try to contact you." I knew this was not true, as the phone number on the file was mine and I had never received any message from the city. I thought about saying something, but concluded that an argument with the government would be futile. I decided it was best to shut up if I wanted to ever get this project approved and didn't argue the point.

My wife, being the voice of reason, smiled at the clerk and asked what other information was required to complete the submission. I don't recall all the items he listed, but I do know that none of them had been on the original checklist the HOA provided us with when we made our submission in the first place. I could feel myself free-falling into one of Dante's inner circles of hell. This was not going to be easy. We were going to have to stay on top of these people if we ever wanted to get this project done by summer. We had started demo in early January; it was now mid-March.

You learn a lot working with your local government permitting agency. First, they never tell you *everything* you need to know. They leave things out. My theory is it's a question of control combined with personality. Code enforcement is often arbitrary and inconsistent. You get one story from one person and another on the same subject from someone else. And the progress of your project as it goes through this system is often affected by the mood of the person with whom you speak on any given day. You can complain, but then you can be loaded down with additional resubmissions requests that only further delay your project—and, of course, cost you more money as every resubmission is accompanied by another fee.

We ended up resubmitting three versions of the plans over the next two months. By then, it was May, a full five months after we began our ill-fated demolition. We had to live with a half-destroyed deck hanging off the back of our home the entire time. Just before the calendar struck June, the city issued their preliminary approval to the HOA. Now, it was in the hands of the HOA to conduct their review and give their okay so the city could then issue the final permit. It took the HOA another month, but they, too, gave their approval and sent the plans back to the city for a final okay. I remember watching the 2008 Olympics in China, and recalled a comment about the incredible airport they'd built in Beijing. I mentioned this to my wife one day.

"Do you know that the Chinese built one of the world's largest, most modern airports in less time than it's taken us to build a fifteen-by-eighteen deck? How does that happen?"

"Relax," she said. "We're almost there. And we did it the right way. It will be smooth sailing from here." If only that were true. In early July, we returned to the city office to obtain our permit. When we got to the counter, the guy there said, "There's a problem."

My wife saw that I was about to jump over the counter, so she interceded. "What's the issue?" she asked.

"It looks like you have a 'setback' problem," he said.

"What in heaven's name is a 'setback' problem'?" I said.

The man explained it as follows. "When you look at the deck dimensions inside your property lines, any addition to a structure must have a minimum setback of fifteen feet from those property lines."

Let me explain what this meant to us. We lived on the top of the hill, and our property included a slope that went many feet down the hill. But for the purposes of "property lines," ours ended at what's called the "top of the slope." Our deck, to be in compliance with the city ordinance, could extend no further from the home than to a point fifteen feet from the top of the slope. The agent could not approve the final permit as it looked to him from the property map that our project would put our deck past that point. My wife asked for more details and if the man would please photocopy the pages in his codebook that addressed "top-of-slope" compliance.

Before we left, I asked the man, "How does the city verify and approve the actual top-of-slope line calculation?"

"We usually rely on property maps and photos," he said. "So, bring me those."

"How old are the property maps you used for our residence?" my wife asked.

It turned out that they were more than thirty years old. So, I said, "A lot can change with a slope line in thirty years, right? So, what do you need from us to get the permit?"

"Bring me a diagram and photos showing the deck in relation to the top of the slope line." He even gave us a photocopy of our residence property map with a dotted line drawn representing the approximate *top of the slope.*

We rushed home and got to work producing the information he wanted so that we could put this nightmare to bed once and for all. We oriented the property map, made our best vertical approximation of the top of the slope, and painted that line in the dirt. Then, we taped out the profile of the new deck dimensions on the ground and discovered we were . . . not in compliance. The deck was two feet "over the line."

I looked at my wife and asked, "Now, what do we do?"

"We lie," she answered.

"We lie?" I asked.

"Yes, we lie." It was at that moment that I fell in love with her all over again.

"You know, I said, "that this is against all the rules. You know that you just crossed over into the dark side and the world of little white lies, don't you?'

"Don't push it, buster. Let's just do this," she replied.

"You know that *I'm* good with that," I said. "But I'm going to remember this moment for a long time."

So, we lied. We lied about the placement of the top of the slope line. We took the city clerk's property map and realigned the top of the slope line three feet further from our home, in such a way that if you were there, you would see that the line was now clearly on the *downslope*. We drew it exactly where it needed to be for the deck to be in compliance with the city's codes. Then we got creative with the pictures we took of the new line. We took pictures lying on the ground, which gave the impression that the new line was indeed *at* the top of the slope and not *down* it. Those pictures and the new top of slope line on the property map looked pretty convincing.

But then my wife started backtracking. "What if they come up here and actually check this out?" she asked.

"Honey, he'll never some up here to check this out. I think this guy is just covering his rear end. He will never leave his office to come up and check these dimensions. In other words, if we say it's good, he'll sign off."

We drove right back down to the city office and submitted our proof. I did not want my wife second-guessing her decision. The guy looked our stuff over, and we got the approval stamps and permit. The guy never came by to check—anything. During the project, we decided to install some lights in the deck, too. We lied about that, too, as code demanded that any *new* electrical installation get another set of approvals. When the city inspector showed up for the final sign-off on the completed deck, he looked at the lights we'd installed that were *not* part of the original plan, and asked my wife if that electricity had been part of the original construction. My wife looked him dead in the eye and said, "Yes." Another lie.

Ten months after we started our little project, we had our new deck. What had begun as a simple $5,000 replacement job had ballooned to twice that amount. I looked at the deck and thought about an earlier time in my life when a project like that would have taken me, two friends, and a case of beer, two weekends to complete. But it was done. And more important, my wife, the rule follower, had told more than a few white lies. She'd come all the way over to the dark side, my side, to complete the project.

The first time we sat on that new deck, looking at the city lights, I said, "I'm proud of you. . . . All those little lies helped get this done."

She looked at me and said deadpan, "What lies?"

I took a sip of wine, and thought, "Wow! I hope I haven't created a monster here.

Final Note: I'm not condoning lying. I am condoning common sense. If an occasional white lie is necessary to cut through the crap we create disguised as rules . . . then it is an act of mercy sparing us all from the numbing mindlessness of the rule followers and enforcers. Today, the deck is still there. It hasn't fallen down or burned up due to faulty wiring. And the views are *killer*.

CHAPTER 26

Penny's Pens

"How do I love thee? Let me count the ways."
—Elizabeth Barrett Browning

We learn how to *receive* love from our parents, if we're lucky. And I was. How we learn to *give* love is less clear. Certainly, our parents teach us something about this, by example, but we each have to find our own way. My parents did teach us something about this. They rarely fought. And so, to this day, I don't like to argue too much with loved ones. My mom and dad were never outwardly hand-holding affectionate, either—at least not that I could see. But they were devoted and loyal to each other. I guess that's why I've never been a big hand-holder or affectionately demonstrative in public with my wife. But if you'd interpret that as "not being in love," you'd be far wrong. I am fiercely loyal and devoted to her. But I know even she wonders sometimes. She thinks I tease her too much instead of hugging her. I try to tell her that's the way I show my love. I know where I learned that, and that's just how it is with me.

I am very protective of the people I love but far less protective and caring about the stuff I own. Stuff is replaceable—people aren't. But I understand people who *are* very protective of their stuff. I think they have good reason to be, especially with people like me around. The fact is, *their* stuff is not *your* stuff, and lacking permission to touch their stuff, you should respect it and leave it alone. I know people feel this way, but I have crossed the line, forgetting this basic rule, at times.

You may recall I departed Florida, looking for a new direction in my life. I returned to New York and applied to MBA programs, ultimately getting accepted at Southern Methodist University in Dallas. During my last term at SMU, I interned at a restaurant company that was once owned by Norman Brinker. I needed the internship to help defray tuition costs, and to accumulate the necessary credits for my degree. Mr. Brinker was the man who created Steak and Ale, Bennigan's, and Chili's restaurant chains, and he eventually sold Steak and Ale and Bennigan's to the Pillsbury Company. I had the opportunity to intern at his company and to meet him one day at the office. He made a deep impression on me. At the time I was new to the business world. I imagined that the people who ran big companies had to be larger-than-life supermen. Mr. Brinker wasn't like that. He never acted like a superman. He was cordial and humble. He seemed like an average guy. And though I haven't modeled my personal approach to people entirely on his management style, he certainly influenced the way I've dealt with people. I've tried to emulate his humility, and the way he treated people with respect. I combined those things with hard work and a little luck, hoping I might go as far in my career as Mr. Brinker did in his. I guess, to me, he *was* a superman, simply because he didn't act like one.

As a new intern with his company, I was assigned to work in the financial analysis department because my course credits were designated for the area of finance and accounting. The financial analysis department was comprised of about a half dozen people. I worked with almost all of them at some point in my time there and liked them all. I also liked the work, as it was both interesting and enjoyable. I discovered I had an affinity for that type of work, and it showed in what I produced. As a result, I got a lot of recognition, which further motivated me to do even better work. It was then, and still is to this day, one of my favorite job experiences. For the first time, I could see that my decision to return to school and get a business degree was a good one, and it reinforced for me that I was on the right track.

Since I was hired as a temporary intern, there was no separate office space available for me. The department manager set me up in the same cubicle as Penny, one of the other financial analysts, and we shared that space when I was in the office, which wasn't every day. Penny had worked for the company for many years. She was kind enough to make some room, in her space, for me, the new guy, the short-timer MBA golden boy. I knew she wasn't overly impressed with my golden boy halo, and I knew for certain she wasn't thrilled with the new seating arrangement. But she never said anything about it. So, I settled in and made it my new home.

I haven't spent much time working in office environments throughout my business career. This was true then and has remained so for most of my business career. For the most part, I've worked from home or on an airplane. As a result, I'm no expert on office etiquette. I am aware, however, that personal space is important to people, and that they can be territorial, especially when sharing small confined areas.

At the time I was taking a class in organizational behavior at SMU. It was one of the most valuable classes I ever took as part of that MBA program. The material we discussed in class revolved around theories of human nature in the workplace, and how these theories affected conflict management and decision-making. It was very interesting stuff. One of the theories discussed was proposed by a researcher named David McClelland. McClelland's studies suggested that human behavior was driven by three basic motivations. And understanding these motivations could help newly minted MBA types understand *where people were coming from*, and not just act productively to manage conflict but ultimately make better decisions.

In the interest of brevity, allow me to summarize McClelland's ideas, because they have a lot to do with Penny and me. Instead of there being two types of people in the world, McClelland argued for three types: those who were motivated primarily by a need for *affiliation*; those whose primary motivation was a desire for *achievement*; and lastly those who were primarily driven by a need for *power*. It turns out that I'm an achievement type, and Penny, I'm convinced, fell into the affiliation category. According to McClelland, Penny and I would naturally experience some level of conflict as—owing to our basic natures—we would approach situations with different motivations.

What does this mean for Penny and me? In simplest terms, *affiliatives* are team players and sensitive to the needs and space of others. Their primary drive is to *get along*. I, as an *achiever*, was more likely to act as a loner. Achievers are less sensitive to space and others, as our primary motivation is to *win*. Power people, according to McClellan, just want everyone's space for their own, as they are primarily motivated by a need to *control*. Although Penny and I were never involved in a *hot war* about her space, there was always an undercurrent that I was an invader who needed to be repelled. And my actions supported these natural feelings—I didn't make things any easier for her as time went by, and I settled further into *her space.*

Here's what I mean. When I was hired, I was never issued my own office supplies. In fact, I never even thought to request any. As I saw it, I would go without those things, not make a big deal by requesting my own stuff, and simply borrow Penny's stuff when I needed it. This seemed like a perfectly normal way of doing things to me. So, it began. I'd borrow a ruler or a pen from her, and neglect to put it back where I'd taken it from. I didn't do this intentionally. I'd borrow Penny's stapler and forget it in the mail room, or I'd take a pen to sign something and leave it on someone else's desk. I'd use it and forget about it. Penny wasn't thrilled with me and mentioned my habit of taking her stuff without permission and leaving it somewhere else. I agreed that she had a very good point, and that I'd change my ways. But I'd still occasionally borrow and misplace one of her things.

I think she grew increasingly frustrated with me, and determined that she had to do *something.* She took the step of labeling all of her stuff. She actually typed her name—yes, she had to use a typewriter—on a sheet of paper about one hundred times, line after line, from the top of the sheet to the bottom. Then, using her scissors, she carefully cut these into narrow slivers, each with the word "Penny's" on it. Then she Scotch-taped each of the labeled slivers onto the things that were hers. By the time she was done, I could pick up her stapler and clearly read "Penny's" on top of the stapler.

I wasn't offended by her labeling program. Not at all. Those were, after all, her things. In fact, I remember coming in the next day and mentioning to her how impressed I was by the level of effort she put into labeling all that stuff. I was fascinated by it, as I would never,

ever do something like that. At that moment, I realized that I was not only reading about organizational behavior in class, I was living it in the real world right there in that financial analysis department with Penny. From that day until the time I left, I did my best not to mess with Penny's stuff.

Two weeks before I graduated with my MBA, I gave Mr. Brinker's company notice that I was moving on. The day after graduation, I was scheduled to depart Dallas for Phoenix, where I had one more term to complete at what is now known as the Arizona State University Thunderbird Management School. When my manager heard the news, she scheduled a going-away party for me on my last day. I was touched and appreciative as I had very much enjoyed my time with those people. We actually had the party in the office, consuming adult beverages and swapping stories. Can you even imagine that happening today? It was a great party. When it finally broke up, and we'd said our good-byes, good lucks, and stay-in-touches, I hugged everyone and stayed behind in the office to handle a few last-minute affairs.

"I have a few things I need to pack up before leaving. You guys go on ahead. I won't be long." I thanked everyone again, and the office was empty. I then walked back to the cubicle I'd shared with Penny for the past few months and looked around, and thought about all those people and how sad I was to be leaving, and then I got to work. I spent the next hour *relabeling* every one of Penny's pens, staplers, calculators, and rulers. I had prepared all the paper slips a week earlier. It was then just a simple matter of removing Penny's labels and applying my own "Kevin's" labels. I stayed until I replaced every single one. The pencils were the toughest. I felt that the opportunity Penny had presented me with her labeling was just too good to pass up, and I wanted to return the favor. I wasn't being vindictive in doing this. I was teasing her. In fact, I wanted to let

Penny know how I felt about her, so I also left a brief note on her desk before I left. It read:

Dear Penny,

Thanks for putting up with me. I enjoyed working with you, and I will miss you.

Kevin

PS: Thanks for letting me use YOUR stuff.

As I said, I'm not a hand-holder or given to public displays of affection. Instead, I like to tease the people I love. I can't explain exactly why I do this. Maybe because when I was growing up, that's what we did in my family. We were sharp-tongued and sharp-witted, and we teased one another endlessly with humor and digs. Maybe through that experience, I came to associate love with teasing. I *was* teasing Penny by relabeling her pens. I wasn't *in love* with Penny. But I guess I had grown to appreciate her, and teasing her was my way of communicating that. Penny, if you are out there somewhere today, and you read this, and remember any of this, I hope you know that I was teasing you. And I hope you also understand that I tease those I love. And the ones I love the most, I tease the most.

CHAPTER 27

The Heisman

"Beautiful things don't ask for attention."
—A line of dialog from the movie
The Secret Life of Walter Mitty

I wrote about Norman Brinker and how his humility and common touch were something I admired and wanted to emulate in my life. I had the pleasure some years later of meeting, under very different circumstances, another man with similar traits. He, too, was humble, with the common touch, but he was arguably *famous* as well . . . but you'd never know it by the way he acted. He is one of only eighty-five people on the planet who own a Heisman Trophy, an annual award given to the most outstanding player in college football. That's a very select group, and winning it is a great accomplishment. It's always an honor to meet men and women with the common touch, but meeting this guy was even better because I'm a very big college football fan, and the Heisman is familiar to every collegiate football fan. But I'm getting ahead of myself here.

I left my first consulting job to take a position with one of our clients. You may recall I was working in Dallas at that time. The business I joined was another family business, also with two brothers. The two of them actually ran separate companies, but they were close, and in the same kind of business, and in the same geographic market. They appeared to be friendly competitors. It was the older brother, the Heisman winner, who introduced me to the younger brother. It was the younger brother who hired me. And it was ultimately the younger brother who fired me. And he had every right to do so, as I screwed up and deserved it.

I deserved it because I was too rash, trying to make too many changes, and I didn't think through the consequences of my decisions and actions. I've learned from the mistakes I made with him, and applied them to the way I work now. Today, I'm humbler, with more of a common touch, though I'm still direct and to the point. I always do my best to be a "trusted go-to guy," and to do what I say I'll do. I prefer to fly below the radar and give credit where credit is due. I like people who are like that, too. I like people who do good things, without calling attention to their good works. I think we have enough of that in our celebrity-crazed culture, where we celebrate many *not so nice people*, who do nothing but call attention to themselves.

I've experienced all types of people during my years in business, and I've concluded that the world would be a better place with more people like Mr. Brinker and the Heisman winner, and with fewer people like the guy at a certain Florida airport. Before sharing what happened at that airport, I'd be remiss if I failed to note that in regard to the story I'm about to relate, I've heard several different versions over the years. In fact, when I tell the story, I've had people tell me they've heard it before. It seems these events may have taken place in some version more than once. But I did witness the following between one very important man and a gate agent in Florida: My flight was delayed due to weather that day. There were lots of people in the gate area who were unhappy about this, of course, and many were trying to rebook their flights. The gate agent was overwhelmed and working as hard as she could to satisfy everyone. I noticed a guy approach the agent. He did not get in line—he just walked up to the counter and started asking her questions.

"When will we be boarding?" he wanted to know.

The agent replied, "I don't really know right now." She was busy assisting another passenger at that moment.

Then the man said, "How can you *not* know?"

She replied, "As you might have noticed, the weather is still very bad and Operations has not released any departure information as of now."

The man said, "Well, I have to get to Chicago for a meeting this afternoon."

"I understand, sir, but as you can see, so do a lot of other people, and I'm doing the best I can here to accommodate everyone, as it's likely this flight is going to be cancelled."

"Then put me on another flight," the man replied. Keep in mind the situation here. The man had already cut to the front of the line where other people had been waiting, and now he was monopolizing the agent's time and attention. So, she said to him, "Sir, if you can get in line with everyone else, I will do my best to get you to Chicago." This was apparently the wrong thing to say. The man escalated the conversation.

"This is unacceptable. I purchased a first-class seat with the stated promise that *your* airline would get me to my meeting on time." The agent didn't say anything, but she did give him one of those quiet, withering "I wish I could kill you right now" stares. And that, I think, made him more furious.

The man glared at her and shouted, "Seriously? This is how you handle things? Do you have any idea who I am? Do you? Do you know who I am?" By this time, everyone close by was watching the two of them. There was silence before the agent responded. Maybe she'd lost her patience, or maybe she was a natural wiseass, but talking to everyone in the area, and nobody in particular, she said, "No, I don't know who you are. Maybe someone in line here knows who you are. Can any of you help this gentleman out? It seems he doesn't know who he is."

Be careful what you ask for. The man asked for that. Trust me, I could understand his frustration at that moment. But what I cannot understand was his need to call attention to himself. He wasn't the only one with a problem that day. I think you get more done with humility than you do with self-importance . . . even if you are an important person.

I've heard it said that any of us could follow someone around for a year, observing them in many different situations, in an effort to understand what kind of person they really were, but that it would be more telling to observe them in one single moment, like the one with that guy in the airport, and you'd know exactly the kind of person they were. I had one of those moments one evening with the older brother, the Heisman guy I mentioned earlier, when he extended me an invitation to join him and his family for dinner.

Let me provide some more background about the Heisman for those who may not follow college football. Since 1935 when the first one was awarded, the Heisman Trophy is presented each December to college football's best player of the year. It is *the* most prestigious award in college football. In 1935, it was awarded to Jay Berwanger of the University of Chicago, and was actually called the Downtown

Athletic Club Trophy after the New York City organization that awarded it, as it does to this day. The following year, 1936, when the award was presented, it was renamed in honor of the club's former director, John Heisman, who had died that year. The first winner of that trophy was Larry Kelley, from Yale. There have been eighty-one winners as of 2020.

I was invited to dinner at the home of what was at that time one of the fifty winners. I was looking forward to the dinner, but I was really excited about being able to see the actual Heisman Trophy. Sure, I'd seen pictures of it, but the actual trophy? In real life? That would be a dream. When I arrived, he introduced me to his wife and kids and poured some wine. We made small talk. I didn't want to appear impatient about seeing the actual trophy, so we continued to chat until we came to a break in the conversation, when, as casually as I could manage, I asked, "So, where do you keep it?"

"Keep what?" he asked. Seriously? Keep *what*?

"Where do you keep your Heisman Trophy? I'd love to see it," I went on.

"I think it's in the den," he said, pointing down a hallway.

"Okay if I go take a look?"

"Sure, go ahead," he said, as he pointed down the hallway. I thought the trophy was so important that he'd want to escort me into his trophy room, and tell me all about how he won it, and what it was like to do that. Hell, I wanted to know all of that!

"Okay, then." And I set off alone down the hallway to the den. When I got there, I looked around but there was no trophy case. "Weird," I thought. I was looking for something where the Heisman was displayed behind glass with little pin lights highlighting all the features of that iconic pose. Maybe there's another "den." Maybe I'm in the wrong room? I thought.

I called back down the hallway, "Am I in the right room?"

"Yeah, you're in the right room." The man paused for a moment and then said, "It might be on top of the TV." These were pre–flat screen TV days. This was the time of the big console TVs that sat on the floor. I adjusted my eyes to the light in the room, and looked across the room to the TV and, sure enough, there, on top of the TV, was the trophy. And draped over the straight arm, the lifted knee, and around the neck of the sculpted football player that make up the trophy were pieces of his family's tennis gear. There was a visor. There were headbands and some wristbands. They were all hanging and drying on the trophy. The Heisman was being used as a clothesline.

I shouted back to the kitchen, "You know that there's tennis stuff hanging on your Heisman Trophy, right?"

"Yeah, I know." he said. "I really do need to find a better place for it. I just haven't had the time to do that."

I looked at the trophy and picked the gear off so I could see it clearly. "Is it okay if I pick it up and hold it?"

"Sure, go ahead" he answered. I stood in that den, holding something that, at the time, only fifty other people on the planet had in their possession—guys like Roger Staubach, Archie Griffin, Tony Dorsett, Earl Campbell, Herschel Walker, Doug Flutie, and the most recent winner, Bo Jackson. The trophy is amazingly light. I could tell that he wasn't coming to the den to tell me about the trophy. So, I just held it for a minute before I placed it back on top of the TV and hung the various pieces of tennis gear where I'd originally found them. I walked back to the kitchen. Dinner was almost ready. "Thanks for just letting me hold it," I said. We sat down to dinner, and my host never discussed the Heisman at all. We talked instead about his family, his tennis game, and business. It was a very pleasant evening.

Driving home that evening, I thought about my host. . . . Here was a guy who had done something great, and yet he didn't make a big deal about it. He never called attention to his accomplishment. He was the antithesis of the guy at the airport. He was the rarest of things, a guy who *could* call attention to himself, but didn't. If only, I thought, there were more guys like my host that night in the world, and fewer of the guys I saw at the airport. . . . I let that idea trail off, and thought, it'll never happen. But a guy can dream, can't he?

Final Note: Confession: Had I ever gotten the Heisman Trophy, I'd have at least one pin light installed in my den to illuminate what I think is one of the prettiest awards in sports.

CHAPTER 28

Mount Fuji

*"To see the world, things dangerous to come to,
to see behind walls, draw closer, to find each other,
and to feel. That is the purpose of life."*
—*From the movie* The Secret Life of Walter Mitty

I nearly died on a mountain in Japan. I even briefly considered including the circumstances of this story in the chapter "Nine Lives," but in the end I felt the events fell short of meeting the qualifying criteria. In other words, it could have been worse than it was. I lived in Japan for six months. I was on an international exchange program as part of my course work for what is today known as the Arizona State University Thunderbird School of Global Management. The campus where the program was conducted was located near a little town named Fujinomiya, on the northeastern slope of Mount Fuji, about one hundred miles south of Tokyo. From my dorm room window, I could look out and see Mount Fuji. It was right *there*.

This was my first trip overseas. I was excited. That excitement soon turned to disorientation. And to say that what a lot of us suffered was culture shock would be an understatement. The "lot of us" included exchange students like me who were from the United States, and others who came from Canada, France, and Thailand. We were housed and attended classes together, and integrated with a large group of Japanese students. Many of these Japanese students had very basic English skills, making communication a challenge at times, but even those skills were more than the language skills most of the *"gaijin"* (*See the definition at the end of this chapter*) had, which was close to none.

For the entire time we were there, we experienced some level of cultural disorientation. Yet by the end of the semester, most of that culture shock had faded into a simple desire to return home where things were, well, more normal and homelike. The Japanese, in general, were very structured and very polite. In fact, the Japanese language reflects that. It has different words for the same thing, depending on whom you might be speaking to. There's a social hierarchy that is both rigid and mystifying at times. It is a thing foreign to Americans, so it was hard to get accustomed to. Not only the language but the food was very different and hard to get used to. Restaurants were not at all like what we knew at home. At home we'd go out to a restaurant on occasion, at least that was the case for me back in 1981. But Japanese businessmen spent almost every evening during the workweek going out to dinner with their co-workers. It was normal and *expected*. The first time I experienced one of these dinners, I was with a group of Japanese students from our dorm. They took a few of us to a traditional Japanese restaurant. We, of course, could not read the menu, so they insisted on ordering everything for us. "Do you like fish?" they asked. I grew up near the water and I'd always liked seafood. "Sure, I like fish," I said.

They ordered fish. When the fish was served, it appeared to me that the chef had neglected to put it on the grill. "It looks like it's undercooked." I said. I got the strangest looks from our hosts, and then they all laughed. "Oh, Kehoe-san, you are funny guy making a great joke. This is, of course, the best sashimi in Japan. You Americans, are so witty, *neh*?" (*Again see definition at end of this chapter – you didn't know you were going to get a Japanese language lesson, did you?*). I had no idea what they were talking about.

When they said "sashimi," they might just as well have said, "This is a sequential bilateral genome sequencing." I had never heard of sashimi. "It's *supposed* to be raw—that's what sashimi is," one of the other American exchange students whispered in my ear. I looked at him and quietly asked, "And people eat this?" He gave me the Ugly American look, and I said to myself . . . *Okay, when in Rome. . . .* It *was* delicious, of course, and I love sashimi to this day. But how did I miss that little detail in the pretrip briefing about Japanese culture and food? This was not my last cultural faux pas. It was exhausting trying to figure out the proper thing to do in so many of the social situations we found ourselves in over there. And even when I was aware of the things I was *supposed* to do, I had to focus hard and "do them," even when those things make little sense in American culture.

Food did become an issue for us, as many of us missed some of the American basics. There were some foods you simply could not get in Japan, without going all the way to Tokyo. And even when we found them there, they were expensive, and not as good as the versions we knew at home. I am speaking specifically about pizza and peanut butter. For the entire six months we were there, we were on a constant quest to find the best pizza and peanut butter. We never found the best pizza, but we did find a little import shop in Tokyo that sold Jif. We bought up all they had in stock.

Mount Fuji is also an important part of Japanese culture. It is Japan's sacred mountain. It is the highest peak in the country, at 12,398 feet. It's classified as an active volcano, though it has been dormant for centuries. It is famously known and loved for its perfectly symmetrical snow-covered cone. On a clear day, it's visible from the outskirts of Tokyo, a city of 20 million, about sixty miles away. The mountain has always played an important role in Japanese culture. Through the centuries, it's been the subject of poems, music, rituals, and paintings. In ancient times, it was used as a samurai training ground. In more recent times, a scientific weather station was installed on the rim of the crater at the top to better forecast the fickle weather Japan experiences. And in September 2004, that weather station at the summit was closed down after seventy-two years of continuous operation. I only mention this minor news item because the station plays a small part in my story.

The mountain is covered with snow for at least ten months of the year. But when the snow completely melts, as it can do during July and August, the mountain becomes one of the most visited places in Japan. Families make the pilgrimage there, the old and the young, men and women, and they make the hike up to the top of Fuji. It's not an easy trip, as the trail switchbacks up Fuji's cinder- and pumice-covered slopes, but it is a manageable hike, on a marked trail, during those months. But in winter, when it's cold and snow blankets its slopes two thousand feet from the top, it's a difficult and dangerous climb. Mount Fuji, therefore, was often a topic of discussion among the students. We discussed whether we might have the opportunity to climb it before we returned to the States. But since we were leaving at the end of May, and there'd been more than the normal snowfall that winter, the possibility seemed remote, yet two American students claimed they'd made it to the summit in the first week of May. They came into the cafeteria one evening, boasting that they'd made the hike that very morning. There was little proof to back up their claim. Even our Japanese hosts doubted their story, especially the assertion that they'd made the roundtrip in under eight hours.

The day before we were scheduled to depart for Tokyo, where we'd planned on staying one night before catching our flights home, we spent a good deal of time packing, saying our good-byes, and listening, for the last time, to the morning wake-up anthem that played every day over the campus PA system. I'll tell you more about that morning wake-up anthem in the next chapter. On that evening, the last formal campus event was held. It was a graduation ceremony, followed by cocktails and a dinner. The party after dinner continued until around midnight. I left the party, returned to my dorm room, and went to bed.

I was tucked into bed, when my friend Keith showed up in my room and shook me out of my sleep.

"How did you get in here?" I asked him.

Ignoring my question, he said, "We have to climb the mountain."

"It's after midnight, right? You know we're getting on the bus in eight hours, right? You go ahead. I'm going back to sleep."

I tried to hike up the blankets and roll over and go back to sleep, but Keith pulled me and my blankets onto the floor. "This is our last chance to do it," he said.

"Great. Then go do it and leave me alone."

I was hoping Keith would leave, but I knew I was fighting a losing battle with this guy, so I sat up and tried to talk him out of it. He's the kind of person who once a thought enters his head, there's no reasoning with him. I reminded him of the story we'd heard from the guys who claimed they'd been to the top of Fuji. "It's at least an eight-hour round trip, and that's when the sun's up."

I reminded him that we were scheduled to leave in about eight hours, and, worse, we'd have to find a vehicle to actually drive the fifteen miles just to get to the trailhead before we could even start the climb . . . not to mention that it was still pitch-black outside and the middle of the night.

Keith then said, "We'll do it in five hours and have plenty of time to make the bus."

"Five hours?" I asked in disbelief. "Where'd you get that number from? Did you pull it, like one of your answers in finance class, out of the air?"

"We can borrow Nanahara-san's motorcycle to get to the trailhead. What's with all the whining, anyway?" he said. (*Note: "san" at the end of a name in Japan is an honorific*)

"Whining? Listen, you stroll in here half in the bag at one a.m., pull me out of bed, and announce that we have to climb a twelve-thousand-foot mountain in the dark. This isn't whining. This is my way of expressing reasonable disbelief and skepticism, not to mention my way of saving you from yourself."

I could feel that any further argument was going to be hopeless, so I relented and agreed to go. I didn't want to go—I just agreed to go.

"Does Nanahara know we're taking his motorcycle?" I asked.

"No, not yet. But it won't be a problem. He leaves the keys in it, and we'll be back before he wakes up, anyway."

"Okay, so far so good. What about clothes, water, and food?" I asked. "It's going to be cold up there. I don't have mountaineering gear. Do you?"

"Just put on as many layers as you can. I've already packed some food and liquid," Keith said.

I'd already packed for the Tokyo bus ride, so I had to unpack and rummage through my bags to come up with something to wear.

I ended up with an outfit that included two wool caps, three pairs of gloves, three pairs of jeans, three pairs of socks, three sweaters, a ski jacket, and a pair of tennis shoes. That was all I could muster, and by the time I put all that on, I looked like the Michelin Tyre Man.

Sure enough, Nanahara *had* left his keys in his motorcycle. We decided not wake him and ask permission, so we rolled the bike out of the parking lot before starting it and driving off to the trail-head. About twenty-five minutes later, we were at six thousand feet in a pitch-black parking lot, pawing the ground looking for the trailhead, so we could start climbing. It was cold and dark. At this point, the lunacy of what we were doing was hard to ignore. "Are we seriously going to do this? We can't even see three feet in front our faces?" But we'd come this far, and I guessed we felt committed.

We couldn't locate the trailhead at all. Instead, we just started crawling up the hill in the dark. In short order, we had to resort to scrambling on our hands and knees, groping about in hopes of finding the trail. We weren't having any luck. We had only one small flashlight to illuminate the biggest mountain in Japan, so it was useless. It felt like we were on the dark side of the moon.

Gradually, however, as the sky began to lighten by about 2:30 a.m., we were finally able to locate the trail and stand up and walk, instead of crawling over the sharp rocks. We hiked for another hour until we reached the end of the trail, where the snow and ice field began. The snow and ice essentially buried the rest of the trail to the top under several feet of snow. Now we began the slog through the snow straight up Fuji. But before we started, I asked, "Can I get some of the water you packed?"

Keith handed me a fifth of Canadian Club Whiskey.

"Whiskey?" I asked. "Seriously? *This* is the liquid you referred to earlier? Let me guess. The food you packed is dry ramen noodles, right?"

"Yeah, it was all I could find on short notice."

Perfect.

We started slogging straight up through the snow and ice. It was nearly four a.m. when we were able to make out what looked like the summit above, and what looked like a structure with antennae and such on top of it. The climbing was hard because the snow was deep, and the rising temperature was making conditions slippery, especially for me as I only had tennis shoes on. It took us another thirty minutes to get to the top . . . the rim of the volcano crater.

There was indeed a building there. It was located right on the lip of the crater, and we were now looking down into its depths. Fuji's crater is about a quarter-mile wide, and about two football fields deep. I looked over at the building and said, "Let's see if they have any coffee. That would really hit the spot right now." We walked over and knocked on the door.

"It looks like a weather station or some science thing," I said.

We knocked a few times and got no response. Any thought of getting a hot cup of coffee evaporated. To this day, I'm certain that somebody was in that weather station. I'd swear that I heard what sounded like footsteps coming from inside. But I could understand the person's unwillingness to answer a knock on the door at 5 a.m. He was alone, and there were two wildly dressed *gaijin* outside. He probably decided to just stay in bed. Remember my earlier reference to the minor news item about the weather station that closed in 2004? We had just knocked on the door of that very station.

By now, the sun was rising over Tokyo off in the distance, and we could make out some of the city. It was a true *"wow"* moment.

"Was it worth it?" Keith asked.

I took in the spectacular views and just said, "Shut up. Yeah, it was worth it." It had taken us a little under four hours make the climb to the top. But it was then close to 6 a.m., and our bus to Tokyo was leaving in less than four hours. We needed to get down and back to campus—fast. In general, the fastest way down a mountain is on skis. And if you don't have skis, the next-fastest way is by glissading. Glissading is like skiing, but without the skis. One simply sits on one's butt, aims oneself downhill, and pushes off. It is way faster than walking. And far more dangerous if you cannot control your rate of descent. To control one's rate of descent, some kind of ice ax is required. We, of course, didn't have one of those.

I set off down the hill first, and Keith followed. I picked up speed, and then a little more speed. I cannot say for certain, but my guess is, I approached a downward velocity of twenty-five to thirty miles per hour that morning. I was flying past boulders and rocks, trying to use my tennis shoes, gloves, and whatever else I had to slow down. Nothing worked. I could then see the end of the snow-field approaching, and I tried to jam my feet and hands into the snow to stop, but I kept on flying right off the snow and into the cinder-and-rock field. I managed to get myself upright, and on my feet, but that only got me airborne, taking lunarlike leaps down the hill, trying to keep myself from a train wreck of somersaulting end over end. It was a boulder that finally slowed me down. I hit it, I somersaulted, and then I rolled to a stop. I was on my back, looking up into the morning sky, when Keith finally caught up with me. I was sprawled out in the pumice and ash, bleeding.

"That," he said, "was the most spectacular thing I've ever seen." Keith is a man of many understatements.

"Don't you want to know if I'm all right?" I asked.

When I hit the boulder, the impact ripped through the three pairs of jeans I was wearing, opening a gash on my thigh. The wound wasn't deep, but it was nasty-looking and bleeding. The friction from glissading had worn out the seats of the three pairs of jeans such that my underwear was showing. That was the only cloth now between the snow and my skin. The same thing happened with the three pairs of gloves. The friction from using my hands to slow down the velocity of my descent had left the palms of my hands raw and bleeding. Other than that, I was perfectly fine, I told him.

There was no time to waste tending to the damage to my body. We had to hurry to the trailhead, get on the bike, and hustle back. The sun was fully up by the time we reached the trailhead and the bike. We started the bike and it barely fired up because the gas tank was just about empty. Perfect!

"We passed a gas station about ten miles back on the way here," I said. "Maybe it's open."

We sat on the bike without starting it, and aimed it downhill. We glided and coasted downhill around curves and hairpin turns until the road straightened and leveled out. We ran out of momentum about fifty yards from the gas station, and it *was* open. We got back to campus by 8 a.m.

When we walked into the cafeteria at 9 a.m. for breakfast, after showering and dressing, neither of us looked worse for the wear from the night's exertions. We then sat down next to the guys who'd claimed that they had climbed Fuji and struck up the conversation, "You guys do anything after the party last night?"

"No, nothing really," they answered. "What about you guys?"

"Oh, nothing . . . except we climbed Fuji."

"Sure, you did!" They laughed.

I asked them, "How long did you say your roundtrip journey took?"

"We did it in eight hours."

"We made it in six hours," I said.

They laughed again. "Right!"

"Yeah, maybe you're right. Maybe I just dreamed the whole thing up."

We made the bus to Tokyo. It took two weeks to heal my wounds, bumps, and bruises. And all I recall of my flight back to the United States, in coach, was that it was one long drunk to dull the pain.

There are times in life when the foolish and the ill-advised turn out to be anything but, and in fact those events become personal landmarks. There are times when what on the surface appears to be lunacy is, in fact, destiny. Some of life's most memorable and meaningful experiences begin just as they did that night in Japan, when one of your friends shakes you out of your bed . . . and you end up on a mountain witnessing majesty and you come away with an experience that binds you to that person in perpetuity. Sometimes it pays to do a crazy thing or two in life… and to feel fully alive.

Definitions:

Gaijin: Japanese word meaning "foreigner." Though I spoke more Japanese than most of the exchange students, I still knew I was a foreigner. Today I can recall very little of my Japanese. And the times when I can usually start with several bottles of sake at some sushi joint, where for some reason my Japanese language skills magically reappear.

Neh: A Japanese word generally used at the end of a sentence, like the English word "right," as in "That was a great time, right (*neh*)?" The Japanese use this word… all the time.

CHAPTER 29

No Harm, No Foul

"No harm, no foul."
—*The* Hartford Courant *first employed this phrase in 1956.*

I did one other thing in Japan, the day before we climbed Mount Fuji. But unlike the spontaneity that accompanied the Fuji climb, this thing required planning, a little bit of spying, and some ninja special-op activities that culminated on the morning of our last full day in Japan. Our lives as students in Japan were very structured, especially in terms of time and schedule. Our class sessions started and ended on time. Our meals were scheduled and conducted on time. The trains in Tokyo always seemed to run and stop on time. This was very unlike my experiences in New York and with the LIRR, where schedules were regularly missed. In fact, the trains on Tokyo's central loop were scheduled to go *out of service* every night at exactly 11 p.m. Wherever a train was at that time, when the clock struck 11 p.m., the train parked at the nearest station, and everyone got off and hustled to find another way home. I experienced this "fire drill" one night. When the train stopped, no one said anything negative about the obvious inconvenience—they all simply ran off into the night and found another way home. It was a *nightly* ritual to which all Japanese in Tokyo were apparently accustomed.

On campus, we had *daily* rituals. The primary one I remember was the music that played every morning and evening at exactly 6 a.m. and 6 p.m., respectively. The PA system would come to life with a short, static warm-up buzz, and then the same music came on, one song in the morning, and another in the evening. It happened every day, right on schedule. Wherever you might have been at those hours, whether inside your dorm room, outside in the quad, in the library, or in a classroom or the cafeteria, you would hear that music. After about two weeks of this routine, the music became a topic of conversation among the students. Why do they play the same songs every day? Why not change it up a little? And what is that music, anyway? No one knew. By the time we'd been on campus for two months, we didn't even hear it anymore as the monotony and tedium of it turned into background noise that we could almost ignore. That is, until the last day of the semester.

I'm not certain when the idea came to me, but I decided that something had to be done about the music. I wrote a letter to my dad. That's what you did in those days, as there was no email or Internet, and international phone calls were far too expensive for a poor student. I wrote my father a letter, and in it I requested that if he could locate it, would he send me a cassette tape recording of a dance club song that was popular at the time called "Turning Japanese," by The Vapors. Then I waited. I had almost forgotten about my letter, when two months later I received a package from him, and in it was the cassette tape I had asked for. I checked it out and it sounded pretty good.

With the cassette tape in hand, I decided it was time to move ahead with the rest of my plan. First, here's some background. When I originally arrived on the campus, I'd signed up as a volunteer to participate in a cross-cultural program that would help improve my conversational Japanese language skills. The program involved working in the campus administrative offices for a few hours a week, alongside the Japanese staff, doing things like paperwork, filing, and other like jobs. The staff not only needed the help but they, too, were interested in improving their English skills and learning about American culture. The arrangement was a good deal for everyone.

As I worked with the staff, I got to know my way around the administration building. And as the people there grew accustomed to me, I was granted greater access to the office, with less supervision. I was filing papers one day in a cubicle adjacent to the audio-visual (AV) equipment room, the place where the music was located. I wanted to understand how the system worked.

"Why do you play the same music every day?" I asked.

"I'm not certain. We've just always done that." Watanabe-san told me.

"What are the names of the songs that are played? I've asked and no one seems to know."

"Well, the morning song is a kind of Japanese national anthem . . . and the evening song . . . well I'm not really certain what that song is."

I pointed to the tape machine and said, "It looks like a complicated piece of equipment."

"Not really," Watanabe-san replied. "It's pretty simple. We just insert a cassette tape here, set the timer, and the rest is automatic."

"Looks pretty easy," I said. As the weeks went by, I noticed that the door to the AV room wasn't always locked, as there was really no need to do that. But there were some days when it was. I asked and learned where the keys to the room were kept. They were simply hung on a kind of key-hanging board with various keys to other parts of the office on little hooks. The board was easily accessible in the front office, and each hook was neatly labeled with the description of the key's use. The only problem for me was that each was labeled in Japanese. So, I asked for help in reading the labels. After all, I was volunteering to work in the office so I could improve my Japanese language skills. I memorized the location of the hook where the AV room key was hung.

I also knew I might need help executing the final phase of my plan. I shared it with one other person, someone who I knew could keep a secret, and enlisted his help. Otherwise, I wanted it to be a complete surprise. On the evening before our last day on campus, I said good-bye to everyone I'd worked with in in the office. We hugged and wished one another well. It really had been fun working with them. Many of the Japanese could be a little quiet and remote, but once they got to know you, especially the Americans, they seemed to loosen up. They enjoyed our irreverence and humor. A few, in fact, said they found us a breath of fresh air in their, sometimes, overstructured lives. The last thing I did before I left was to stop by the AV room. I noticed it was locked.

It was late May. The weather was beautiful and warm. That evening, I needed to get back into those offices. I knew the AV room was located at the back of the second floor of the administration building. When I walked around to the back, I noted that several windows on the second floor had been left open to let the warm air in. This was good. Just after the sun set, I visited my friend, the one I'd let in on my plan. "It's time to do this," I said. "I've found a good place to get in, too. Are you ready?" I changed into a dark-colored shirt and pair of pants, and met my friend outside the administration building, in the back. There was an open window on the second floor, directly above some kind of heating/AC unit, which was located almost directly underneath it. We determined that if my friend stood on top of this unit and hoisted me up onto his shoulders, I could reach the window ledge.

I had the cassette tape my dad mailed in my pocket. My friend hoisted me up, and I managed to get myself on his shoulders. I grabbed onto the ledge, and without too much trouble pulled myself up and slid in through the window. The rest was easy. I knew where everything was. I retrieved the key from the key board, opened the AV room, took out the 6 a.m. morning music cassette tape from its slot, inserted the Vapors "Turning Japanese" cassette tape, and placed the 6 a.m. tape on a desk. I attached a note to that tape with a smiley face drawn on it, then I turned up the volume knob, locked the AV room, returned the key to the board, and exited through the window the way I had entered. The mission was accomplished.

I rose early the next morning—our final day on campus—and found a seat on a bench in the middle of the quad area. I sat down at about 5:50 a.m. I had a good view of most of the dorm rooms, many of which had an external balcony. At exactly 6 a.m. that morning, instead of the same tedious song we'd all come to ignore, a new song came on the PA system. I could hear it loudly and clearly from where I was sitting in the courtyard. It must have been really loud in the dorm rooms. The sun was coming up, and slowly, a few groggy heads poked out of a few windows, and a couple of people appeared on the balcony to investigate. I sat for a moment, taking in the scene, listening to that dance club tune, before I got up and walked back in the direction of my room on the other side of the quad. As I walked, doing a little dance to the beat, I sang along with the chorus line: "*I think I'm turning Japanese. I think I'm turning Japanese, I really think so,*" as it played over and over, until the end.

I have to imagine that someone in the office must have concluded who the perpetrator was. There were only two exchange students who worked in the office. I did have some level of plausible deniability, but I was certainly the more likely candidate of the two of us. But I wasn't worried. I knew that my Japanese hosts wouldn't conduct a search for the guilty. They were too nice, and I'm willing to bet they, too, got a good laugh that morning. Even if a search yielded me up, so what? What punishment could be meted out? Send me home? I was leaving the next day.

I sat down for breakfast next to my friend—not the guy who'd helped me get in through the window, but the guy with whom I would scale Mount Fuji in less that twenty-four hours.

"Was that you?" He wanted to know.

"Was what me?" I said.

He gave me the "you know what I'm talking about look."

"What would make you think I was responsible for that?"

My friend didn't say another word, and went back to eating his breakfast, and I did the same.

Of course, later the next morning, huffing and puffing up Mount Fuji in the dark, I did say something like, "Wasn't that just the coolest thing this morning—the wake-up music?" He knew for certain then who was the culprit, and he just looked over at me and said, "Only you. . . . ."

My wife will often tell me, after I play a prank or make a smart comment, "You know nobody likes a wiseass!" And I will look at her in mock surprise and say, "Are you serious, sweetie. It's just the opposite—everyone *loves* a wiseass." I think that's a fact. And since no one got hurt by my stunt that day, all was well with the world. That's how it has to be in life sometimes, if we are to get any enjoyment and separate ourselves from those joyless zero-tolerance "scolds" of the world. We laugh and say, "play on"—*no harm, no foul.*

Final Note: You can go on the web, type the words "The Vapors" or "Turning Japanese," in the search window and you'll find several ancient-looking, early 1980s MTV videos of the dance club song. And if you close your eyes while you listen to it, and picture a campus in the shadows of Mount Fuji, with the sun rising in the morning and hungover students blinking their eyes open while this tune blasts away—it might just put a smile on your face.

CHAPTER 30

Crazy Beautiful

"Happiness is health, and a short memory."
—Audrey Hepburn

Being a lovable wise guy is one thing, but being stone-cold crazy and lovable is quite another. There are people like that in the world. And they fascinate me. They're fun, but only from a safe distance. They're a car wreck happening in real time. They fly, they crash, and get right back up in the air again. They forget, recover, and move on. They live in the present. They're crazy, tragic, beautiful, and – yes - even lovable. I've known a few, but not very many. And if you get too close to them, God help you. But they make me smile, well, because there is something beautiful about watching someone live in the moment with nary a fear. Here's a story about one of those people.

You know I was a business consultant. I'd ride into a new town every week like a gunslinger hired by a village to rid them of the bad guys. It was a lonely way of earning a living, but it was always fascinating because I got to meet the most interesting people. One of these people was a guy I'll call Mike. I first met Mike at a conference where I was the keynote speaker. I was speaking to an audience of business owners on the topic of "Increasing Your Bottom Line." Mike was one of those business owners. He sat up front, and I noticed that he was paying close attention to what I was saying, and took lots of notes. He approached me after the program as I was packing up my computer and speaking notes. He was excited and started talking at a high rate of speed.

"That was really great!" he said. "It was really good information!"

"Thanks, I'm glad it was valuable for you."

"Very valuable, and let me tell you why."

And Mike rolled right into a description of his company, his problems, and how he was looking for a consultant to help him fix these things. Would I be interested in working with him as a client? I told him that I was always interested, but that at the moment I had a "full dance card," and my schedule was booked for the next several months. I suggested that he and I follow up in the coming weeks to "see what might be possible." We parted and I thought that I'd never hear from him again, as that was the normal routine after a conference. People got excited at the conference, ready to make changes, but all that faded away when they returned to work, and the day-to-day demands of running a business put them right back in the old grind. I expected that Mike would be no different. Yet, I did intend to follow up with him. However, that proved unnecessary, as he called me the very next week.

"When can you come here?" he wanted to know.

"Before we discuss that, let's discuss your business first. I only want to work with you if I can really help you. You might have some problems for which I may not be your best resource," I said.

"Oh, you're the right guy, all right. I checked up on you," he fired back.

For the next twenty minutes we discussed his business and what he wanted me to do. He shared that he wasn't making the kind of profits he once had. He didn't know exactly why that was. But many of the things I had spoken about at the conference resonated with him. He sounded in earnest, and wanting help is often half the solution.

"Can you help me get my company on a profitable footing again" He asked, referring to what he'd told me about the challenges he was having in his business.

"Sure," I answered, "but what you're describing will take time. We need to conduct a detailed analysis, determine a few practical recommendations, and then work together to execute the changes. Are you okay with that?"

"That's not a problem," he said. "I'm ready to get started. When can you get here?"

"Before we schedule anything," I said, "let's discuss fees, the contract, and a work plan."

I explained my fees and contract, and outlined a work plan. When we finished the call, he told me to send him the paperwork, and provide him with a scheduled start date. Two days later, I got the signed contract back, and the down payment for my fees. We scheduled our first on-site meeting.

I do not like to rent cars when I travel for business. It's an inconvenience. It also always added an hour to the trip from the airport to the hotel, as it seemed like all the rental centers were located miles from the terminal. Worse, I'd gotten lost so many times driving at night from the airport to the hotel in the cities and towns unfamiliar me that I avoided rentals whenever I could. And you know now how I can treat a rental car . . . just ask Avis! I told Mike to arrange a pickup for me at the terminal, and a ride to the hotel. When I arrived, I was expecting a guy holding a sign with my name on it and being ushered into a hired car. (Note: I use Uber now but, then, Uber did not yet exist, and cabs were sketchy especially in more rural areas.) Instead, Mike met me in the baggage-claim area and led me to his truck parked curbside. He was my ride.

Mike drove a large white Dodge dually-type pickup truck. It was so high off the ground that I had to climb up some steps just to get in it. The truck was equipped with every imaginable mid-1990s communication device then available. Mike had two pagers, a flip-type cell phone, a truck-mounted cell phone, and a CB radio. We set off for the hotel, and he began a monologue that was only interrupted by his pager going off, or a call coming in on one of his two phones, or some squawk from the CB radio that connected home to his work crews. These interruptions were incessant. Mike would talk to me, and then talk to someone else at the same time. I just sat in the passenger seat, observing the madness.

He told me that we'd take the "back way" to the hotel as it was shorter and, as I was about to discover, scarier. We were driving on dark, narrow, and twisting roads that felt barely wide enough for his truck and another vehicle to pass simultaneously. He was driving at a high rate of speed while answering and making calls and, in between, talking to me. He barely watched the road. I was so distracted by thoughts of impending doom, in some spectacular and fiery car wreck, that I couldn't focus on anything he was saying. Mike seemed oblivious to my situation, and merrily drove on.

At one point during the drive, we approached an interstate junction where'd we'd pass over the highway. There were the standard traffic lights at the ramps to manage vehicles exiting and entering the interstate. As we approached, the light turned yellow. We kept barreling along. Then it turned red. We were at least thirty yards from the intersection when the light had gone red. Mike never slowed down. He never touched the brakes. We flew through the red light. I closed my eyes, waiting for the sound of impact. But the only thing I heard was Mike's voice talking about something else. He never said, "Sorry about that red light—my bad." Or: "I didn't mean to scare you. . . ." Nothing, no explanation at all.

When we arrived at the hotel, Mike informed me that he'd be busy in the morning, and that he'd arranged to have one of his people pick me up and bring me to the office. "How's eight o'clock for the pickup time, and a start time of eight-thirty for the meeting? The guys will have coffee and muffins ready."

I said, "That sounds like a plan. And what's the guy's name who'll be picking me up, just so I know?"

"It will be either John or Steve. I'll see you in the morning." And the big white Dodge dually rumbled off into the night. As Mike left, I thought about kissing the ground before entering the lobby to check in. I felt like a survivor of something.

The next morning, as promised, one of his guys showed up and met me in the lobby. When I strapped into the passenger seat, he looked at me and asked, "I heard Mike picked you up from the air- port last night. How was the drive?"

I looked at him and said, "It was harrowing."

"Ah, welcome to town! You've now been baptized by the White Specter of Death." The guy explained that this was a description used by the local townspeople who were familiar with Mike and his truck. And although Mike had never been in a vehicle accident, there'd been enough scary close calls to warrant the name, and warn anyone on the road of his approach.

"You were never really in danger, though," he said, reassuring me. "When the White Specter of Death comes down the road here, we can all see it, and we just stand back until he passes. It's just safer for everyone that way." That at least explained the empty roads and lack of traffic the night before. I made a mental note about Mike's driving, and guessed that he just might run his business the same way—heedlessly and pell-mell. I wasn't too far wrong as it turned out.

We met for the next two days in his conference room. They were exhausting days. Mike was such a high-energy guy that it was hard for him to stay focused on a single topic. He would jump from one thing to the next. He obviously had a short attention span. He talked over the top of his people and me, constantly. But when he did this, it never felt like he was being an arrogant, know-it-all. He was just genuinely excited—about everything—and whatever popped into his head had to be said. Despite my growing frustration with him, I found myself liking him . . . and at the same time thanking God that I didn't have to spend every day with him like his people did. I could see why he had problems, and why his business wasn't executing efficiently.

Mike was a big part of his own problem. He was unable to focus on anything for long periods of time, and as a result neither were his people. They sat around, waiting for his next brilliant idea. From day to day, the priorities changed. That, of course, is the recipe for inefficiency. On top of all this, Mike ran more than one business. His other business was the *real* source of his income . . . a collection of real estate rentals. He was also in the business of acquiring beaten-down single-family homes. He'd clean them up, and then he'd lease them out and collect the rents. He had mortgages on top of mortgages to fund all these purchases, but he was making good money in that business.

At the end of the first day of meetings, Mike said, "Let me take you out to dinner so we can talk a bit." I said that was okay by me. In fact, it was a standard practice for me. I'd go out to dinner with my client at the end of the first day's meeting to debrief with them. I was always a cheap date. I preferred not to go to fancy restaurants serving rich food. I also made it a practice to order only one glass of wine at dinner. I learned early on that if I did more than this on the road, I would end up trashing my body and growing old long before my time. Besides, I liked to get to bed by 10 p.m. at the latest.

We ate dinner. I had two glasses of wine. Then Mike suggested that we visit one of his favorite places for a nightcap. "I'll take you to the hotel right after that," he promised. Off into the night we went in the White Specter of Death. That night we visited more than a few of his favorite places. I did not get back to the hotel until 2 a.m., and then only after I said I'd call a cab and he could stay as long as he liked. Mike relented and drove me to the hotel. I don't recall much of the evening, but at one point I do remember him drinking "flaming shots" of Sambuca with something else, and buying drinks for everyone. The second day of meetings was tough. My head ached.

After we concluded the meetings, Mike invited me to dinner at his home. "Please come over and meet the family and see my home. It will be an early evening, I promise." How could I say no to an invitation to meet the family? I accepted. When Mike's guys heard about the invitation, they smiled and told me I was in for a real treat . . . but they'd say nothing more than that.

For the fourth time, I climbed into the White Specter of Death. When we turned into Mike's driveway past the ten-foot-high iron gates, I couldn't see the home. It was set *way* back somewhere on the property. When we finally pulled up to it, Mike parked in what looked like a still-unfinished paved courtyard. The entire property looked like a construction site. There was work being done everywhere. The home was at least ten thousand square feet. The backyard was a dirt pit. I learned at dinner that Mike was installing a pool, a cabana, and a tennis court back there. We walked from the courtyard into his home and he led me into the kitchen: "Let me introduce you to my family." We ate dinner with the kids. His wife was charming. I was thinking, watching the two of them together, that it would take a special woman to handle this guy day in and day out.

After dinner, Mike asked, "Would you like to take a tour of the property?" *Are you kidding?* I thought. *Of course!* We started inside. He was building a top floor in one part of the home to add bedrooms for the kids. The master suite was being enlarged. It was awe-inspiring. Then we went to the garage. Mike was making the garage even bigger . . . big enough to house an RV bus and all his toys, which included cars, motorcycles, jet skis, and boats. He was like a little kid building a tree house, showing his friends how cool it was going to be when it was done.

We were on our way from the garage to the pool-cabana-tennis complex—what else can you call it?—when we walked through the paved driveway area and courtyard. In the center of it, there was a circular, framed stacked-stone outline of what looked like a fountain. It wasn't as large as a public Roman fountain, but it was large enough to be impressive. In the center of the fountain there was a raised stone platform. I could see that something eventually would be mounted on top of that platform . . . like a statue maybe.

I walked behind Mike and beside his wife throughout most of the tour. I could sense that she was a little embarrassed by the whole thing, as it was a lot to take in. But far from being irritated by her husband, she seemed to be endlessly patient with him. Later on, after I had time to think about it, my guess is that she knew that he was crazy, but she loved him in spite of that or maybe even because of that.

I was walking next to him when I asked Mike, "What's going on that pedestal in the fountain?" I think he heard me, but before he could answer, his wife said, in a complete deadpan, "A statue of Mike." She said it without any trace of meanness. In fact, she said it, sighing, patiently teasing him, and ready to be done with the tour. I could see that she'd done this before. Mike said nothing, like he hadn't heard what she said, and kept right on going to the backyard complex. I looked over at his wife. I was laughing, as I thought her line was one of the funniest I'd ever heard. Yes, you had to be there, but it captured her and Mike perfectly. As I watched the two of them, I found myself liking him. He was dangerous, but he was fun.

I worked with Mike for about a year, before I became so frustrated that I discontinued him as a client. It's the only time in three decades as a consultant that I did this. When I did it, I told him that I liked him very much, but that he was crazy, and more than a little unfocused. "You're wasting your money with me. You are frustrating your own people, too. They want to make changes, but they can't. When you're ready to focus on this, call me. Okay?" Mike expressed some surprise, but he had no hard feelings. He even said that he understood.

Several years later, around 2008, I learned Mike had suffered a major financial setback. By that time, he had amassed more than two hundred homes. They were all mortgaged to the maximum. When real estate prices crashed, the rental income was not enough to compensate for the home price crash. Mike went belly-up as they say in business. I did not hear from him during this time. Several years after that, I was on a stage, preparing for a presentation as part of a conference program whose topic was something about "recovering from the downturn." There, in the front row, sat Mike. He looked different. He looked older and thinner. I came down from the stage and walked over to him.

"Mike, how are you? How's your wife and your kids?" The kids were grown and his wife was fine. They were still living in the same town, but in a much smaller home. "What are you doing here?" I asked him.

"What do you mean?" he asked me. "I'm here to hear you speak and learn and get some ideas for my business." Although he'd lost everything with his real estate holdings, he still had his other business—the one he'd hired me to work on all those years ago. He was as excited about it as ever. Here was a guy who went from rags to riches and back to rags, and he was ready to put it all on the line and roll the dice again. I looked at him. "If anyone can do it, Mike, it's you." And I meant it. If there's one thing I've learned from crazy lovable people, it's that you never bet against them. That's what I love about them. I wish that we all had a little more "Mike" in us.

CHAPTER 31

Twisted Sister

*Twisted Sister is the name of a 1970's glam
rock band... and the chapter title comes
from my brief experience with the band...
not from my experience with the nuns.*

Have you ever played the game where you and your friends have to answer the question, "What job would you most want to have—if you could choose it—when you come back in your next life?" The question makes for great conversation, especially with a bottle of wine or two. My answer to the question hasn't changed much over the years. I've concluded that I either want to come back as a ninth-inning closer and relief pitcher for the New York Yankees, or as my sister. The sister answer is, of course, my form of dry humor, but the ninth-inning closer dream is real. I ask you, Is there a better job in the world than throwing twelve pitches, three nights a week, for six months with, maybe, the playoffs, and making $10 million dollars doing it? As for my only sister, Deirdre, whom I love, my brothers and I like to tease her, saying that she lives a pretty good life, staying at home with two good boys and playing tennis. We tell her that we'd trade our busy working lives, anytime, for her home life. If we only really knew, she tells us.

There's a long roster of sisters who've played a role in my life. My mother's three sisters and my father's two sisters have always been around for us and involved in the lives of my brothers and me when we were growing up and even into our adult lives. I went to Catholic schools with sisters—in this case they were Dominican nuns—attending class with them almost up through high school. And my little sister, nine years my junior, thought her big brother walked on water until she knew better. And once upon a time, I got to sing onstage with the once-famous rock-and-roll band, Twister Sister. There were always sisters around, shaping my life.

I was born in Forest Hills, Queens, New York City. We moved to Farmingdale, Long Island, New York, when I was two years old because child number two was on the way, and the apartment superintendent had had enough of my energy, and said so to my parents. We stayed in Farmingdale for ten years, where my sister was born, before the expected arrival of child number six made it necessary to move out of that little house on Intervale Avenue. That was our last move as a family, and it took place in 1967. That home, in Smithtown, New York, remains the home where my mother still resides to this day, more than half a century later.

I started my school days in Farmingdale, attending kindergarten at Woodward Parkway Elementary School. Mrs. Hanken was my teacher. I wasn't a standout student or kindergarten prodigy. My first report card, sent home by Mrs. Hanken, stated that I didn't know my right from my left hand, and that I didn't like to dance with the girls in class. But being who I am, I took Mrs. Hanken's feedback to heart, and I've worked really hard on both those holes in my résumé. Today, I am happy to report that I have mastered both those things.

I attended first grade at St. Kilian's Catholic School with Dominican nuns. These sisters wore those black-and-white habits, with that severe head covering cowl and veil that made them look a little scary to a first-grader. It wasn't until fifth grade that we began to wonder what was actually under all that cloth. Like, is there an actual female person underneath that like our mother and our aunts? My first teacher, for both first and second grades, was Sister Maurice. She was a tall and lean woman, with a thin face, a beak of a nose, and dark, piercing, brown joyless eyes. Her presence exuded sternness and discipline. She was a no-nonsense teacher. When Sister told us to do something, we did it. We learned that during the first week of school.

For Sister Maurice's first homework assignment, we had to go home and learn and memorize our home address, and be prepared to write it, and spell it properly, by the next day. We lived at 128 Intervale Avenue, which was located about three miles from the school. I know that distance because over the years I'd made that three-mile walk a hundred times to attend choir practice. The next day in class, Sister Maurice pointed to a boy who sat at a desk the next row over from me. "Donald," she said, "please go up to the blackboard and write and recite your home address." I knew Donald, and I knew he lived on Staple Street, as I had walked past his home many times. His actual address, I learned that day, was 249 Staple Street. Donald walked up to the blackboard, took a piece of chalk, wrote the numerals "249," and then, instead of spelling out the word "Staple," he drew a line picture of what a wire paper staple looks like—you know, the upside-down, squared-off letter "U." He turned and proudly smiled at Sister. I thought it was creative, but

Sister appeared less appreciative of Donald's creativity. To this day, I'm not exactly sure what Donald intended with that little stunt, but Sister, I think, saw it as the insubordinate act of a wise-guy class clown. And she was about to let us all know what she thought of class clowning.

As Donald did his thing at the blackboard, Sister had been standing off to the side of the blackboard about fifteen feet away or so. She then moved, with amazing speed, toward Donald. What happened took place so fast that all I can recall definitively was Donald flying through the air, over my desk, and landing, with a thump, back in his seat. The sister actually *threw* him there. There was no anger or rage involved. She didn't yell or get red in the face with anger. This was just her version of calm classroom discipline and control. Fifty first-graders just stared. Had that actually just happened? Donald wasn't even crying. I think he was in shock, too. But if the sister was intending to send a message about how her students would comport themselves when in class, it was clearly heard.

When my mother picked me up from the bus stop that day, she asked what I'd learned that day. I related the story about Donald, thinking she might be shocked. She just nodded and said, "Well, maybe he *was* being disrespectful." Maybe he was, but I thought turning him into a flying object seemed a little excessive, and I said as much to my mother. My mother nodded again, "But you know, Sister has a hard job with fifty of you in the same small classroom. She doesn't have any help, either." I just thought about that a bit. Then she asked me "So, what did you learn from this?" I said something like, "That you should never, ever, mess with Sister Maurice." And for the next two years, I never did.

After Sister Maurice, all the other nuns were more relaxed. I think Sister Maurice's classroom management approach was based on the "broken window" model of urban decay. Let broken windows remain broken, and you will have more broken windows. Fix the broken window, and then you will have fewer broken windows but, more important, more order and less urban decay. The sisters I had after that did not practice the Sister Maurice style of management, so I decided to see what I could get away with in the new and less regimented classes. I wasn't the only one testing boundaries. Lots of the other kids were trying to see what they could get away with, now that they weren't in Sister Maurice's class. As a result, I got into trouble for the first time.

What happened was I took and hid Judith P's lesson book. She was a girl that sat right in front of me. I swiped her book and hid it under the tabletop of my flip-top desk where she could not find it. This was my way of showing my love for Judith. I guess I had a crush on her, and this move, I thought, would certainly demonstrate that love and endear me to her. How could it not? That day, Sister Alberta called on Judith to read from her book, and she, of course, had to tell the sister that she didn't have her book. This was a no-no. Sister questioned her about responsibilities and lack of preparation for the lesson. Judith then started crying and pointed her finger behind her at me, and said, "It's not my fault. Kevin took it." So much for true love.

"Kevin, is that true? Do you have Judith's book?" Sister asked, staring me down.

I'd been conditioned by Sister Maurice for the previous two years that "honesty was always the best policy," and that George Washington always told the truth, especially about that cherry tree. I admitted the theft. Sister sent me downstairs to the principal's office. We all knew from horror stories that you never, ever, wanted to be sent *there*—ever. If you were, you would face the "Board of Education." The "Board of Education" at St. Kilian's was an actual board. More specifically, it was a wooden paddle about two feet long and six inches wide. It was a flat, sturdy, one-half-inch thick piece of wood with holes drilled through it. According to school legend, the holes prevented the build up of any compressed-air "cushion" that might protect your rear end from maximum contact. I know this about the "Board of Education," because I had it applied to *my* backside that morning by Sister Monica, who was the principal. It hurt, but not enough to make me cry. I was more embarrassed than anything else.

After my paddling, I was sent back to the classroom after promising no further bad behavior and delivering an apology to Judith. I did that, but as I handed her back her book, I said something like, "Thanks for being a rat." And so ended my first childhood crush. I smoothly moved from that first one to many more failed crushes. Maybe Mrs. Hanken *was* on to something when she reported that I did not dance well with the girls in the classroom. Hmm . . .

The sisters could be stern, but they could be kind, too, especially Sister Alberta. She was my third-grade teacher. Of all the sisters, I recall her with the greatest fondness. She actually smiled. It's amazing the effect a simple smile can have on a third-grader, like me. And oddly enough, her smiling, and the compliments she gave out, never resulted in chaos and classroom disorder. Maybe there were alternatives to Sister Maurice's classroom management style? Let me tell you, a strategically placed compliment can be as powerful in motivating a student as a well-placed thwack of the "Board of Education" on the backside. I know, because I remember one compliment to this day.

At that time, St. Kilian's had a world-renowned boys' choir. It was a celebrated part of the New York City classical music scene. The choir had originally been formed by Father Raphael for the purpose of singing at Sunday and feast-day formal high masses. Then Father Raphael took it a step further and hired a respected choirmaster from Hungary, Árpád Darázs, to train the boys' choir professionally. Within a few years in the early 1960s, the choir became a professional-level group, performing with people like Leonard Bernstein, Seiji Ozawa, and Andre Kostelanetz, at venues like Tanglewood, Carnegie Hall, and Lincoln Center, and singing works by Britten, Mahler, Mozart, and Beethoven. The St. Kilian's Boys Choir became as good, and was talked about in the same terms, as the world-famous Vienna Boys Choir.

Almost every second- and third-grade boy dreamed of being in the choir. I certainly did. Making it into the choir was considered a major accomplishment. Choirboys were treated like gods at St. Kilian's. I, of course, knew about the choir by the time I was in second grade. I was friends with some of the older boys who were members. I was also hooked on the Disney movie *Almost Angels*, which was about the lives and training of the boys in the world-famous Vienna Boys Choir. All I wanted to do was to sing in the choir. I dreamed about it all the time.

The choir seated about thirty-eight to forty boys. The boys were divided into four approximately equal sections: Soprano I—the highest voices; Soprano II's; Alto I's; and Alto II's—the deepest voices. Each year, during the second grade, any boy who wanted to be in the choir auditioned. It was a long and rigorous audition process, and, in the end, only a few new boys were invited to join the choir, usually replacing six to eight older boys who were "voicing out"—in other words, puberty had arrived and they were sopranos no longer. If you passed the initial audition, you were asked back for subsequent ones. The more you got called back, the better your chances of being asked to join, and the more excited you got. I was asked back several times during my second-grade year. The final selections were made in June, but were not announced until the following fall when you started third grade.

That's how it came to be I was in Sister Alberta Marie's third-grade class when the new boys were announced. The PA system crackled to life as it always did every morning with announcements from our principal. Sister Monica Jeanne's voice slowly read the names of the six new boys who were being inducted into the boys' choir. And I heard my name as if in a fog. It was true! I was in, and I don't remember much else that morning aside from looking at Sister Alberta smiling at me. She motioned for me to stand up and said to the class, "Congratulations, Kevin. Class, let's show Kevin how proud we are of him for making the choir." No one had ever clapped for me before, and I wanted to kiss her for that kindness and compliment. That's all I can say about that, though I wish I were a better writer and had the words to explain just how much that meant to me. I am simply not that kind of wordsmith.

It would take a whole other book to share all that happened to me in that choir over the following three years. We traveled a lot to perform. We trained with our new choirmaster, Hermann Furthmoser, the very same choirmaster who'd appeared in the Disney movie *Almost Angels* with the Vienna Boys Choir. Those years, without becoming overly serious, were among the most memorable of my life. But they ended when we made our move from Farmingdale to Smithtown to our bigger home. And though I did join the school chorus at my new public school, and I received the honor of being designated as a tenor in the All-State chorus, things were just not the same. After my experience at St. Kilian's, singing in a public-school chorus was *unfullfilling*. (how's that for a lame snobby description?). After that I simply drifted away from all those sisters and the world of music I loved so much. But life has funny ways of repeating the past, and there was one more group of sisters that would bring my music past back into the present one last time.

I played football in college for SUNY Stony Brook. My football teammates and I would frequent a night club called the Mad Hatter, usually on a Thursday night. The Mad Hatter was one of those Long Island clubs popular back in the 1970s where local rock bands played. We were regulars on Thursday night because drinks were half-priced before 10 p.m., and when you're in college, twice as much for the dollar is an easy decision. A band called Twisted Sister played at the Mad Hatter pretty regularly. We knew the band, and the band had a big following who liked their brand of glam rock. They usually drew a big crowd, and this night was no different.

We were up near the stage when they started playing one of their standard covers—Lou Reed's "Sweet Jane." Maybe we had consumed too many half-priced drinks by then, I don't recall exactly, but we started mocking Twisted Sister's rendition of "Sweet Jane." Maybe we felt their rendition wasn't as good as Lou Reed's, or maybe it was just something to do. Whatever it was, we started heckling the band. At some point, Dee Snider, the front man for the band, had had enough. He waved to the band and stopped the music. Here's a guy dressed like it's a KISS Halloween party with makeup and platform shoes, chastising us like Sister Maurice did, and loud enough on the mike so the entire crowd could hear, "Okay, how about you bozos come up here and show us how it's done!" We didn't move. "What's the matter? Just all talk? C'mon. How about you four," pointing at me and three of the other guys, "Come up here and show us. We'll have a contest and let the audience judge who's better. What do you say?"

We joined the band on the stage. The crowd was loving it. Dee announced the rules of the contest: "Each one of these guys will get the chance to sing the 'Sweet Jane' chorus line with us. You guys have to cast your vote after each one. Cheer for your favorite. Good. Is everyone ready?" One by one, each of us had to solo the chorus line. I was the last guy up. It was almost like the old days. I'd been one of the two soloists in the St. Kilian's Boys Choir during my final year. I was accustomed to being onstage. I liked being onstage. Heck, I loved that part of my life as you know . . . I loved singing in that choir. That night, I won the inaugural of what became Twisted Sister's "Sweet Jane" contest. So there you have it . . . I was a rock-and-roll star for a night. Better than never being one, I suppose.

And afterward, my teammates asked, "What the hell, Kehoe? Where did you learn to sing like that?"

"It's nothing," I said, "I used to sing a little when I was a kid. I guess it just came back to me."

For the rest of the year, wherever Twisted Sister played, they did the "Sweet Jane" contest. It became popular across Long Island and was advertised on the radio all the time. The band became a bigger draw because of the contest. "Sweet Jane" contest nights drew all kinds of people, many of whom were trained singers. It was like *American Idol*, before there was *American Idol*. During the first months of the mania, I'd follow the band around occasionally, and whenever I did, Dee would invite me up to the stage for the chorus line. It felt like Sister Alberta Marie all over again.

Most of us have memories of "perfect times" in our lives. We remember how good they were, and how unlikely they are to ever come back. But it's important to keep those memories alive and give the past some power in the present to create a future that is more perfect. If nothing else, it can make us smile when we tell the story, and provide us with hope that perfection resides within us and is possible still, even with the passage of time making us very different people. We can, and should, live many lives in our one life. It's true that "our memory is a more perfect world than the universe: it gives back life to those who no longer exist." I don't know who, or where, I'd be without all those sisters in my life. Here's to their memory.

CHAPTER 32

Drinking the Kool-Aid

The phrase "drinking the Kool-Aid"
was coined after Jim Jones led his cult
to mass suicide by drinking grape Kool-Aid
laced with cyanide.

My cousin got married in 1982 with two thousand other couples in a ceremony by the Reverend Moon at Madison Square Garden. The reverend's followers were known as Moonies—a moniker they disliked as it suggested they were members of a cult. I'm not rendering any judgment about the reverend and his flock, but that ceremony was not your traditional family wedding. And it does suggest that those involved were something more than just followers. For the unenlightened, like myself, it did look like a cult. I am not a joiner—in general. And I am not a loner; I just hate being labeled as, well, anything. I like to go my own way. But I do join organizations and such. However, when I do, I like to maintain a healthy distance from organization politics and the most overly zealous members. I don't like drinking anyone's Kool-Aid.

I worked as a consultant for a CPA firm in West LA in the late 1980s. I was responsible for bringing in new clients. I was very average at doing this. This frustrated the managing partner of the firm so much that he enrolled me in a sales training program. He wanted to sharpen my selling skills, since I, like most consultants, was more disposed to "doing" the work than "selling" the work. I guess we thought selling was beneath us, and something that only used-car salespeople did.

The program consisted of classroom sessions followed by, what felt like, very stressful role-play sessions conducted with the managing partner acting as the prospect. The trainer who was hired to facilitate the program was a young woman who'd been successful in sales and was a good communicator. She would set up the role-play situations, providing the background and the scenario. Then she'd observe and at the end debrief us on how we did. I guess I wasn't very good at these things, mainly because both she and my boss told me I wasn't.

They both felt I was "defensive" and argumentative during the role play sales call, especially when the prospect raised objections. Instead of listening to them and charming them, when challenged I would defend my point of view and show them how they were wrong. When the trainer told me this, of course I argued with her about it, proving her point. I challenged her about her conclusions. Then she showed me the videotapes of my role-play sessions. I don't know about you, but for me, it feels weird and a little disturbing, to watch yourself on tape. When I viewed the tapes, I realized that what I thought I was doing, and what I was actually doing, were very different things. I decided after watching the tapes that I wouldn't buy anything from me, either, so I had to agree that the trainer was right and that I could do better.

"Okay, what should I do? Do you have any suggestions?" I asked.

"I think you'd benefit from understanding why you approach sales the way you do," she responded.

"I don't know what you mean. What should I understand about why I do what I do?"

"Your approach to sales seems to come from a place of anger. That's why when the prospect asks you a question, you see it as a challenge, and you respond defensively." I'm paraphrasing here what she said, but it's a fair summary as I recall it.

"A place of anger? I am not following you. You've lost me. And what has that got to do with closing a sale, anyway?"

"It has everything to do with it. I think your anger is deep, and might be rooted in what you learned early in life."

I told her to stop right there. "Is this a sales training session, or a psychotherapy session?"

"This is what I'm talking about," the woman said. "You're arguing with me right now. Do you want my help or not?"

"Okay, what do you suggest, assuming you're right about this?"

"I belong to a self-improvement group that might be very good for you," the trainer suggested. Of course, just the word "group" and the inference that I would join one got my *spidey-senses* tingling (think Spiderman). "Great . . . I thought: a cult! That's all I need."

"It's not a cult." The trainer answered as if she was reading my mind. "Professionals from all walks of life have participated in the group."

"Why did you join? Are you an angry person, too?" I asked.

She smiled, "The one thing you have going for you is your humor . . . and, yes, we can all be a little angry." Then she handed me a brochure for something called "How to Make Love Work," by Barbara De Angelis, PhD.

I looked at the title and thought about how this would ever work in the business world and said, "What's love got to do with it?"

The trainer smiled. "See, you can be charming when you want to be, and if you did more of that on a sales call, you actually might be pretty good at it. Why don't you come to the meeting as my guest next week, and see if it's for something you might like. It can't hurt, and it may help, right?"

I went to the meeting with the trainer. She was deeply involved in the group. In fact, she was one of what was known then as Barbara's "angels." I'll explain what an angel is, but first a little background. This was the late 1980s, and the Westside of LA was *the* mecca for the self-improvement and spirituality movement. The region was teeming with self-improvement programs and new-age prophets and gurus. Barbara was one of those gurus. There were others such as Werner Erhard and his est program, and Barbara's ex-husband, John Gray, who wrote *Men Are from Mars, Women Are from Venus*. But Barbara was very popular. She had her own radio show and book deals, among other things. But her big claim to fame was a weekend workshop she facilitated called "How to Make Love Work." Assisting Barbara in managing this workshop was the focus of the group my sales trainer had gotten me involved with— Barbara's angels. That's how I came to enroll in the workshop for the first time, and ultimately become one of Barbara's angels, too.

Here's how the workshop worked. You arrived and took a seat at 5 p.m. on Friday evening. You were in a big room, along with two hundred other people. The workshop was organized into "modules," each of which began with a lecture by Barbara. This was followed by small group "breakout" discussions, each of which was led by one of Barbara's angels. The breakouts were then followed by a large group debriefing led by Barbara. These debriefing sessions were like testimonials. Individual participants would walk up to the stage where Barbara sat and share some "breakthrough" they'd experienced during the breakout discussions. This sequence continued until about 1 a.m., at which time you left for the evening—usually to a hotel close by. It's a long first night, but it was only a start. The angels assisted Barbara throughout the weekend, working with the participants as I've described, facilitating Barbara's breakout sessions.

You arrive on Saturday at 8 a.m. to start day two. The flow of the day was much like the night before: lecture, breakout, debrief, testimonials. You got quick breaks for lunch and dinner, and you'd be dismissed, again, at about 1a.m. Sunday was a repeat of Saturday. Sunday started at 8 a.m., but wound up a little earlier, around 10 p.m. It was a long and intense weekend for anyone. The sessions, led by the angels, were designed to break you down, and then build you back up, new and hopefully more self-aware. Everyone was spent by the end of it on Sunday night. And if you're wondering—yes, I've seen grown men cry throughout the weekend . . . a lot.

I was raised Roman Catholic. That was my religion. It was a good way to be brought up. But this thing Barbara was doing was something new to me. It wasn't a religion exactly, but it had some of the same trappings. There was the revered leader figure, there were tenets and beliefs, there were deacons and acolytes, rites and ceremonies, and of course the donation and collection of money. I didn't see any conflict between these two "religions," so I enrolled in a second workshop two months later. I ultimately attended a dozen of them—the last ten of which I worked on as one of Barbara's angels. I joined the angel group after one of the weekends. I don't recall how it came about—whether I was asked, or I asked them—but I was recruited into the group. I was now on the "inside," and I suppose I could be categorized as a follower of Barbara.

As I've stated, I'm not a joiner or a follower. But I'm a good team player. There's a thin, but clear line, delineating these two things, at least in my mind. Followers don't often question things. Good teammates always do. For example, were my team to go off in a bad direction, I'd say something. I simply wouldn't keep quiet and not rock the boat in the interest of "team unity." The way I look at it, a pile of dead lemmings at the bottom of a cliff, who've all died following the leader, are not much of a functioning team. Some lemming should have said something, in my opinion. Anyway, I'm pretty certain suicide is not a requirement for being a good team player. But I've been labeled "negative," and not a team player for thinking this way. Teammates should be able to disagree without becoming outcast.

I started this story with my lack of selling skills, remember? Now, I was working as an angel in a new-age group on the Westside of LA, and I liked it. I learned a lot from the time I invested in the group. In fact, I had become a better salesman because of it, almost to the point where I preferred *selling* the work to *doing* the work. I absorbed what I needed from the group, but I kept my distance from the politics and the overly zealous members. Then one day everything changed. At the start of a weekend workshop, the angel team was gathered for the prebriefing meeting. A few months earlier, Barbara had married a guy whom she'd spoken about frequently. She referred to him as her soul mate and "the love of her life." Their marriage was a big deal inside the angel group.

Barbara stood up and told us she'd strayed from her new husband . . . and that she'd done this with one of the other angels. In other words, she was telling us she'd cheated on her brand-new husband, her soul mate, and the love of her life. I listened, and thought . . . some soul mate! Then it got weirder. The chief concern seemed to be that her husband might come to the facility during the weekend and make a scene. Heck, I'd hardly have blamed him if he had. I'd have been upset, too. Barbara seemed to be downplaying the cheating. I cannot recall exactly what was said, but she suggested that she hadn't really betrayed him, but instead had found, unfortunately late in the game, the *real* love of her life . . . and that we all should have the same courage to pursue true love, even if it meant—well in this case, I guess—cheating.

Let me be clear. I admired Barbara. She was great at what she did. I benefited from her program. She's a wonderful salesman, and has more chutzpah than a platoon of sergeants. But, that day, I wasn't buying what she was selling. Where I grew up, cheating was cheating, and she just should have said that and owned up to it, and said it was wrong. I thought it was wrong. *I* thought her speech was wrong. And throughout the weekend, I said so to many of the other angels. A few felt as I did. But most insisted that *I* was wrong.

"You just don't understand, Kevin."

"That's not the way it is."

"You're not being a team player."

I was pretty certain that I *did* understand and that things were *exactly* as they were . . . in this case, wrong. The Tuesday that followed every weekend workshop was a time for the angel group to meet with Barbara and debrief the weekend. Word about my concerns regarding the weekend's drama had by that time become broadly known within the group. I was asked why I was not on the same page as everyone else with Barbara on the situation. I told them why. I suppose my feelings on the matter did not go over terribly well, and, without too much drama or argument, my career as an angel came to an end shortly thereafter.

I've tried to imagine what it was like in Jonestown when they handed out the Kool-Aid. What were those people thinking? Would they all mindlessly follow Jim Jones, their prophet? Or did some of them sense that something was wrong? There were survivors at Jonestown, you know. There were those who did not drink the Kool-Aid, some of them by sheer luck of time and place, and just a few by choice. Those few escaped becoming lemmings in a pile at the bottom of the cliff.

I am not suggesting Barbara's group was a cult at all. It wasn't. She was too nice to be that kind of prophet. But, in that one instance, the group did exhibit the trappings of a cult— *group think* being the primary one. Group think is dangerous. It can be used to justify almost anything in the name of team unity. I've witnessed the damage group think can do. And I've witnessed the aftermath of the disaster and the absence of good answers to the question, "Why didn't anyone speak up and say something?" I don't like conflict, but I really hate preventable disasters. Silence for the sake of team unity is, for lack of a better word, complicity. There are times in life when common sense, and principles of right and wrong, demand that you *rock the boat*—not only because saying, "I'm sorry," afterward doesn't cut it but because calling 'bullshit" is an act of bravery that reminds us that one person can make a big difference. There are situations in life that are not "gray"—they are black-and-white. God help you if you can't figure out the difference.

Final Note: As for my Moonie cousin and her marriage to her handpicked groom, the union survives very nicely to this day, thank you. And for all you Kool-Aid drinkers of the world in the 1960s, here's the list of the original Kool-Aid flavors from those days; Choo-Choo Cherry, Goofy Grape, Lefty Lemon, Rootin' Tootin' Raspberry, Freckle-Face Strawberry, Jolly-Ollie Orange, and Loud-Mouth Lime. I remember them well.

CHAPTER 33

Marriage Advice

"Wise men don't need advice. Fools won't take it."
—Benjamin Franklin

There's a long-standing tradition that the best man makes the toast before the wedding party starts in earnest. It's a real honor to be a best man. At least that's how I've always felt. I've been one a few times. The best man's toast is important to the bride and groom, so there's a lot of pressure to do it well. Over all, I did pretty okay with my toasts. I had some moments of brilliance and some moments not so brilliant, like my first one. I was new to the toast game then, and really did not understand what was required. Specifically, I had a few too many tequilas before I made my appearance on stage and I rambled on too long. So it goes. As a result I learned from that and over the years developed a few rules for delivering a good toast. These rules are outlined at the end of this chapter under the heading "Suggestions for a Wedding Toast."

I've been the best man at a few interesting celebrations. One was on a boat in the Whitsunday Islands in Australia, another in my parents backyard in the rain, a third was for my brother, Michael, another for my friend John who drove off with his bride in her wedding gown on a Harley, and one was in the middle of the desert at Joshua Tree National Park. That particular wedding featured a shaman who performed the ceremony among the desert scrub, boulders, and Joshua trees. But no matter how crazy the proceedings, a good toast is critical, and it must fit the couple and be appropriate to the audience.

The ceremony at Joshua Tree is a good example of this simple rule. There were only seven people there: the couple, the maid of honor, my ex-wife, the couple's four-year-old son, the shaman-minister, and me. The couple chose the location because—and this is my opinion of the lovely couple—they have a streak of hippie counterculture in them, and they try to avoid doing anything that might smack of traditional or mainstream. The toast had to fit them, the location, and the small audience, including the shaman. I needed to avoid any of my traditional and mainstream dry humor, as that would have been out of place for this celebration. The toast had to be simple, and reflect where we were. I thought the best way to do that was not to make a speech but to involve the bride and groom in the toast itself.

Here's what we did: When the shaman completed the exchange of vows, I stood in front of the couple and said, "If you will allow me, I want to include you in my toast." I handed each of them a stick about three feet long. I asked them to face each other and not to use the stick on the other person—at least not for the present. The two were standing about four feet apart. Knowing me, they seemed to be wondering how weird the toast might get, so I allayed their concerns: "Don't worry. You know me. Nothing weird is going to happen here."

I then directed them to use their stick to etch a circle in the dirt around their feet.

"That circle you drew is how we are before we are married. We live in our own separate worlds. Before marriage we are alone, and our circles are smaller before love works its magic and makes us bigger.

"Now I want you to draw another, larger, circle outside the first one you drew." At this point, the circles were touching each other.

"Now draw one more, even larger than the first two. Now, you can see that your circles are overlapping and beginning to merge. At some point, as you continue to draw larger circles, they will merge into one circle. Two will become one." I stopped for a moment before I continued.

"And this is my wish for you—that you grow together into one happy couple. I don't know a lot about marriage, but I think that's the purpose of a union. Here's to you two—now bride and groom." That was the toast, and they are still married. So, all's well that ends well, right?

My friend Scott, whom you've already met in the "Best Day Ever" round of golf in Scotland, and whom you will meet again in the last chapter, had one son, Caleb. When Caleb married, I was unable to attend his wedding because I was going through cancer treatments, and I was not up to the cross-country trip from California to Maryland. My wife and Caleb's mother, Sandie, asked me if, in my absence, I might write something as a kind of "toast" for the couple. They wanted to include it in a book they were gifting the couple on their wedding day. I said I'd be honored, but what did they want me to say?

"Whatever you want. We trust you to get it right."

No pressure there, right? I've known Caleb since he was an infant. As he grew up, we'd played golf together with his dad, we'd raced ATVs, and rafted rivers. I didn't know the bride, but I knew Caleb understood my sense of humor, as well as he knew my love for him and his father. If this girl was marrying into that group, I concluded that she, too, might appreciate what I had to say. I offered the couple the following marriage advice as a toast of sorts:

"To the newly married couple, I have to be careful giving advice because as it's been said, wise men don't need it, and fools won't heed it. Yet if you will allow me to offer some, here's some of what I've learned through almost twenty-five years of two marriages:

- You are allowed to tell little lies, but not big ones. Omissions count as little lies.

- "I forgot" works.

- Remember: "Happy wife, happy life."

- Learn how to say, "Yes, dear." This is for both of you, but mainly for the groom.

- There can only be one boss, and here's a hint: it's not you, the groom.

- Learn how to argue. A marriage without the occasional battle is not really a marriage. It's more like a polite date.

- A man marries a woman thinking she won't change, but she does.

- A woman marries a man thinking he *will* change, but he doesn't.

- Take this reality into consideration when you look at your partner and wonder why they did what they did.

- A hug in the morning and a kiss at night is a good idea. I should do more of that myself.

- You will disagree about things. That's normal. It's not a crisis.

- When things look bad—which they will at times – try to remember why you married in the first place. If you can't do that, then you have a crisis.

- Kids will drive you crazy and test everything you think you know, but never allow them to divide you. Get on the same page and stay on it.

- "No" is a perfectly good answer to a spouse's request.

- Allocate the chores fairly. Write them down if you have to. This establishes good boundaries and a sense of teamwork. After all, that is what you are—a team.

- Don't throw things!

- Develop activities that you enjoy doing *together*: hobbies, sports, something.

- Lose with grace, and don't hold grudges.

- Decide who handles the money. Do that on day one. No, do it right now.

- Take some time to dream about what you might become, no matter how crazy it may be. Life is a progression of self-fulfilling prophecies.

- Make the bed together in the morning. It's a good way to start a new day.

- Write each other little notes. It's nice. Everyone likes a love letter.

- Groom, remember to tell her how pretty she is—like I tell my "my pretty wife."

- Occasionally, dear bride, think like a man. Groom, likewise: try to think like a woman. Yes, groom, her mind is a scary and foreign place. You will likely never truly understand her. As Jack Nicholson's author character said in the movie *As Good as It Gets*, when asked how he as a male author wrote about the women in his novels so well, said, "I think of a man, and I take away reason and accountability." It's a joke, okay?

- Remember that a marriage is a long journey. It's a marathon. Take your time and enjoy the ride.

- Perfection is the enemy of the good. Strive to be good, but not perfect.

- It follows to then be accepting.

- If you marry someone who does not share your values, well, God help you.

- Be on the same page politically. Maybe left versus right can work in love, but why mess with those probabilities?

- Say you're sorry and mean it.

- Say you love her/him, and say it often.

- The toilet paper rolls over, not under.

- Spoons go in the spoon slots, knives in knife slots . . . you follow me on this?

- Finally, in any argument, the woman will have the last word. That means, dear groom, that anything you say after that is merely the start of a new argument. Just know this."

A wedding toast is an act of love and generosity. Could you imagine how different life might be if we toasted the people with whom we work, live, and love at the start of every day? Wow! We might all just be bigger and happier. Would that be so bad?

Final Note: Suggestions for a Wedding Toast

To deliver a memorable toast, you must prepare and do some research. Understand who the couple are, and keep in mind that parents and old folks may be in the room. Be careful with humor as it doesn't always work. It can, but not all the time. Here are some suggestions in no particular order.

- Write it down.

- Practice it out loud.

- Keep it short at three minutes—maybe four maximum.

- Avoid sarcasm and really dry humor—again it can work sometimes, but go easy.

- Tell the audience your name and relation to the couple—they may have never met you.

- Don't bring up *anything* you did with the groom "in the old days."

- Say something about the bride . . . relate an incident or memory—maybe something she said.

- Do the same for the groom after you make the bride look better.

- Don't get all weepy and say stuff like "*I love you, man.*"

- Keep the drivel about soul mates to a minimum.

- Use a funny or classic quote about marriage or love.

- Make the closing line a wish on behalf of all the guests, as in "We, all of us, join to. . . ."

- Finally . . . don't drink five shots of tequila or ten beers before giving the toast.

Of course, if you are an actual stand-up comedian, you can forget some or all of this advice.

CHAPTER 34

No Such Thing as a Free Lunch

"There's no such thing as a free lunch."
—Phrase popularized by Economist Milton Friedman

Professor emeritus Friedman is often associated with the quote above, but according to my editor, the phrase has its origins in the 1930s Depression era, and the actual source is unknown. If nothing else, I have to concur with the quote, regardless of its origin. And I will tell you why. I like to do work around our home. I don't hire contractors to do everything. I like to build and fix things. Although I have limited talent for things like auto, electrical, and plumbing repair and maintenance, I'm good at woodwork, tile work, painting, and landscaping. I learned these trades by helping out around the house with my father. That's what he did. I remember working on cars, dryers, washing machines, plumbing leaks, and tile floors. And whether he did the job himself because we didn't have the money to pay a contractor, or because he wanted to teach his boys these skills, or because he actually liked doing it, doesn't matter. We all grew up fixing and building things around our home, only calling a contractor when absolutely necessary. I have retained my father's mentality in that regard.

Yet when I have to hire a contractor, I will. I've learned that they are much better at performing certain types of work than me. I've also learned—the hard way— that you get what you pay for, too. A low price is almost always the promise of low quality. Low price is like a shortcut on a road trip—it's too good to be true and you pay for it in lost time, worn tires, and spousal anger. Here's what I mean: You might recall that I traveled almost every week for many years. And even though I enjoy working around our home, the challenge I faced was that there simply wasn't enough time on the weekends to surf, motorcycle, hike, spend time with my family, and pay attention to the mowing, weeding, trimming, and watering of the landscaping. My wife, knowing this, suggested I contact one of the many landscaping companies that prowled our neighborhood, and have *them* do the work. "You don't have to do everything, you know!" she told me.

After mulling it over, much as I didn't want to, I relented and called three local landscape companies, requesting a quote for their services. Contractors have proved to be an interesting breed, for me. "Interesting," as in these guys can be more trouble than they are worth. Of course, there *are* excellent contractors, yet it seems a large percentage of them have, let me say, significant business management "issues". And this makes me hesitant to hire them, at all. The first issue seems to be that they don't show up when they say they will. And the second seems to be that they lack the concept of "lead time" when it comes to ordering parts and materials for a job, so often miss deadlines they promise, by weeks. The third is that they can be, well, slobs. They leave crap everywhere and seem to create more work in cleanup than is actually required to do the real work.

All three of the landscapers I contacted scheduled appointments with me to review my property and provide a quote for their weekly services – services like mowing, weeding, trimming and watering. One of the three simply never showed up and never called again, ever. I met with the other two, and each quoted me a monthly price. The prices were very different. I asked each of them separately, "Why should I use *your* services?" The first guy said something like, "I'm not the cheapest in the neighborhood, but I'm the best." His price was 50 percent higher than the other guy's. When I asked the other guy the same question, he didn't actually say he was the cheapest, but he did say that my job wasn't "rocket science,' and therefore he could do it easily at a much lower price. Now I had to make a decision. That low priced guy seemed okay, but I had the sense that the more expensive guy would actually do a better job. He seemed more caring and competent, and his truck was shinier and newer.

I said that I'd get back to each of them in a day or so. I then told my wife about the two meetings with the landscapers. "Well, you talked to them—what do think?" my wife wanted to know. I told her they both seemed okay, but also that there was a clear difference in price.

"The first guy was really expensive, but I think he'll do a better quality job. The second guy was less expensive, and I was worried about how the landscape would look because I thought his work would be not as good. It's the classic choice," I continued. "Do I pay more to get more, or do I pay less and hope he exceeds my expectations?"

"I know what I'd do," my wife commented.

"What would you do?" I asked.

"I'd hire the more expensive one and not have to worry." My wife is very excellent at spending my money.

And that's what I did. I called them both back with my decision and asked my new landscape guy when he could start. He said that he could start the next week and wondered if Tuesday would be a good day for the regular weekly work visit. I said that schedule would be "fine." And so, we started. I no longer had to work weekends on my landscape. He was now in charge of that.

The man did very nice work and he was reliable. But soon I noticed that my monthly bills were more than he had quoted. I asked him about this. Here's what he said: "Yeah, I inspect your property every time I'm on site, and when I find something that needs to be repaired, I fix it for you. That's what those extra charges are about." Not wanting a confrontation or to dim his passion and initiative, I politely said, "I really appreciate your attention to detail and taking the time to address these issues. And if it's okay with you, it would be good for me that before you fix things, you simply contact me and give me an idea of the cost in advance. I have a monthly budget in mind, and that would give me the opportunity to consider whether I want to do the work that month. That way there will be no billing surprises."

The man seemed a little miffed, like I didn't appreciate his service model or something, but I reassured him that wasn't the case, and he also agreed that I had a point about the extra charges. For the next few months, he was good about sticking to our agreement. Then he reverted to his old practice, and again my monthly invoice was more than I expected. I paid it, and I also reminded him of our conversation a few months earlier. Again, I related how much I liked and appreciated the quality of his work, but that I didn't want to deal with any more surprise bills. For the next two months, there were no surprise bills. Then three months after our second "talk,"

I got an invoice with extra charges on it for things he had fixed on my property for me. And since I didn't want to engage in yet another discussion, I paid him, and I let him go. I was sorry to lose him, but it seemed unlikely that we'd ever get on the same page.

I did not call or hire a new landscaper, immediately. I let the property "go" for a few weeks. The grass grew and the plants went untrimmed. I did this intentionally, knowing that the local landscapers driving by would see this, and deposit their business cards in the mailbox, or on my front doorstep. And that is what happened. I called three of the guys, one of whom was the same low-price guy I didn't hire the first time around. I scheduled appointments with all three. This time, the only landscaper who showed up for the appointment as scheduled was . . . the original Mr. Low Price and Unknown Quality Guy who I hadn't hired the first time. As a result, the man won the work by default. I recalled thinking at the time, "Really, how bad could low price be, anyway?" So, I mentally lowered my expectations a bit, and we agreed to start the work.

The new guy showed up the first few weeks on schedule as promised. The work was acceptable though it was nothing like, or as good as, the work the other guy had delivered. On about the fifth week, he did not show up as scheduled. I didn't call him. I was waiting for him to call *me* with an explanation. I was willing to listen, as perhaps something had happened to him. But the call never came. He did, however, show up the following two weeks, as if nothing had happened during the missing week of service. What developed from then on can only be described as random work scheduling. It seemed like he'd show up whenever he wanted. Neither my wife nor I ever saw him, as we both worked during the day, so we could never nail him down and discuss his lack of reliability.

Four months after hiring him, I arrived home, hoping to catch him, but I just missed him. I parked in the driveway, and noticed that he had only edged the lawn *halfway up the driveway*. I studied it, and wondered to myself, "What happened here? Did he just run out of gas in his edger, or did he run out of interest?"

I told my wife about this.

"Call him," she said.

"I would, I said, "but there's a little problem."

"What's the problem?"

I explained that Mr. Low Price and Quality had never sent me a bill. For the entire time he'd been our landscaper, I hadn't paid him a dime. I was getting the work done for free. "I don't know why we haven't been billed," I told my wife. "But I can only guess that somehow we fell through the cracks of his billing system. It seems he's about as good at business management as he is at landscaping."

"So, what's the problem with calling him?" she asked again.

"You don't see my dilemma?" I asked.

"Not really."

"Okay. The guy is lousy, but we're getting *free* landscape services. And if I call him and complain, he might discover his billing oversight . . . and then I'll have to have argue with him about payment."

In the end, I decided not to call him. I guess I hoped that he'd just simply stop showing up. And just a few weeks later, he did stop coming. He never billed me, and although I was getting the service for free, all I was really getting was a headache. By now, almost a year had passed since we'd decided to hire a contractor. First, I'd paid top dollar and had problems. And then I paid nothing and had even bigger problems. In the end, guess who ended up doing the weekly landscape work again? Right . . . me. We'd come full circle. And that's how it remained for the next fifteen years. From time to time, a landscape guy would drop off his business card and tell me, "You're a busy man. I can do it for you, and for a good price!"

I thanked them all for stopping by, and would say, "I'll think about it." But every Saturday morning, I'd get up early and I'd be in the yard, mowing, weeding, trimming, and watering the landscaping. I could state the obvious—that you get what you pay for, but there's a little more to it than that. The real truth is, that there's no such thing as a free lunch. Someone always pays. In this case it was me. And sometimes, it's as simple as . . . if you want something done right, you might have to do it yourself.

Final Note: My sister-in-law grew up in Soviet-controlled Hungary. She and her family escaped to the United States. She has shared stories about what it was like to live in that USSR-dominated economy. She'll tell you, "Sure, health care was free. The problem was, you could never get to see a doctor. You'd wait for months, and if you finally did see one, the quality wasn't very good.

"It was that way with everything. We ran a restaurant, and the supply of food was not reliable from the state stores. Instead of going to the state stores, we instead bribed the state officials—those in charge of the supplies, as these people operated in the 'black market.' We paid really high prices, but we got what we needed. That was the way things were done. You have no idea how good you Americans have it."

CHAPTER 35

Look Up, Not Down

"Look up, not down, Look forward, not back. . . .
—Joel Samuel (some guy whose quote I found on the web)

People are funny about money, especially when they don't have any. It's true—when you don't have it, it's all you think about. But those who do have it never seem to obsess about it—as it just always seems to be there. I know. I grew up without money. All I ever thought about for years was how to get it. I'm going to give you my two cents about money, as it is central to the human condition. There is nothing crass about money. Money— at least in the business world—represents the value you provide to someone else. The more value you provide, the more money you earn, unless of course you're a crook and a con artist. For better or for worse, we're not just human beings—we are economic ones. In fact, outside of love, sex, and power, money drives all human relations.

When it comes to money, we tend to think in extremes, dividing the world into two types of people: the *haves* and the *have-nots*. Of course, that analysis is far too shallow, and in fact misses the essential point about money, and that is that most people do not exist at either end of that spectrum—they can be found somewhere in the middle of it, constantly *moving* closer to one end or the other. In other words, the poor do become wealthier, and the wealthy do become poorer, not by taking money from one another, but by providing or failing to provide value. That means the distribution of money is not a zero-sum game. Both you and I can make more money at the same time working together.

Having or *not having* are two sides of the same coin, and these conditions are not static. They are always changing. When it comes to having it or not having it, there is *the now condition*, and then there's *the future condition*. I can have *nothing* today (and I did that for a long time), but I might have *more* tomorrow. That all depends on the value I provide to others. Also, there is a strong likelihood that the money I have in the future will depend on my *expectations about the future*. What I mean is, if I think of myself as poor, and expect that not to change in the future, I will likely have that future. And if I think of myself as wealthy, and expect that to continue, I will likely achieve that future, too. There's no guarantee about this—just a very high statistical probability. I've noticed that those who have money think they will always have it. And those who don't have a hard imagining that they will have ever it. *That* is a big difference between the so-called *haves* and *have-nots*. They think differently about money. I know, as I have lived in both worlds.

Enough economics. Let me provide a concrete example. When I was a consultant, one of my areas of expertise was sales training. One of my clients was a landscape contracting company that sold big-ticket landscape renovation work. The projects they sold to their clients could range in cost to the client from $50,000 to over $1,000,000. The owner hired me to help his sales team improve the way they sold and closed these projects. I set up a training schedule and we began the program. I have some basic principles I teach in my training programs. One of them is that it's a lot easier to sell the big expensive jobs than the smaller, less expensive, ones. As soon as I said this, I got "pushback" from all the sales reps.

"You don't understand how hard it is to sell those big jobs to those people," I was told.

"Unless we lower our prices, no one is ever going to spend that kind of money. It's not fair." They also told me I was full of crap. So, when I countered, telling them that they were wrong, and it was a lot easier to sell a million-dollar job than a $10,000 job, they said, "Prove it!"

"I thought you'd never ask." I countered. "Let's talk with some-one who *has* purchased a $1,000,000 project and hear what they have to say. How about that. I'll arrange it."

"You're on," they said. And that's what I did. I called one of the company's recent $1,000,000 clients, John, and made the arrange-ments.

I told John, "I'd like to bring a few sales reps to your place for a tour of your new backyard. I'm trying to teach them about sell-ing and thought you might provide them some insights about *your* decision-making process. I think we'll need an hour of your time." The client agreed to do the tour and talk with my young sales reps.

We arrived at John's home in the early evening. He lived in a ten-thousand-square-foot home on a hill. He invited us in, and we walked to the backyard to see the project. The company, for which these reps worked, had designed and installed a pool, a waterfall, a hot tub, a cabana, an outdoor kitchen, and TV room, as well as all the decking and gardens. The place was spectacular. He then took us inside his home, showing us around before he finished the tour in his "man cave." He poured beer from the taps on his bar and said, "Fire away with your questions. What can I tell you?"

For the next few minutes, the reps asked questions. Then I said, "Tell us about yourself." John told us that he wasn't born into wealth. In fact, his early life was quite the opposite. He'd built up his small manufacturing company over a period of twenty-five years. The money he made in that business paid for everything we'd seen on the tour. He talked for five minutes or so, and the last thing he said was, "I'm just a normal guy, living a normal life like everyone else. And when it comes to buying anything, I know what I want, and I'm willing to pay the price for it."

I couldn't let that comment pass unanswered. I said, "John, for most of us here, there is nothing normal about any of this—your home, your backyard, any of it. It's beautiful, and much thanks for sharing your home today." And we left.

The next day, I asked the reps, "What did you learn about John, and selling to him?"

There were a few wisecracks about the man cave, but one guy asked, "Why don't you tell us what we *should* have learned. How *is* it easier to sell the million-dollar job than a $10,000 one?"

"I was hoping you might have seen that it *is* easier. Did you hear what he said about being a normal, regular guy?" I asked.

"He really believes that," I went on. "For you guys, none of that was remotely close to normal. But for him, it is. He just lives in a world with more zeros than you do. Your mistake is that you're trying to sell to him using your zeros frame of reference, which right now, today, can't afford to buy that kind of backyard. In other words, you're seeing his budget through your budget lens. He has more zeros than you do right now. You heard what he said. "When it comes to buying, I know what I want, and I'm willing to pay for it." For the guy buying a smaller project, he may have fewer zeros to spend, so he thinks hard about parting with his money. That makes it harder to sell the smaller job.

I continued on. "Here's my question: If you buy into my belief about this, what then would be the best way to sell to a guy like John?" We discussed approaches for a few minutes; then I said. "It's simple. You do not have to *sell* John at all. You simply need to ask him a question like, "John, what is it you really want?" And then listen to him. Forget about how much money it might cost and especially forget about how much money *you* have. Then tell him you can do it, if you can. Then give him the price. Let him make the decision about price, not you!" And as Sean Connery said in *The Untouchables*, "[A]nd therein endeth the lesson." I liked Sean Connery.

I wasn't born into wealth, far from it. So I was accustomed to thinking of money in terms of very few zeros. When I was in college, spending ten dollars was a big deal for me. Likewise, earning ten dollars was a big deal. I thought about money in terms of *single* zeros. That's what $10 is—a single zero. After graduation, I got a job and my zeros changed. I grew accustomed to thinking in terms of *two* zeros, instead of one zero, and naturally my thinking and my expectations about the future changed. I could write a check for $100 without too much stress, but not for much more. I went back to school and got an MBA, and then I took a chance and called Dr. Churchill (the professor who got me into the consulting business) who helped me get into my consulting career, and they paid me more for the value they expected and I provided. I could now experience money in terms of *three* zeros. I could buy things that cost $1,000 without getting too stressed out. I was working for people making four or five zeros and could envision that might be possible in my future.

Then I got lucky. I got divorced. You may recall that story in an earlier chapter. That divorce forced me into a decision. I decided to start my own consulting business, and I hung out my shingle. I began to make more money per day simply because I got to keep *all* the fees I billed, instead of paying a percentage of those to my boss. It was now *my* business, and I worked harder than ever at providing good value to my clients. Within a few years, after a tough start, I was now thinking about money in terms of *four* and *five* zeros. I wasn't stressed about getting enough money just to get by, something I'd done my entire life to that point, and which is an exhausting way to live.

Even though I had money by this time, I still worried about money. Why? Because I was accustomed to that mind-set from childhood. My brain said, it can all go away and you'll be struggling again. In fact, every year around the holidays, I'd go into a money panic. It made no sense, given my situation. But my wife, Lorraine, will attest to this because it was as regular as Christmas around our home. She would refer to those two weeks as my "days of doom." I'd freak out about the coming year, thinking about all the new clients I'd have to find. I'd veer wildly between "I'll be able to have another good year" and "I'll be drinking Ripple out of a brown paper bag on a corner somewhere." My wife would roll her eyes: "Honey, lighten up, you'll be fine. You always are."

"Easy for you to say," I'd mumble, "But what if we're not? What are we going to do? *Aarrggh!*"

And then, like clockwork, during the first weeks of January, my phone would begin to ring, and I'd start booking work again. This process repeated itself every year for the first fifteen years of our marriage. And every year, my wife would counsel me: "Don't you remember you went through this same thing last year, and the year before, and the year before that, and everything worked out just fine?"

My wife was right, but she missed the point. I was accustomed to *not having* money. I'll say it again: it's the way we think about money—specifically our expectations for it in the future that in large part account for *having* it and *not having* it. I was—from habit—looking back *down* to where I'd come from, not forward and *up* to where I could be.

There was a time when I did a lot of rock climbing. I'd scale sheer rock faces with a group of other climbers, using ropes and belays. Even when I was halfway up a small thirty-foot face, it felt like I was clinging to the side of the Empire State Building on the eightieth floor. The ground looked so far away. And in that moment when I looked back down, I'd freeze with fear. I'd become immobilized, almost hyperventilating. The first time this happened, the lead belayer on the ground yelled, "Don't look down—look up." I did, and it changed everything. My fear went away, and I started to focus on climbing up to the top. That's how it is with money and anything in life; look up, not down.

Certainly, having money is better than not having it. As I said earlier, we're not just human beings—we are economic ones. When my grandparents came to America in 1920, they didn't look back. They looked forward. They left Ireland and never went back. I think they'd be proud of how their children, grandchildren, and great-grandchildren have carried on in their footsteps. Upwardly mobile or downwardly mobile are self-fulfilling prophesies that are determined more by one's expectations, energy, and courage than by circumstances. You can ignore this reality, or embrace it.

Final Note: I thought about using another analogy in place of the rock climbing one, and since it is equally as relevant, I will share it here. I rode and raced motorcycles, as you know. There is a cardinal rule in riding and racing: *you go where you look*. If you look at the edge of the track in a turn and focus on that, you will likely go there and off the track. But if you look up and ahead and through to the end of the turn, you will go there and stay on the track. I know. It's simple in life, you go where you look.

CHAPTER 36

Showing Up

"Eighty percent of life is just showing up."
—Woody Allen, Comedian

I show up, almost every day. It's just my way. I only state this because I've learned that many people don't make the effort to show up. As a result, I decided, early on in my business career, that if I just did this simple thing, I'd be way ahead of most of the people most of the time. So, I show up when I'm sick, when I'm tired, and even when I don't feel like showing up. Maybe I'm dumb, or just stubborn, but I felt like I needed to "show up" just to have a chance of competing with the folks who had real talent and could run circles around me.

I even thought like this outside my business life. Like when I competed in 10Ks and other races. You may recall from an earlier chapter that first 10K I ran. That was the start of what might generously be called my road racing "career" in 1980. The end of that career came in 2017 at the Camp Pendleton Mud Run, the last race I ran or will ever run. Between 1980 and 2017, I ran in ten marathons, all them between the years 1981 and 1989. I want to talk about the 26.2-mile marathon because it is an experience like no other for a runner. Like life, the race requires that you show up at every stage along the way to the end. And, like life, it's a long grind, not a short sprint. For anyone who's run a marathon, you know the stages, starting with the excitement you feel at the beginning, through the suffering you endure in the middle, to the triumph, or relief, you experience at the end.

The stages of the race are analogous to the stages of our lives. In life, we experience childhood, the teen years, young adult, midlife, and the senior years. And even though it's been more than three decades since I ran my last marathon, the memories remain fresh. I especially remember my first marathon run. I was more excited than I was scared because I had no clue about what I was really getting into. But by my tenth marathon, I felt differently. I was excited, *but* I was also scared because I knew what lay ahead of me. When we're kids and teenagers, we are bulletproof, immortal, and worry about nothing. In middle age and senior years, we know better. We know we need to be prepared and in theory should be able to run the race better, not faster. If you have never had the pleasure of running the marathon, allow me to provide my version of the stages a runner experiences over the 26.2 miles.

Excitement: From the starting line up to mile 7, you feel great. Your excitement produces so much adrenaline that you feel light on your feet and think you can run forever. But you have to be careful not to "go out too fast." Because if you do, you'll pay for the wasted energy later on in the race. That's not a maybe—you *will* pay for it. But like childhood, the start of the race is exciting and you are full of energy and possibility.

Settling in: By mile 7, the thrill has definitely worn off and the real work begins. From mile 7 to mile 13, you know there's still a long way to go and you can feel some fatigue setting in. That can be a little depressing. The key at this stage is to conserve energy by getting into a mental and physical rhythm. You have to become like a metronome. I used to focus on putting one foot in front of the other, relaxing my breathing, and trying to think as little as possible about how I was feeling.

Grinding it out: From mile 13 to mile 21, it's natural to experience some mental and physical let-down. The reality is, no matter how well you've trained your body, you are wearing it out and fatigue is becoming very real, and you're still a long way from the finish line. It's like a midlife crisis. You've been at the job or, in this case, running for a long time, but retirement and the finish line, though closer, are still off in the distance. You want to stop and rest, but you can't if you want to finish the race. In fact, that's what happened to me in my last marathon. I had a real letdown at mile 17 and I said, "screw this." I had to stop and walk the better parts of miles 17 and 18, before I started running again, as the thought of quitting the race was even more depressing and painful than the hell I was experiencing while I was running it.

Hitting the wall: You hit the wall around mile 21 or 22. The wall is the marathon's version of life's "worst thing that can happen to you"—like a bad divorce or health diagnosis. Everyone hits the wall; some just hit it harder than others. It's your own personal hell. It's adversity. I've experienced the mild version of the wall, and the "death march" version of it. In my first marathon, I was so prepared and well trained that I barely noticed when I hit the wall. But in my final marathon, it felt like the wall hit me. It's called *the wall* for a reason. It almost feels like you hit a physical barrier—like a force field. Your legs stop moving. Your legs feel like hundred-pound weights being dragged through mud. Your brain is telling your muscles to move, but they don't. It's like the two have stopped talking to each other. The brain says, "C'mon, let's go," and your legs say, "Okay, brain, then you do it—we're tired." That's the wall. Your body is failing because it's used up every bit of energy and pasta you consumed the day before, and it's now stealing energy and calories from core organs like your brain. I've witnessed racers lose control of some of their voluntary bodily functions at this stage of the race. I won't describe the details, but you can guess! My last marathon became a survival test for me. I could not control or feel my legs and arms, and ran the last three miles like I was in a dark and narrow tunnel. My vision was so tunneled that I felt like I was looking through a telescope. And if you have ever tried to locate something in the night sky through a telescope, you know how narrow the focal point is. In short, I felt like the finish line was a hundred miles away – though I knew better.

Crossing the line: In that last marathon, when I finally saw the *one mile to go* banner through my telescopic lens eyes, I knew my suffering was going to be over soon. But it still took twelve more minutes to finish, a distance I usually covered in about six minutes. I felt more relief than a sense of triumph in that race, which was very unlike my first marathon. But that's life, too. Sometimes you're just happy to survive and move on to the next thing. That's why I knew that day that I'd never run another race. Later that night, after a few beers, I did feel a sense of triumph, but more like an old guy looking back who feels a quiet sense of completion versus exhilaration.

Okay, what has all of this got to do with "showing up"? That's a fair question. Even in my best marathon finish, I'd only placed in the top 5 percent of my age group. I was never close to winning and finishing first. In thirty years of running in more than three hundred races, I'd never experienced winning. Given that, I felt like I really wanted to finish first, just one time, before I ended my running days. But where could I do this? I was chatting with a friend when he told me about the Camp Pendleton Mud Run. He'd run the race before and was entering it again. I had never heard of the race. But when he described the 6.2-mile course set on the US Marine Corps base just south of San Clemente, California, I was interested.

The course winds through the chaparral of coastal Southern California on the grounds of the marine corps base. For the first mile or so, the runners splash through a sandy swamp, with streams and sand. Then, the course ascends into the hills. The climb is continuous—sometimes severely steep—for the next two miles. All through the first half of the course, the runners also negotiate obstacles like a 20-foot-high cargo net, 2-foot-deep mud pits, and a variety of other challenges. Once you reach the crest of the long uphill, the route turns sharply downhill before entering another narrow section of swamp and flattening out into a series of obstacles like a 50-yard mud pit with a 7-foot-high slippery wood wall to climb. Immediately after that, you have to cross a lake. Depending on the Southern California rainfall the previous winter, the quarter-mile crossing has to be waded through or swum across. The last 1.5 miles of the course include a crawl up a severe and slick muddy hill that's constantly watered down by a guy with a fire hose, and that is followed by a series of mud pits and tunnels, before you finally arrive at heartbreak hill for a final climb along a narrow path.

At the top of heartbreak hill, you turn steeply downhill and emerge into the final straightaway to the finish line. Here you pass in front of a cheering crowd and are forced into a deep water-filled trench. You cannot wade through it—you must get on your hands and knees and crawl through—before emerging on the other side for the final 75-yard sprint across the finish line. That's the Mud Run.

The first time I ran it, I finished tenth in my age group: forty-six- to fifty-year-old men. I noticed that the time difference between me and the winner was less than two minutes. I thought I could run *at least* two minutes faster. And it became my mission that day to win that race. I trained harder than I had in years, and I ran the race for the next five years, finishing third, third, third, second, third.

I got to know the names of the two guys who were consistently finishing ahead of me. I felt like I knew them, though I never actually saw them in any race. They were just the two guys whom I could not seem to beat. But they were also the same age as I was. They weren't going to *age out* of my group, allowing me to outlast them and win. I had to beat them if I was ever going to finish first. The 2008 Mud Run was held on a typical June day in San Diego, sunny and warm. The starting line area was packed with a thousand or more runners, including the usual menagerie dressed in everything from full camo gear and boots to ballerina tutus. I assumed those two guys were there again, somewhere in the crowd. I ran an okay race that day, but when I crossed the finish line, I felt as if I hadn't done enough to win. In fact, I'd run almost a minute slower than I had the year before. I looked at my wife as I came out of the finishing chute and said with a sigh, "*Third again!*"

We walked over to the infield area for the ritual post-race shower. As we did, I asked her, "How many old guys did you see finishing before I did?" She said she'd seen a couple of older guys finish. "There it is," confirmation of third place, I thought. After showering, she said, "Let's go look at the results. They should be posted by now." The results were always displayed on a big board in the infield twenty minutes after the race. I didn't want to look. I just wanted to get in the car and drive home. But my wife insisted, "Let's just go look." We walked over, and there on that board in black and white we read:

Men's 50–54

1. Kehoe, Kevin (53) 53:35.

I did tear up. Twenty-eight years after my first 10K in Florida, I had finally finished first. I stayed for the medal ceremony, of course. That medal hangs in my office to this day as a reminder that you have to show up to have any hope of winning, even just once. Then, ten years later and thirty-seven years after my first race, I ran my last race—also the Mud Run. There was never going to be a first-place finish that day. Instead, there was something better. Four old guys wearing neon lime-green T-shirts emblazoned with the words, *"Cancer, your name is Mud,"* in bright blue letters, crossed the finish line together. That picture hangs right next to the first-place medal. Life is a long race. You need more than hope to make it to the end—you need faith. And if you can keep the faith—who knows, you just might get the glory one day as St. Paul wrote to Timothy:

"I have fought the good fight to the end. I have run the race to the finish. I have kept the faith. All there is to come now is the crown of righteousness reserved for me, which the Lord will give to me." 2 Timothy 4:7-8

CHAPTER 37

Sometimes the Dragon Wins

*"Some days you get the bear,
other days the bear gets you."*
*—The phrase is attributed to an old English proverb.
It means that you win some, and you lose some.*

In the archetypical hero's story, the knight rides out, slays the dragon, and rescues and wins the hand of the fair maiden. But in the real world that doesn't happen all the time—sometimes the dragon wins. My wife always asks, "Honey, how was your day?" And sometimes I will tell her, "Honey, the dragon won today." Even though I'd put in my best effort and thought I'd done all the right things that day, I'd ended up falling short, losing, or just having a bad day. The dragon won. There would be no fair maiden to carry home that day. I was never angry saying those words. I'd say them with a note of resignation, hoping that tomorrow would be a better day, and that it was best not to dwell on the day's disappointments too much. It's not fair, but in the real world, the knight hero doesn't always come out on top.

You know my friend Scott from an earlier chapter. Scott was a true real-life knight hero. At least he tried to live that way every day. Life, however, unfairly singled him out and afflicted him with heart and pulmonary disease at a young age. And as he aged, he had to live with the increasing restrictions that disease imposed on him. At one time, he was an avid tennis player. He had to give that up. He was also an ardent outdoorsman. He had to curtail that activity, too. The reason was simple: he couldn't breathe. His heart and lungs could not keep up with what his brain and body wanted to do. Even when we were golfing in Ireland and Scotland, playing on courses where carts were forbidden, he had to get an exemption to ride in a cart, as he could not walk the 18 holes.

I knew he was suffering, but I didn't realize to what extent until we were touring Arlington National Cemetery one weekend. As we strolled along, he kept falling further and further behind. We had to stop and wait for him to catch up, huffing and puffing. It was obvious that he wasn't in good health. I asked him about it that night: "Scott, what's going on? How serious is your condition, and what are your options?" I was hoping for a good prognosis, but he indicated that his options were limited. The best option was a heart transplant, but the years had so weakened his lungs that the doctors were hesitant to marry a good heart with bad lungs, especially when the limited supply of hearts might be better suited for someone waiting in line with better lungs. The drugs he had to take every day, and there were many, were his best bet to slow down the disease, and only real option, he said. I guess I knew then that he wasn't going to get better. I was just hoping his condition wouldn't get worse. I really wanted *his* dragon to go away.

I saw Scott for the last time in the summer of 2016. We were visiting him for our annual vacation to Maryland. For many years, my wife, my daughter, and I traveled to Maryland to spend a week or so with Scott, his wife, Sandie, and their family. Those were good times. On our last visit, everything was different, though. Scott and I were both unwell. He was suffering from the early stages of congestive heart failure, and I was suffering from the effects of surgery, radiation, and chemo. Instead of golfing, rafting the Monocacy River, hosting big family barbecues, and all the other things we'd always done, neither of us was well enough to enjoy our time together. I was laid up for much of the visit on a couch, hoping for relief from nausea and pain, and Scott was wasting away, losing weight and medicating himself—a process that took hours each day. I watched him do it, unable to offer any help, or even talk about it. It was the second-saddest trip we ever made to Maryland.

As we drove away from Scott and Sandie's home at the end of that trip, I looked back at him, sitting on the porch with his family, waving good-bye to us. I looked at my wife and she was crying. "You realize this is the last time we're going to see him, right?" she said.

All I could say was, "No, he'll pull through. He'll rally." But Scott didn't rally. He died sixty days later. He died on a Tuesday, just another unremarkable day for the rest of the world that didn't notice a good man's passing. He died when his kidneys finally shut down, because his big heart was worn out. His death ended years of suffering for him, and for all those who worried and prayed for him. He left behind his bereft widow and three children, all of whom were present when he breathed his last.

We heard the news that Tuesday morning, and again we boarded a flight, this time to bury a friend, and for the saddest trip to Maryland. I sat in his office in his home, a place where we'd spent many hours together. His "to do list," notes to himself, and his calendar were all open on his desk, waiting for him. It was sobering realizing that all his plans and dreams were simply over. All those "to do's" would never get done. Sandie came into the room, and I wondered aloud if I might say a few words at his memorial the next day. And Sandie, as graceful as always, said, "I was hoping you might." She thought Scott would like that. She was composed, but her sadness was overwhelming. You could tell she'd been "gut punched" by Scott's death.

I spoke at the memorial the next day. I recalled a day five years before that I knew Scott would remember. I told the mourners that he was brave, always game for the next challenge, and had a large but, to our great sorrow, physically defective heart. That day, five years before, began with coffee, a backhoe, a tractor, and chain saws. Sandie wanted us to tear down the old goat house. We turned it into a big pile of wood. When we finished that, we took out the big lawn mowers, and, with his son, Caleb, we mowed the ten acres of his yard.

When we finished that, we changed out of our work clothes, played a round of golf, followed by a quick lunch. Then we loaded up the canoes and rafted through the shallows of the Monocacy River. By the time we returned from the river, it was late. And as the sun set, we barbecued chicken and drank wine with "the girls," having dinner as a family. But before our heads hit the pillows, we set fire to that big woodpile, the remains of Sandie's goat house. We watched it burn—a fire so large and bright that had they been up there, the astronauts on the space shuttle might have seen it. I finished my short memorial by saying, "Now he's gone, and we'll never have another day like that again. None of us will."

I think about Scott often these days. He was one of those rare men who are innately good and selfless. Where I grew up, in New York, we called guys like him a "mensch." It's a Yiddish word that refers to a person of integrity and honor, someone you want to admire and emulate, and someone with a noble character. The term is a compliment that expresses the rarity and value of such an individual.

After the memorial, we assembled in a little graveyard, one we'd driven past so many times on the way to and from his home. We buried him on a nearly perfect autumn afternoon in his town, Woodsboro, Maryland. The world lost a knight hero that week. The dragon won. It wasn't fair. It wasn't "right." He deserved better. All we had now were memories of a friend. Some years before on the occasion of his fifty-fifth birthday I quoted the words of James Boswell, written in 1791, as a toast in that celebration.

> *"We cannot tell the precise moment when a friendship is formed. As in filling a vessel drop by drop, there is that last drop, which makes the vessel run over; so in a series of kindnesses there is at last one, which makes the heart, run over."*

Sometime during the twenty years I knew Scott, the last drop made the vessel run over. Just before we left Maryland, Scott reached out to me one last time from where he was. He did it through his daughter, Whitney. Whitney handed me a cassette tape with a message Scott had recorded for me some months before. She said Scott wanted me to have it. I heard his voice tell me not to fear dying too much. And that when the time came, I should face my death with grace and courage. It was very brave stuff. Here was a man trying to help *me*, while *he* was dying. And, as I listened, I thought that maybe those words were intended for him, as much as they were for me—that it might be his way of facing up to his own imminent death.

I was paging through my high school yearbook recently. I do that on occasion. I was rereading messages my classmates had written almost a half century earlier. I turned to the "Teachers" section of the yearbook, and there was a picture of Mr. Frascino, my favorite teacher in my senior year, and the note he had written me. It said;

"Ave atque vale . . . to Kevin, a gentleman and a scholar for whom I predict great success. It was a pleasure to have you in class."

Ave atque vale is Latin. It translates as "Hail and farewell." I salute you, and good-bye. It was used by the Romans as part of a eulogy to a hero. Dear Scott: Wherever you are, I listened to your message. Thank you for your heroic words. But I'm not ready to go quite yet. I think I'll stay around a little while longer. And in your memory and your honor, I will ride out every day to battle the dragon and rescue the fair maidens of the world, even knowing sometimes the dragon will win.

What else is there to life? I don't know exactly, but I think a big part is *living*, even when you know you're dying; and continuing to try even when you know the dragon might win; and doing your best whether you win or you lose. That's heroic.

Ave atque vale

Scott J. Hall

Born: November 9, 1957

Died: September 2, 2016

CODA

"Coda: Something written or sung that serves to round out, conclude, or summarize."

All things must come to an end. And so, allow me to end my collection of stories with a few thoughts. My life, I suspect, is not too different from yours in many ways. I'm just a guy making his way in the world, trying to be happy and be the best person I can. I've made mistakes—some very bad ones. It seems I've lost more times than I've won. Although I've achieved some things, I might have done better. But the journey certainly hasn't been dull. I was taught to be a certain way, and I've adhered to most of the lessons I learned growing up as well as to those I learned along the way. You know, really simple and timeless things like: "Don't tell a lie. Tell the truth. Don't take what's not yours. Give more than you take. Pull your weight. Don't just say you're sorry—make restitution. Treat people as you want to be treated. Do the right thing. Go the extra step." I don't know any other way. I am, as are we all, a creature of habit.

I am now, after almost seven decades on the planet, a guy who is the sum of his choices, dreams, and values . . . for better or worse. And my journey is not over yet. I hope to have another few years to make new stories and shape myself and the world around me for the better. That's my plan. The big question is, At this stage of life, am I happy? Sure, I'm happy with some things and unhappy with others. Maybe a better question is, Have I made the most of what God gave me, and have I contributed and done enough to make my own little world better for everyone around me?

When I was a boy, long ago in New York, I never dreamed that I'd have the life I've had. I did not think that far forward or know enough to imagine the possibilities. I feel like golf champ Bubba Watson when he was asked by a reporter after winning the Masters Tournament, "Bubba, is winning the green jacket as good as you'd dreamed it would be?" Bubba replied, "I don't know. I never got that far in my dreams." He never thought that far ahead or considered and imagined the possibility. He just went to work every day, taught himself the game, and did the best with what he had been given.

I never dreamed I'd have the life I've had, or be where I am now. Don't get me wrong, I had dreams, but mainly I went to work every day, taught myself the game, and did the best I could with what I was given. And again I had Waylon Jennings to help me make sense of some of it and to learn whom to trust. The rest I learned the hard way. Now, I've shared some of what I learned with you. I hope it was interesting for you and you can do something with it.

I asked my dad on his sixty-fifth birthday, "How does it feel to be sixty-five years old, Dad?" He said, "It's funny, my brain thinks I'm twenty-eight, but my body is telling me a completely different story." I can relate to that now. I feel young, but the reality is, that I'm closer to the end than I am to the beginning of life. That concerns me, of course. But I've faced death and lots of adversity, and survived all of it thus far. So, to answer my "happiness" question, I worry less about my future, and live more in the present. This makes me happy. It's one of nature's gifts for getting older: not only have you forgotten more than you remember but today matters more than tomorrow—if only for the simple reason that there're just fewer tomorrows. Now that I think about it, I wish I'd felt like this when I was younger. My choices and decisions might have been better, wiser, and I would have worried far less. But as it's been said, youth is wasted on the young.

There's a lyric in a David Bowie song that goes something like, "We can be heroes, just for one day." I like the song. I was always a Bowie fan. But why just one day? Why not every day? That's my attitude. Get up to bat and swing hard. Go big. As Marianne Williamson (cited in the first chapter) said, our acting small doesn't serve the world. If nothing else, one day something good is going to happen when you act large. . . you might get the big hit. My ride on life's highway isn't over yet. There are more chapters to be written. But that's tomorrow. Of course, there are a few things I have to address sooner rather than later: like retirement and death. Here's what I'm doing about these two things.

Retirement, though I like the sound of it, it also makes me nervous. What will I do? Maybe you'll feel the same way, especially if you enjoyed what you did for a career. Leaving a career behind is a big adjustment—at least it is for me. Mine defined who I was. Now I need a new definition of me. I haven't figured it out yet. But I know for certain that retirement means fewer dry-cleaning bills. I've spent a lot of money at dry cleaners over the years. I always made sure everything was cleaned and pressed for the coming workweek.

In fact, my shirts became the way I marked the time when I traveled. Some people cross days off the calendar. I counted the shirts in the closet. I'd pack the number of shirts I'd need for the week . . . four days of travel meant four shirts in the suitcase. When I'd arrive at the hotel, I'd hang my shirts on one side of the closet. Each morning, I'd select a shirt for the day. Every evening, I'd hang the one I had worn that day on the other side of the closet. On the last day of my trip, there'd be one shirt remaining: the *last shirt*.

The last shirt said to me, "The job is done, the battle's over, you get to go home today." I felt like Caesar on that last day, looking at the last shirt: I came, I saw, I conquered. In Roman times when the conquering hero returned home with victories for the empire, he was celebrated like a god. He was paraded to the Forum through the streets of Rome, surrounded by adoring crowds. And in the golden chariot in which he rode, there was always a slave holding the hero's golden crown above his head, and it was the slave's job to whisper in the hero's ear—that fame is fleeting, and that he was only a mortal and not a god. My wife would listen to me in the car on the way home, and gently remind me that I was only a mortal.

My wife was doing me a favor. Why? Because you get in trouble when you start to believe your own press. And that always seems to lead to the fall. Maybe because our egos can blind us enough that we forget that the rules of life apply to everyone. I've witnesses this many times. So I just try to keep my head down, work hard, and stay humble. I don't want the gods picking me out for special attention.

Death is a part of life, and we should prepare for it. I had to think about it a lot when I got cancer. We had to prepare for my absence, and get our affairs in order, should the unthinkable happen. One of the things we did was to pay a visit to Pacific View Memorial Park in Corona del Mar, California. When my dad suddenly passed away, a quarter of a century ago, we weren't prepared for it. We had to purchase a grave site in a day. We had to conduct a wake, a funeral, and a burial, and figure out how to do all that in seventy-two hours: notices, eulogy, music, church, graveyard service, and coffin. It was a lot to do, at a very bad time.

I didn't want anyone to experience that when I passed away. That's why my wife and I spent a day at Pacific View Memorial Park, selecting our site and documenting decisions for those who would have to manage our passing. It's an odd experience to do this. But cemeteries are a business like any other, and they are expert at these things. When we met with their sales rep, we discovered just how many things had to be decided and documented. There were options we hadn't considered.

There were standard in-the-ground headstone plots; there were wall slots on a mortuary wall; there were memorial plaques, mausoleums, benches with inscriptions, and simple stone markers. You could even buy your own boulder with a plaque, where your ashes would be interred inside forever. And that's what we ended up selecting: a boulder beside a brook, on a hill, next to a path looking down on the Pacific Ocean.

By the time we completed the paperwork, the sun was setting. We sat by our boulder by the brook, and watched the sun disappear into the Pacific. We talked about how we hoped that one day, far into the future, our friends and loved ones might come, spend a few moments here with us, and recite some of the old stories and memories before returning home to their lives. As far as death goes, our affairs are in order. I'm glad we did it.

One final thought about life and happiness. My wife likes movies and TV shows that are neatly tied up in a bow by the end. And it's a big plus if the ending is a happy one, too. I also prefer shows and movies with happy endings. I don't like dark, gritty, hope-killing, and so-called realistic lifelike endings. I'm not saying these are bad movies. I'm just suggesting that if I wanted that kind of darkness, I could watch the news or attend a city council meeting. I want to have hope and feel uplifted and happy at the end of a movie. Shallow? Maybe, but I'll take fantasy, hope, faith, and the promise of a better future any day over reality.

Here are just a few of the things I've learned, tied up in a nice, neat bow:

- Self-belief is self-fulfilling.

- The early bird gets the worm.

- We all work for someone.

- When opportunity doesn't knock, build a door.

- It's never too late to change a bad choice.

- Be bold.

- Remember who you are.

- Build some permanence and tradition into your life.

- There's no place like home.

- The world doesn't revolve around you.

- Listen to your mother.

- Have a best day to remember.

- Obsession is the road to madness.

- No good deed goes unrewarded or unpunished.

- You will be thrown under the bus.

- There just might be a pot of gold at the end of the rainbow – keep your eye on the prize.

- You're not the only one with problems.

- Take the high road - always.

- Bad things will happen to you for no good reason.

- There is stupid in the world.

- Take one for the team from time to time.

- Common sense is uncommon.

- Thick skin and a short memory are essential for happiness.

- White lies keep the world turning.

- Laugh at yourself.

- Avoid self-important people.

- No harm, no foul.

- Do what you love, if you can.

- Don't drink the Kool-Aid.

- There are no free lunches.

- Showing up is 90 percent of "life."

- Pride goeth before a fall.

- Karma is a bitch.

- Sometimes the dragon wins.

These are not *my* rules for life. These are simply a few lessons that have helped me survive my journey. I wish I'd known them sooner, instead of having to learn so many the hard way. However, had I learned them earlier and more easily, I wouldn't have nearly as many stories to tell. I'm no hero—just trying to live like one.

> *"When your time comes, be not like those who fear death and weep and pray for more time to live their lives over again differently. Sing your death song and go like a hero going home."*

> —*Tecumseh*

ACKNOWLEDGMENTS

I want to thank my wife, Lorraine, for helping me edit this book. She listened to my multiple drafts and always provided great feedback. I want to acknowledge, by first name only, those mentioned and those unmentioned in this book who've made my journey possible: Mom, Dad, Michael, Brian, Timothy, Deirdre, Jeremy, Julia, Vincent, Tommy, Bob, Judy, John-Boy, Lorraine, Greg, Elizabeth, Holly, Janet, Keith, Scott, Joe, Tara, Larry, John, and Toby. You know who you are. It's a short list by design. I could fill a few pages with the names of all the wonderful people I've known and who have made my life richer than I could have ever imagined when I was a young boy, lying in the newly mown grass under the weeping willow tree in Farmingdale, wondering what life might bring me.

CPSIA information can be obtained
at www.ICGtesting.com
Printed in the USA
LVHW092119271021
701713LV00001B/1